METHODS
FOR
TEACHING:
An Overview of
Current Practices

SECOND EDITION

WILLIAM K. ESLER
PHILIP SCIORTINO

UNIVERSITY OF CENTRAL FLORIDA

CPC *CONTEMPORARY PUBLISHING COMPANY*
508 ST. MARY'S STREET, RALEIGH, N.C. 27605—(919) 821-4566

Publisher: Charles E. Grantham
Copyediting: Sheryl D. Thomas
Typesetting: Piedmont Litho
Artwork: Terri Sciortino Koepsell
Printers: Edwards Brothers

Acknowledgements

David S. Lake Publishers for material used in chapter two from Robert Mager's "Preparing Instructional Objectives."

Sterling Park Elementary School, Casselberry, Florida, Jackson Heights Middle School, Oviedo, Florida and Riverside Elementary School, Orange County, Florida for photographs used throughout the text.

Printed in the United States of America.

ISBN: 0-89892-095-7

PREFACE

Welcome to Methods for Teaching! We are sure you will find the information on these pages helpful as you prepare for an exciting and rewarding career in education.

This book is designed on the premise that a body of knowledge, skills, and teaching methods exists which is valuable and common to all those who wish to be the most effective teachers they can be.

Since K-12 students come in a variety of sizes, shapes, and genders, and possess wide differences in cultural backgrounds and mental, emotional, and physical abilities, it is obvious that an effective teacher must possess a repertoire of teaching methods to meet the needs of all students. In Chapter One, "Today's Teacher" you are introduced to the nature and importance of teaching as a profession and asked to consider if this occupation is for you. In Chapter Two, "Educational Goals and Objectives for Effective Teaching," you will discover ways in which our society forges programs for its most important institution, schools. In Chapter Three, "Planning for Effective Teaching," ways of turning desired goals and objectives into quality instruction are presented. The proper and effective use of classroom questions, which many believe to be the primary tool of the effective teacher, are presented in Chapters Four and Five. In these chapters you will learn about kinds of questions teachers ask, how to ask them, and how to manage student responses. The art and science of using classroom questions is brought to its highest level of application in Chapter Seven.

"The Didactic Teacher, The Efficient Purveyor of Information," Chapter Six, demonstrates procedures for maximizing the effectiveness of direct instruction. In Chapter Seven, "Teaching Problem Solving and Critical Thinking Skills," you will find clear instructions for using several types of indirect instructional techniques which are related to the development of critical thinking and problem-solving skills. Chapter Eight describes strategies which individualize instruction for individuals and small groups while Chapter Nine suggests strategies for teaching the whole class at once. The ever present concern of beginning teachers, preventing and dealing with discipline problems, is the subject of Chapters Ten and Eleven. You will find several specific and practical suggestions and examples to help you with this area of concern.

Chapter Twelve treats evaluation of instruction including directions for creating effective teacher-made tests and using a variety of non-test procedures to assess student progress. The treatment of standardized tests and testing in the last chapter emphasizes the nature of such testing as it is found in most of today's elementary, middle and junior high schools. Methods for interpreting student scores to better provide proper instruction and communication with students and parents are also suggested.

For greatest clarity we recommend that the chapters be studied in order through Chapter Seven. The sequence of the remaining chapters is of less importance. We hope you will find reading the contents of this book as enjoyable and rewarding as we found writing them.

ACKNOWLEDGEMENTS

We would like to express our thanks to our wives, Jo and Mary, who contributed to this project as they have long given of themselves to numerous other projects over many years. We are indebted to Dr. Delorys Blume for critiquing the manuscript, and to Chuck Grantham, our publisher, for his advice and patience.

CASE STUDY INTRODUCTION

At the beginning of each chapter you will find a case study that is designed to introduce you to some of the issues of the topic covered in the chapter content. The case study is essentially a presentation of a scenario that depicts a typical problem that confronts professionals in the field of education each day. The scenario will consist of some background information and specific data that would be available to a person responsible for making decisions in a real life situation. You are invited to temporarily step into the shoes of the professional educator, carefully consider all the facts presented, consult with your peers or other interested parties and make the decision required by the exercise. In performing this problem solving activity you will come face to face, and learn to deal, with many issues of the field of education. Test your own decision making abilities before you begin each chapter.

TABLE OF CONTENTS

CHAPTER ONE

INTRODUCTORY CASE STUDY

SHOULD JOHN A. AND SUSAN B. BECOME TEACHERS??

Ruth Smith advises undergraduate students in the College of Education. This morning she has appointments with two students, John A. and Susan B. She will review John A.'s application for admission to the Teacher Education Program, inform him of her recommendation and pass on a written recommendation to a College Standards Committee composed of five faculty members who will make the decision on his admission. Susan B. has stopped by Mrs. Smith's office seeking assistance in making a career decision — to remain in the Teacher Education Program or transfer to a program in the College of Engineering. Mrs. Smith has each student's records and notes from recent interviews.

CASE STUDY 1-1

John A.

Sophomore, second semester
Major: Elementary Education or Middle School Social Studies
Grade Point Average: 2.34 (minimum required 2.5); grades most recent semesters: Spring Term — 2.2, Fall Term — 2.5, Summer Term — 3.0, dropped two courses, retained one course.
SAT score: 965 (minimum required 850)

Interview Responses

Q: Why are your grades this low?
R: I don't know. I just can't seem to stay with a course for a whole semester sometimes. I can do better.
Q: Why do you want to be a teacher?
R: Well, I like working with kids. I've coached Little League for two years. We were lucky enough to win most of our games even though we didn't practice much. The kids seemed to like it.
Q: If the Committee permits you to enter into the program on probation, can you raise your grade point to graduate?

R: I think so. I can take some classes in things I'm good at like sports. Then if I get lucky in one or two others, I'll be OK.

Q: Have you thought of doing something other than teaching?

R: Not really. My dad works in a bank, but a friend got him the job a long time ago. I don't know anyone like that. I just think I'd be good at it.

WHAT IS YOUR DECISION? Would you recommend to the College Standards Committee that John be admitted on probation? What would you say to John when he shows up for the interview?

CASE STUDY 1-2

Susan B.

Senior, first semester.
Major: Secondary Mathematics Education
Grade Point Average: 3.5; most recent grades: Spring Semester — 3.7, Fall Semester — 3.3, Summer Semester — 3.4
ACT — 28 (minimum requirement — 17)

Interview Responses

Q: How can I help you?

R: I have a problem; I don't know if I want to stay in Education or transfer to Engineering.

Q: I see you have completed your first semester of school experience; didn't that go well?

R: It went great. I was able to teach some classes in first year algebra. I feel real good about what I did. That is not the problem.

Q: Well, what is the problem, Susan?

R: It's my parents. My father is an engineer and he wants me to go into engineering.

Q: How do you feel about that?

R: I can do the work; I was in Engineering before I transferred into Education. I thought I would rather work with kids than be an engineer.

Q: Does your mother have any thoughts on this?

R: Mom is big on the feminist issues. She says as a female, I have an obligation to my sex to not work in a traditional female profession.

Q: How do you feel about this?

R: Well, I could make a lot more money and I would like to see females be able to work where they want and make as much as men.

Q: If you went into teaching, do you see yourself in the classroom in say twenty years? Will you still find it challenging?

R: I can only say that I enjoy it now. I think maybe I would want to write some better mathematics books that the kids could read and understand or if I was good enough at it, to help other teachers do a better job.

Q: I don't think I heard you say whether you could enjoy working in the engineering field as a career.

R: I think I would find it interesting. My father has been involved with some exciting projects and has traveled to a number of interesting places all over the world.

WHAT IS YOUR DECISION? What would you recommend to Susan when she appears for her interview? Should she pursue becoming a teacher or an engineer?

CHAPTER ONE
TODAY'S TEACHER

"If I have seen further than others ... it is by standing upon the shoulders of Giants."

-Sir Isaac Newton

GOALS

After reading this chapter the student will:

1. develop an appreciation for teaching.
2. establish a cause and effect relationship between teaching methods and learner behaviors,
3. recognize common methods for teaching and
4. be motivated to develop skills and knowledge related to a variety of teaching methods.

OBJECTIVES

After studying this chapter the reader will:

1. list three positive reasons for the selection of teaching as a career,
2. match the methods of direct and indirect teaching with their likely learning outcomes,
3. match a list of teaching methods with brief descriptions,
4. write a short paragraph that outlines a rationale to support the need for high fate control attitudes among teachers and
5. write a paragraph that supports the need for developing skill with a variety of teaching methods.

"Nothing is more vital for humanity's happiness than good teachers."

This comment was made by Robert Muller, then Secretary of the United Nations Economic and Social Council. Muller went on to say how two teachers had transformed his life. Alexander the Great once said that parents give you life, but teachers teach you how to live. This dynamic young Greek leader had in Aristotle one of the acknowledged great teachers in history. Ann Sullivan, through patience mixed with firmness and creative teaching released Helen Keller, a deaf and blind child, from a life of terrible isolation to become a renowned social worker and teacher. These are only a few teachers among thousands who have made significant contributions to the lives of countless people.

Most of us at some time pause to think about the teachers with whom we have studied. By the time a student has completed high school dozens of teachers have been encountered in the classroom, the music room, the gymnasium, and on the athletic field. Perhaps two or three teachers are remembered in a special way. They were the best; the ones that made a difference in our lives.

Please take a few moments, relax, lean back, and think of your own best teacher or teachers. How many come to mind as being special? Did you know them in the elementary, middle school, or high school? Perhaps it was in college. What were they like? Why are they memorable? Most people say things such as:

"She made learning fun."
"He cared about his students."
"He had us work in groups, discussing problems or doing projects."
"She worked us hard and made us learn."
"She had us do a lot of different things. It was always interesting."
"He always listened to his students; we felt like part of the class."

From comments such as these it is difficult to see anything unusual, anything mystic about great teachers. It appears the best teachers were probably ordinary people who cared that students learned and worked hard to help them achieve. Perhaps someday you will be on many people's list of best teachers.

WHO SHOULD TEACH?

If the ten "best" teachers were lined up in front of a classroom there would probably be nothing visible that would be common to all ten. And if we could observe each one teach we would, no doubt, see a variety of teaching techniques, everything from lecture and discussion to working with materials and participation in group problem solving. There is no best way to teach; no model that may be singled out as the preferred method of instruction. What do these ten teachers have in common, if anything? Another quick scan of the descriptions of the best teachers and a little reading between the lines might reveal a hidden common thread that binds them together. They all appear to find some measure of joy in teaching. Each of them finds pleasure in helping students grow and develop intellectually and as people. The outward signs of this pleasure may be seen in the well-planned lesson, their own intellectual involvement with classroom activities, and the respect they show for students' written and spoken statements. And something special may be seen in teachers' interactions with their students. They are usually warm, but firm, demanding, yet sensitive to students' feelings. Perhaps it is true that all those who find joy in teaching make the best teachers.

SELF CHECK FOR OBJECTIVE ONE

CAN YOU: list three positive reasons that support the selection of teaching as a career?

WHAT IS GOOD TEACHING?

Teaching is both an art and a science. The science of teaching tells us that specific acts of the teacher and certain defined learning environments will cause specific student behaviors. Years of research on teaching have produced a mountain of evidence that supports the judgement that specific, controlled behaviors of teachers produce predictable results. This is the ultimate test of science, that well defined events consistently yield similar results. Therefore, to a degree teaching is a science. But science will not tell a teacher when to be firm with a faltering student, and when to place an arm around the student's shoulder. And science will not tell the teacher how to change the attitudes of students so they accept a newcomer among them who is different. That requires the art of teaching, knowing when to talk and when to listen, when to proceed with a lesson and when to change the total plan. Teaching is feeling as well as knowing; good teaching demands sensitivity to those who are being taught, a feel for the individual and for the mood of the group. For the effective teacher the art of teaching supports the science of teaching and the science supports the art.

WHAT WE KNOW ABOUT TEACHING METHODS

Direct Teaching

Research reviews on teaching show that the way teachers teach does make a difference. Rather than focus on narrow acts of the teacher such as the amount of praise issued to students, or the frequency with which certain types of questions are asked, it appears that it is patterns of practices which account for effectiveness. For example, in the primary grades of the elementary school one pattern or cluster of teacher behavior that results in greater achievement in the basic skill areas of math and reading is called direct teaching. Direct teaching, according to one study, is defined by such teaching behaviors as: selecting specific instructional goals and appropriate learning tasks, setting time allocations for learners to complete a task, and constant monitoring by the teacher while students are engaged in learning

Good teachers are found with a variety of characteristics, but all share one thing in common; that is a joy for teaching. Each finds pleasure in helping students grow and develop intellectually and as individuals. Good teachers are warm, but firm, demanding, yet sensitive, organized, yet flexible.

tasks. Time on task for the student is strongly emphasized. The direct teacher typically lectures, demonstrates and assigns and monitors seat work. Research has shown that direct teaching will work best on all grade levels when the objective is to teach basic skills and facts, and when materials are designed to cause students to be successful. Direct teaching is less successful when used to teach problem solving skills and when children are from a higher socioeconomic environment or have high I.Q.'s.

Indirect Teaching

Indirect teaching, as contrasted to direct teaching, is characterized by student involvement with learning at higher cognitive levels, group discussions, by student contribution to the instructional process, and by student motivation that focuses on internal or intrinsic rewards rather than on a quest for grades, teacher approval, or other forms of external reward. Inquiry, discovery, and problem solving are a few strategies associated with indirect teaching. Learning that results from these teaching activities, especially as they relate to the use of manipulative materials has been researched. Researchers have found that indirect teaching causes improved levels of attitudes, problem solving skills, retention of learning, and thinking skills. A shift in the style of teaching from direct to indirect results in a new cluster of learning outcomes for the student.

Any single teaching style has limitations and cannot be expected to produce the entire spectrum of learning that is associated with a well-rounded school program. In today's schools teachers are expected to provide students with a variety of learning experiences.

SELF CHECK FOR OBJECTIVE TWO

CAN YOU: match the methods of direct and indirect teaching with their likely learning outcomes?

TEACHING METHODS: INSTRUCTIONAL STYLE OPTIONS

History has described many fine teachers. Great teachers of various religions of the ancient Middle East employed revelation and parable as methods of instruction. Socrates taught by structuring questions to lead his students step by step through problem solving processes. St. Thomas Aquinas constructed logical arguments that convinced and instructed by reason. Maria Montessori, a native of Italy, developed a highly structured set of activities for use with retarded children. They have been adopted throughout the world as model programs for many instructional purposes. Madeleine Goutard, a Canadian teacher, developed a program that used

Table 1.1
COMMON METHODS FOR TEACHING:
WHOLE CLASS OR GROUP INSTRUCTION

Method	Description
Lecture	The teacher directly tells students the information to be imparted. Telling may be accompanied by audio and visual aids, manipulative materials and fact related questions.
Discovery	The teacher structures the learning environment or set of data so the learner forms conclusions. This method is often associated with divergent questions asked by the teacher and manipulative materials in the hands of the learner.
Inquiry	Independently, in groups, or directed by the teacher, the learner defines a problem and structures an investigation of the problem, forms conclusions, and reports results. The investigation may be a search of related literature or use of physical materials.
Seatwork and Drill	Activities designed to reinforce learning of a well-defined body of facts. Common procedures include oral question and answer sessions, flash cards, games, written seatwork, and puzzles.

manipulatives called Cuisenaire Rods to teach mathematics concepts. Her materials are used extensively throughout Canada, Europe, and the United States. Each of these teachers is recognized as having been great. They used different methods while teaching students. Since each one was a very effective teacher and was able to inspire others we can conclude that there are many ways to teach effectively. Table 1.1 and Table 1.2 list and briefly describe a number of common teaching methods used in classrooms.

Each of the methods listed and described in Tables 1.1 and 1.2 will be discussed in greater detail later in this book. The tables provide an overview of the most used and researched methods employed by teachers. In practice, each of the methods is often modified by classroom teachers and blended with other methods to serve special instructional needs. While no teacher is likely to use all methods listed in the tables, many teachers have the knowledge and ability to use several of them.

School programs at all levels usually incorporate learning activities designed to develop learning such as memorization of basic facts, development of problem solving skills, and systems of values suitable for living in a

Table 1.2
COMMON METHODS FOR TEACHING:
INDIVIDUALIZED INSTRUCTIONAL TECHNIQUES

Method	Description
Programmed Instruction	Independently the student self paces work through content that is organized in small increments of information. The student checks work with provided answers.
Learning Activity Packets (LAPS)	Characterized by a system which involves carefully organized, sequenced learning activities which are varied. The LAP includes objectives, self-evaluation, and student record keeping. It sometimes contains diagnostic and posttests and offers students options selecting learning tasks.
Management Systems	A highly systematic learning environment. Contains a hierarchy of objectives, evaluation instruments, instructional materials, and student profiles. It is generally used in the teaching of basic skills of reading and math.
Learning Centers	A location in a classroom that contains self-directing learning activities where a group of students works independently. Learning activities may be related to basic skills, problem solving or inquiry.
Independent Study	Individual students work on assigned or contracted projects. Projects may involve library research, report writing, model building, reading, etc.

democratic society. This requires a skilled teacher to possess competence with a variety of teaching methods. As stated by Marjorie Powell:

> Teachers need to have available and need to be able to use a variety of patterns or clusters of teaching behaviors; they need to know how to teach in small groups, to lecture, to conduct effective drills, to monitor student work when seat work has been assigned. In addition to having a repertory of patterns of teaching behaviors, teachers need to select among those patterns or methods to use.

In addition to the methods cited by Powell, others should be added that are associated with the use of materials and equipment to solve problems and create products. All teachers who wish to provide variety in their classroom activities, or who will teach more than one subject, should possess a broad spectrum of instructional skills. Since they often teach several subjects, elementary school teachers have a special need for developing a broad base of teaching skills. This book is designed to introduce the reader to the variety of teaching methods employed by teachers and assist in the development of the skills required in the classroom.

SELF CHECK FOR OBJECTIVE THREE

CAN YOU: match a list of teaching methods with their brief descriptions?

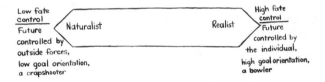

FIGURE 1.1
FATE CONTROL

FATE CONTROL AND THE TEACHER

Studies have been conducted concerning the perceptions of individuals regarding the amount of control they have over the events that shape their lives. The findings of these studies have implications for teachers. Individuals tend to fall somewhere on a continuum that begins with the belief that all major events that will transpire in one's life will be unaffected by his own actions, to the belief that events can be controlled and one's life can be shaped by an individual's efforts. Naturalists believe that events which occur in their lives are preordained or random, and the individual is merely a "leaf blown by the wind," that events are directed by forces greater than themselves. They believe that they possess a minimum of power in their ability to control their own fate. Figure 1.1 illustrates this.

Realists believe they are in control of their futures. They believe that major events of their environment are controlled by their action. They have a high level of fate control. Teaching effectiveness is impacted by the individual teacher's fate control level.

A CONTINUUM OF FATE CONTROL

Research has shown that children with low fate control tend to show little goal orientation because they believe they are unable to influence their futures. They react to immediate needs and do not put aside the need for gratification to achieve long range plans. Naturalists tend to be poor problem solvers and to have short attention spans. The Realist, on the other hand, sees the world as manageable. These children tend to size up the system and set out to manage it. They will put aside immediate rewards to achieve long range goals. Realists tend to be good problem solvers and to finish tasks.

What are some implications of fate control for the teacher? The result of this highly personal view of the world will have an effect on both the individual's preparation to teach and behavior in the classroom. The realist will accept the challenge of the long range goal of acquiring the skills and knowledge necessary to become a complete and competent master of the classroom. This person knows that teacher actions cause predictable behaviors of students. And knowing this, the realist will plan and execute strategies to accomplish goals. The naturalist, on the other hand, having little faith that what teachers do will really matter, will tend to rock along, utilizing the experiences which he has had as a student or teacher, making no concerted effort to acquire the skills that will make him a better teacher. The naturalist tends not to set goals or plan because the naturalist believes that a teacher's actions will make little difference in their lives or the lives of students. The naturalist, after ten years in the classroom, does not have ten years' experience, but has had a one year experience ten times.

Because you are reading this, it may be assumed you are interested in becoming a teacher. Take a moment to assess your position on the fate control continuum. Do you tend to set personal and professional goals? Do you think that what you will do as a teacher in the classroom will make a difference in your own future and in the lives of your students? You will probably not fall at either end of the fate control continuum, but somewhere in between. Generally, it may be inferred that those who believe in their ability to control their own destinies will profit most from any program of training or self improvement.

Research has demonstrated a cause and effect relationship between teacher behavior and student achievement. To a great degree your future success as a teacher rests on your belief in yourself and the development of a positive attitude toward the profession of education.

You may find it interesting to work through the following brief activity. It may serve to invite you to reflect on your own beliefs related to the locus of fate control.

The Way I See It

Circle the number that best describes your feelings.

	Strongly Agree		Neutral		Strongly Disagree
1. Setting goals and working to achieve them is a good idea.	5	4	3	2	1
2. Luck has as much to do with success as hard work.	5	4	3	2	1
3. Most successful people probably had someone to help them.	5	4	3	2	1
4. It is more fun to achieve a planned goal than to hit it lucky.	5	4	3	2	1
5. I can control my future.	5	4	3	2	1
6. What happens to a person is probably pre-ordained.	5	4	3	2	1
7. Life is just a series of ups and downs a person cannot control.	5	4	3	2	1
8. When I read that a person has achieved success I know he probably was very lucky.	5	4	3	2	1
9. I can improve my chances for success with hard work.	5	4	3	2	1
10. I regularly practice an activity in which I become involved.	5	4	3	2	1

Analysis of Your "The Way I See It" Responses

CAUTION: This activity is designed only to provide data for discussion purposes. It should not be used as an assessment instrument for individual evaluations.

To analyze your responses to the items of "The Way I See It":
1. Add the numerical responses for items 2, 3, 6, 7 and 8. (Group One)
2. Add the numerical responses for items 1, 4, 5, 9, and 10. (Group Two)
3. Find the difference between the sums of the two groups.
4. Note which of the group sums was larger.
5. Place an "X" on the continuum below at the point that represents the difference between the two group sums.

← Low Fate Control   High Fate Control →

20	15	10	5	0	5	10	15	20

(Place the "X" on this side if sum of Group One responses was larger.)   (Place the "X" on this side if sum of Group Two responses was larger.)

The "X" on the continuum indicates the value of your "fate control index" as derived from this activity. It might be interesting to obtain the "fate control" indices of as many of your peers as you can. How do they cluster on the continuum? Discuss the meaning of this data.

IS TEACHING FOR YOU?

You have in this chapter become acquainted with the attributes of the "best" teachers, discovered the variety of instructional methods that are the tools of teachers, and learned of the importance of teachers' attitudes toward students and the profession in determining their success. You may already possess some of the skills and attitudes that are the foundations of quality teaching, others you may work to develop. Some students may not be suited to the special requirements of this very demanding profession. If you are considering becoming a teacher it would be appropriate at some point early in your professional training to give serious thought as to whether your own goals, aspirations and values mesh with the nature and demands of the profession. If the answer to that question is yes, the information contained in the following chapters will provide a firm foundation for your development as one of the "best" teachers in the memories of many future students.

SELF CHECK FOR OBJECTIVE FOUR

CAN YOU: write a short paragraph that outlines a rationale to support the need for high fate control attitudes among teachers?

SELF CHECK FOR OBJECTIVE FIVE

CAN YOU: write a short paragraph that supports the need for a teacher to develop skill with a variety of teaching methods?

SUMMARY

If we were to survey the "teacher of the year" for each of the fifty states we would discover a wide variety of personal characteristics and teaching methodologies. The common thread among the 50 teachers would be an interest in students and a zest for teaching.

Most often specific clusters of teaching behaviors result in predictable behaviors and learning outcomes of students. Direct teaching techniques appear to be best when teaching basic skills and facts. Indirect teaching techniques appear to enhance the acquisition by students of higher level cognitive skills and positive attitudes. A listing of common teaching methods may be made under the general headings, Whole Class or Group Instruction and Individualized Instructional Techniques. A proficient teacher should be able to use several methods to provide proper learning experiences in the classroom.

Teachers who have a strong belief in their own ability to determine their destiny and shape the lives of their students are much more likely to be successful teachers than those who demonstrate an attitude that what they do is of little consequence in controlling their fate and the learning of their students.

ACTIVITIES

1. Write a paragraph that describes the best teacher you have ever had in school. Include in your description the teacher's personal characteristics and the activities that took place in the classroom.

2. Write a description of each of the three whole class or group instructional techniques. Select one of the three techniques and describe a lesson as it might be taught using the technique.

3. Place yourself and two or three of your peers on a continuum of high fate control to low fate control. Privately assess the implications of your position on the continuum. If you choose, discuss with a friend the strength of your belief in your ability to determine your own destiny as a teacher.

BIBLIOGRAPHY

Cohn, M.M., Kottkamp, R.B., & Provenzo, E.F. Jr. (1987). *To be a teacher, cases, concepts, observation guides.* New York: Random House.

Derr, R.L. (1984). Education versus developing educated people. *Curriculum Inquiry. 14*(3), 301-309.

Ellis, S.S. (1979). Models of teaching: A solution to the teaching style/learning style dilemma. *Educational Leadership, 36*(4), 274-277.

Florida Department of Education, *Beginning Teacher Program Training Manual:* Tallahassee, FL, 1985.

Fuller, F.F., (1969). Concerns of teachers: A developmental characterization. *American Educational Research Journal, 6,* 207-226.

Gage, N.L. (1985). *Hard gains in the soft sciences, the case of pedagogy.* Bloomington: Phi Delta Kappa.

Good, T.L. & Brophy, J.E. (1984). *Looking in classrooms.* New York: Harper and Row.

Hunter, M. (1982). *Teaching* (Videotape). University of California at Los Angeles.

Klein, M.F. (1986). Alternative curriculum concepts and designs. *Theory Into Practice, 25,* 31-35.

Los Angeles County School District. (1980). *Teacher expectations and student achievement.* Bloomington: Phi Delta Kappa.

Ornstein, A.C., & Miller, H.L. (1980). *Looking into teaching.* Chicago: Rand McNally.

Renner, J. (1973). An evaluation of the science curriculum improvement study. *School Science and Mathematics, 73*(4), 291-318.

Rowe, M.B. (1973). *Teaching science as continuous inquiry.* New York: McGraw Hill.

Shulman, L. (1986). Those who understand: Knowledge growth in teaching. *Educational Researcher, 15*(2), 4-14.

Shulman, L.S. (1987). Knowledge and teaching: foundations of new reform. *Harvard Educational Review, 57,* 1-22.

Sowell, E.J. (1987). Developmental versus practical lessons in the primary grades. *Arithmetic Teacher, 34*(7), 6-8.

CHAPTER TWO

INTRODUCTORY CASE STUDY

CASE STUDY 2-1

SHOULD ELEMENTARY SCHOOLS TEACH ABOUT SEX?

Tawnya Jackson, a former middle school social studies teacher and current President of the Summerset Township School Board has a problem. There have been strong protests in recent weeks over the new fifth grade health curriculum which contains materials on human reproduction and related issues. The protests have been organized principally by Reverend Joseph Smith, the pastor of the Church of the Holy Sepulcher, a small Protestant church in the community. Tonight there will be a public hearing before the Summerset School Board, and she expects a very lively and emotional gathering. Tawnya plans to listen carefully to the presentations made by the townspeople and make a decision based upon the arguments, free from political considerations.

That evening she was not disappointed, the interaction was lively and often passionate. To enter the school cafeteria where the meeting was to take place, Tawnya had to pass through a small crowd of shouting, placard toting people. During the proceedings she took notes of the important points made by each speaker and afterward carefully amended and added to them from her memory, always attempting to be objective and unbiased.

Tawnya's Notes:

Reverend Smith, Pastor, The Church of the Holy Sepulcher — Eleven year old children should not be exposed to issues of sex; sex education will promote curiosity and experimenting; the church and family should be the children's sources of information on these issues; quotes from the scriptures; presents a petition with 300 signatures.

Mrs. Sylvia Mulfoot, a member of Rev. Smith's congregation — repeated many of Rev. Smith's points; presented examples from newspapers and magazines of children being negatively influenced by the media.

Dr. Hyatt Gene, M.D., Pediatrician, parent and member of the community

—cites medical and lay literature concerning the need for sex education for elementary aged children; many pregnancies of ten and eleven year olds; increasing incidents of v.d. in this age group; danger of AIDS transmission; stated education of these young children about these dangers was urgent.

Mrs. Hilda Gavel, President of the middle school Parent-Teachers Association — as a parent she supports the sex education program; many parents do not take the time or see the need to inform their children about such things when they are young; the increase in pre-teen pregnancies shows the churches and homes are not doing the job needed; reads a resolution of the PTA Executive Committee which supports the sex education components in the fifth grade program.

Ms. Victoria Eran, fifth grade teacher in the middle school — worries about teaching the curriculum in question; repercussions, backlash, teacher liability, tenure; Can the topics be taught properly? Are materials available?

Mr. Frank Workman, community resident — If you lived in my area you would see the need for this sex education program; children, young children, walking around pregnant, some acting as prostitutes.

Dr. Arnold Reason, Professor at the Community College — Where is the evidence that all of this education works? Religious issues aside, we know that teaching about drugs sometimes increases drug experimentation; this could possibly increase sexual promiscuity among our young children. Any Board Member that votes for this curriculum will not get my vote in the next election.

There were a number of other speakers, but Tawnya found them to be repetitious, offering little light but considerable heat on the subject.

WHAT IS YOUR DECISION?
WHAT WOULD YOU DO IF YOU WERE TAWNYA?

Is there a real problem? Should the school system get involved with the issue? Are such issues decided upon their merits or is political pressure a factor? In general are schools a proper place to deal with community issues?

CHAPTER TWO

EDUCATIONAL GOALS AND OBJECTIVES FOR EFFECTIVE TEACHING

"Society undergoes continual changes; ... it acquires new arts and loses old instincts."

-Emerson

GOAL:

After reading this chapter the reader should value educational planning and objectives.

OBJECTIVES:

After studying this chapter the reader will be able to:

1. discuss the dynamic nature of the development of school programs,
2. state a rationale for the need for educational goals and objectives,
3. list the parts of the formal objective,
4. write a formal objective when given an informal objective,
5. list and describe the three taxonomic domains with all subparts and
6. write informal objectives in a variety of levels for each taxonomy.

INTRODUCTION

"LEGISLATURE ORDERS SCHOOLS TO TEACH AMERICANISM"
"SCHOOL ADVISORY COMMITTEE URGES A RETURN TO BASICS"
"GUNSHOTS MAR THE OPENING OF SCHOOLS"
"COMPLY WITH TITLE IX OR LOSE $ FED TELLS SCHOOLS"

Headlines such as these appear almost daily in newspapers across America. They express the intense interest that Americans have in the operation of their public schools. Less sensational, but just as important in shaping the curricula of the public schools are secondary headings of articles of local interest, such as: "Parents Demand Class Sizes Be Reduced at Central Middle School" or "State Testing Program Takes Effect In September." In print and electronic media the constant stream of commentary on the affairs of public education is but a continuation of the historic importance of schools in American society. The tone of many of the headlines indicates also that the American public is not merely a passive user of public education, but an active shaper of policy in educational matters. School programs in this country are considered by many to be the direct products of the cross currents of public concern and actions.

THE CONFLUENCE OF FORCES

Instructional programs used to teach students in the public schools are developed from educational goals set by public policy-making bodies, chiefly state legislatures and local boards of education. Public policy related to education grows from the complex interaction of a wide variety of forces that exist in a democracy (see Figure and Table 2.1). These forces represent the historical experience of the nation's people.

The analogy of the model is one of separate streams of social forces, each flowing from its headwater to join with other streams to create a river of public policy. Public educational policy leads to the creation of educational goals and objectives, and ultimately to the development and implementation of school programs. In the Confluence of Forces Model, the headwaters of the various streams that influence public policy are fed by the showers of values and beliefs that shape the nature and energy levels of the various social forces. At the confluence of these streams, there occurs a turbulent mixing of all these forces, each exerting influence in proportion to its energy as it empties into the confluence. Emerging from the confluence is a stream of public policy created by governmental bodies, local, state and federal, which define the purpose and direction of public education. According to the model it is easy to extrapolate that policy regarding public education is not a final product, but is a dynamic process, continually affected by changes in relative energy levels of the various streams that feed into the confluence. As the public policy stream feeds into a second confluence basin, it is joined by streams representing the forces of professional education, those of educational research, learning theory, and instructional methods. These pedagogical forces have the result of turning public policy statements into educational goals, then into objectives, and finally into complete instructional programs. Thus, programs that exist in the public schools are the end products of a complex, dynamic, and often turbulent process that is affected by all society's past and present forces. School programs are not the seemingly placid and static entities that they appear to be in the minds of many.

Table 2.1
FORCES THAT SHAPE SCHOOL PROGRAMS:
SOME EXAMPLES

Force	Examples of Influences
Subject Matter	Traditional subject matter such as mathematics, language, science, and social science have been a stabilizing force.
History	Colonial experiences and democratic traditions have resulted in free, universal, and compulsory education; comprehensive high schools, vocational education, non-traditional subjects.
Pressure Groups	Special interest groups have continuously affected issues of religion, sex education, economic and political education; in more isolated instances nearly every facet of schooling may be influenced by such groups, i.e., "back to basics"; adding chorus, band, sports, school calendars, etc.
Local School Boards	Local school boards have generally lost much of their historical power to operate the nation's schools as state and national governments and various pressure groups have increased their influence.
State Governments	Centralized authority of many states' educational systems has increased. Some examples are: state testing programs for students and teachers, mandated courses and programs, funding decisions affecting school programs, etc.
Federal Government	From a base of negligible influence in the nation's schools in 1950, the federal government has, through funding programs, extended its powers over local school authorities. Examples are: programs for the education of migrant children, low socioeconomic group children, exceptional children, female and other minority children, school subjects such as science, mathematics, computer education, and others.

Confluence of Forces Model for the Development of Educational Programs

Table 2.1 contains a brief list of examples of ways in which various forces have shaped school programs in the United States. Although the purpose of this discussion is only to provide an overview of the basic concept of the dynamics of school program development, it may be of interest to discuss some of the examples in the chart as well as any others that might be cited.

SELF CHECK FOR OBJECTIVE ONE

CAN YOU: Discuss orally or in writing the dynamic nature of school programs citing the major forces that affect them and examples of the changes these forces have caused?

The Development of Programs in the American School System

The Confluence of Forces model (figure 2.1) illustrates the complex and dynamic nature of the process whereby programs and curricula are generated for the schools of the United States of America, a process which is unique to the American experience. Historically, the education of the country's youth has been primarily the responsibility of the individual states. And the states for much of this country's history, while assuming some responsibility for the funding of the educational systems in the cities, towns, townships and counties left much of the actual operation of the schools to the local school boards. But over the nearly four centuries of the American experience, starting with the earliest days of the first pilgrim settlement in Massachusetts, the forces of an open democratic process have rendered constant change in the educational systems of the country and caused the creation of an educational institution which is unique in all of the world. Because of the dynamic nature of the democratic process, the schools have been responsive to the needs of local, state, and federal governments and to the wishes of the citizens.

According to the Confluence of Forces model the process of creating school programs begins with the wishes of the people. And since our society has in its history undergone many swings and shifts in the mood of its people on various issues, it follows that school programs have changed constantly also. Table 2.1 provides examples of some of the forces that have affected the nature of what is taught in our schools. One can use the recent experience in this country with the AIDS and teenage pregnancy issues to apply to the Confluence model to serve as an illustration of the shifting values and changing needs of our society and how they affect the acceptance of sex education in the public schools. The tremendous impact of these problems has come to overshadow the concerns and influence of the traditional conservative pressure groups at all levels of public policy making, and for the first time in at least several decades the inclusion of sex education in the school curriculum is not only permitted but mandated. School programs in sex education grew out of the dynamic, democratic process that established public policy and the concomitant societal goals.

Educators have worked hard in the recent past and are still working to translate the societal goals into educational goals and programs. At this stage in the development of school programs, educators apply their knowledge of child development, learning theory, educational research, and teaching methods to create the daily activities which are designed to satisfy the requirements of the variously stated societal goals.

At this time it might be good to take a look at how educators create educational goals and objectives and turn them into school programs.

FIGURE 2.1
CONFLUENCE OF FORCES

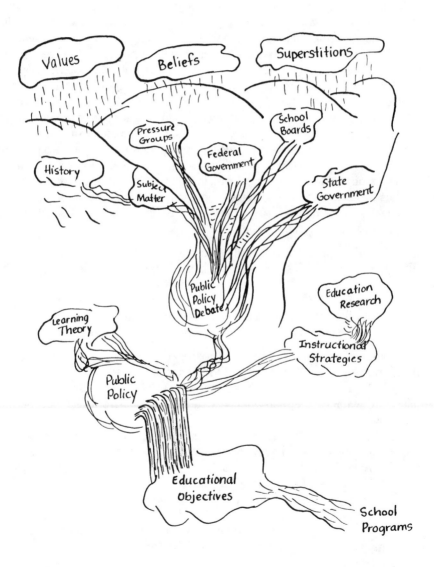

EDUCATIONAL GOALS

According to the Confluence of Forces model, public policy as defined by governmental bodies results in the creation of societal goals. From public policy and societal goals educators create educational goals. An illustration of a societal goal is "citizens should be literate." An educational goal which flows from this societal goal is "students will understand and use language appropriately."

Although both societal and educational goals are to be valued, neither can be directly used when teaching a group of students a specific set of skills. Even the more specific educational goals are too general to be useful to teachers on a day to day basis. If either of these types of goals were used as the basis for teaching a lesson it is likely that neither the teacher nor the student would know specifically what was to be accomplished as the result of a given hour of instruction. It is important for a teacher to know exactly where she and the students are going during each class period. Specific statements on the desired learning outcome of students that is to result from a lesson are called objectives. For the previously stated educational goal we can write objectives such as: (1) students will dictate grammatically correct sentences and (2) students will determine the main idea stated in a paragraph. For each of these objectives there is a stated or implied observable means of evaluating the learning outcomes. An example of a hierarchy of societal goals, educational goals and objectives is:

SOCIETAL GOAL: Citizens will be literate, one of many societal goals.
EDUCATIONAL GOAL: Students will understand and use language appro-
priately.
OBJECTIVES: Students will dictate grammatically correct sentences. And, students will determine the main idea stated in a paragraph (two examples of many possible objectives).

From these examples you can see how goal/objective statements progress from the very general societal goal to the specific objective.

A fable from Robert Mager's book *Preparing Instructional Objectives* illustrates what can happen when teachers do not plan from a base of specific objectives.

Once upon a time a Sea Horse gathered up his seven pieces of eight and cantered out to find his fortune. Before he had traveled very far he met an Eel, who said,

"Psst. Hey, bud. Where 'ya goin'?"

"I'm going out to find my fortune," replied the Sea Horse, proudly.

"You're in luck," said the Eel. "For four pieces of eight you can have this speedy flipper, and you'll be able to get there a lot faster."

"Gee, that's swell," said the Sea Horse, and paid the money and put on the flipper and slithered off at twice the speed. Soon he came upon a Sponge who said,   "Psst. Hey, bud. Where 'ya goin'?"

"I'm going out to find my fortune," replied the Sea Horse.

"You're in luck," said the Sponge. "For a small fee I will let you have this jet-propelled scooter so that you will be able to travel a lot faster."

So the Sea Horse bought the scooter with his remaining money and went zooming through the sea five times as fast. Soon he came upon a shark, who said,   "Psst. Hey, Bud. Where 'ya goin'?"

"I'm going out to find my fortune," replied the Sea Horse.

"You're in luck. If you'll take this short cut," said the Shark, pointing to his open mouth, "you'll save yourself a lot of time."

"Gee, thanks," said the Sea Horse, and zoomed off into the interior of the Shark, there to be devoured.

The moral of this fable is that if you're not sure where you're going, you're likely to end up someplace else — and not even know it.

Mager's seahorse fable suggests one of the repercussions of teachers not knowing where they are going when they begin a lesson. In another analogy, if goals are like destinations when traveling by automobile, ("I'm going to Atlanta") then objectives are the mileposts along the interstate highway that let the driver know exactly how far he has come and how far he has to go.

For a number of reasons objectives have found a prominent place in the daily lives of classroom teachers. Some of these are:

1. The most appealing reason to teachers is that objectives provide a basis for their teaching direction.
2. Another appealing reason is that an objective provides a firm basis for evaluation of student performances.
3. Teachers can use student performance in relation to an objective as a measure of teacher effectiveness.
4. A reason which appeals to students is that an objective, if communicated to them, gives them a sense of direction.
5. Students can assess their success through a comparison of the objective and the result of their work.
6. Principals who must evaluate the performance of teachers have the hard data of the objective itself as well as a record of the students' performance. This is one aspect of teacher evaluation.
7. Objectives, if written in advance, are helpful to substitute teachers who must cause as little disruption as possible in student learning when teaching in place of the assigned teacher.

SELF CHECK FOR OBJECTIVE TWO

CAN YOU: state a rationale for the need for educational goals and objectives?

American schools are the product of a dynamic process which reflects the energy of a variety of groups and individuals. As such, the schools change as the needs of society change. The job of the educator is to bring society's goals to fruition through the development of school programs and classroom curricula.

WRITING OBJECTIVES

Formal and informal objectives

The most common form of objectives used in teachers' plan books and publishers' and school systems' curriculum frameworks is the simple statement of the desired learning outcomes typified by the example: "Students will dictate grammatically correct sentences." When used in the context of a particular classroom, such an objective is sufficiently specific to serve as a guide for the teacher when planning and evaluating learning outcomes. Simple statements of desired student learning outcomes imply, but don't specifically mention, certain factors related to student performance such as: the student's grade level, the level of expectation of the teacher, and the conditions under which students are to perform the desired behavior. Objectives that contain all four parameters will be called formal objectives. We will briefly examine the nature of formal objectives so you know which elements are implied when you read the more commonly used informal objective statement.

Formal objectives.

They are written in four parts:

1. The person who is the learner must be named. Illustrations of learner identifications are third grade physical education students, fifth grade art students and seventh grade mathematics students.
2. The expected behavior of the learner must be indicated. Illustrations of expected behaviors are throwing (a ball), drawing a picture, and solving a problem.
3. A criterion for acceptable performance must be stated. The following criteria may be used: (throwing a ball) ten feet without hitting the floor, (drawing a face) with two eyes pictured, and (solving) without error.
4. The conditions which the learner will encounter must be indicated. Illustrations are: given a basketball, on completion of a sketching lesson, and given a pair of two digit numbers which do not require regrouping.

As stated above the learner must be named. The learner may be a particular individual such as Susan or Elvey. Or the learner may be a group if the objective is a whole group objective. Illustrations of whole group learners are social studies students, or second grade reading students. When individualized instruction is being used, the learner is specifically identified if possible.

Since observable behaviors are required by objectives, verbs that indicate such behaviors must be used. Students in school are frequently required to indicate learning outcomes by performing one of the following actions:

> write,
> choose,
> throw,
> find,
> solve,
> match, and
> evaluate in writing.

Each of these requirements is an observable behavior; each uses a verb. Verbs are to be used to indicate an expected student performance. Illustrations of words to be avoided when indicating student performance are: understand, know, appreciate, and believe. These words do not communicate directly observable behaviors.

If a specific performance is the desired outcome of a formal objective, the quality of that performance should be evaluated. A criterion for acceptable performance must be stated in each formal objective. The criterion will be stated in such a manner to indicate an expected minimum performance. Typical criteria are:

> "at least 80%" and
> "two feet high"

The condition of a formal objective describes the circumstances of the behavior and the restrictions that will be imposed. Some examples of conditions are:

"given 20 spelling words,"
"without the use of a map," and
"using the metric system."

A well written formal objective contains the four elements: the learner, an observable behavior, criterion of acceptable performance, and the conditions under which the learner will demonstrate the desired behavior. As mentioned earlier, although not specifically stated, the same elements are implied by the more simply written informal objective.

The following are illustrations of formal objectives:

1. Given 15 words the fifth grade student will place them in alphabetical order within five minutes without error.
2. The third grade student will use a period to punctuate all simple declarative sentences when given a ten sentence sample.

SELF CHECK FOR OBJECTIVE THREE

CAN YOU: A. identify the learner from the list below:
   fifth graders
   a computer
   teachers in Lake School
   list
   confer
   Jane

B. identify "action" verbs from the list below:
   list
   know
   identify
   distinguish
   like
   understand
   learn
   describe
   appreciate

C. identify appropriately written conditions from the list below:
   given tools
   within the semester
   given 20 drawings
   without aid of...

D. choose criteria of acceptable performance from the following:
   name all...
   solve without error...

80% of...
within 15 minutes without error
E. list five learners excluding those named in this chapter?
F. name five verbs not named in this chapter?
G. create five conditions not in this chapter?
H. name five criteria for acceptable performance not named in this chapter?
I. critique each of the objectives below. Be certain that each one has four parts, appropriately written.

1. given five addition problems the student will solve each without error.
2. given 20 words on the Thursday pretest each student will spell at least 15 correctly. The words will be taken from the class spelling book.
3. each seventh grade student will draw a map of his or her neighborhood (four blocks in every direction from their house). Every street, school, church, store and club should be included. Graph paper should be used.
4. given ten tries the second grade music student will identify pitch relationships as higher, lower or the same in at least eight.
5. the physical education student will bounce the basket-ball ten times in succession from three instructor selected positions.

J. If any of the objectives above did not have four parts, rewrite them so that all parts are present.

Informal objectives.

After examining and writing formal objectives the economy of using the informal objective may be appreciated. The informal objective, "students will solve simple equations," which might appear in your lesson plan book might mean, "Eighth grade students, when given twenty simple equations, will correctly solve a minimum of fifteen with no student solving fewer than twelve." Remember, all four parts of the formal objective are implied in the informal objective. Informal objectives are statements of observable student behavior typically found in the four part formal objective.

Some other examples of informal objectives are:
The students will:
1. identify facts and propaganda,
2. write grammatically correct sentences,
3. demonstrate knowledge of the rules of kickball,
4. write a poem and
5. construct a salt map model.

In the literature and workplace of education informal objectives are also called teaching objectives, planning objectives or behavioral objectives.

SELF CHECK FOR OBJECTIVE FOUR
CAN YOU: write a formal objective for content of your choosing for each of the following informal objectives?

1. Students will solve two digit addition problems.
2. Students will identify the meanings of regular plural nouns.
3. Students will demonstrate the ability to write a properly composed paragraph.

CLASSIFYING OBJECTIVES

Systems have been developed to classify educational objectives into categories according to certain domains and by levels of complexity. The three most commonly expressed domains are the cognitive domain suggested by the work of Benjamin Bloom, the affective from the work of David Kratwahl, the psychomotor as created by Anita Harrow.

The Cognitive Domain

Table 2.2 below summarizes Bloom's cognitive domain by defining each of its component categories and suggesting some action verbs that might be used to write objectives. Examine the cognitive domain while noting its hierarchical nature; each level in the domain is believed to encompass more complex cognitive skills than the preceding one.

The Affective Domain

The affective domain deals with student attitudes. The majority of school time is spent in instruction which emphasizes the cognitive domain. This is particularly true of instruction at the middle and secondary school levels. Therefore, it would be accurate to state that affective objectives exist less frequently in the school setting than cognitive objectives. However, most teachers strive each day to help students to develop positive attitudes and a consistent and viable system of values. Teaching the affective domain is an important function of education today.

The Affective Domain is organized into five parts in a hierarchy of complexity, from the least to the most complex. It is assumed that for a person to engage the more complex behaviors he should have acquired the less complex. This means, for example, that before a person can integrate a system of values into a personal philosophy, awareness of those values and willingness to integrate them must be present. Table 2.3 presents the affective domain by defining each level and listing verbs which may be used to write objectives.

Table 2.2
THE COGNITIVE DOMAIN

Knowledge	The ability to recall or bring to mind appropriate content. Verbs: list, name, select, identify, match, etc.
Comprehension	The ability to use the ideas of a communication without having to relate it to other ideas. Verbs: translate, classify, define in his own words, give examples, explain, rewrite, etc.
Application	Taking a new idea and using it in a new situation. Verbs: use, employ, solve, construct, apply, demonstrate, etc.
Analysis	Breaking the whole into its components while understanding the relationships of the parts. Verbs: analyze, separate, distinguish, infer, see relationships, compare, contrast, etc.
Synthesis	Putting together parts into a new whole. Verbs: construct, organize, perform, compose, write, design, create, originate, etc.
Evaluation	Making judgments using criteria. Verbs: tolerate, value, judge, choose, criticize, etc.

The six informal objectives below use appropriate verbs for each level of the Cognitive Domain.

Knowledge:	Students will list the seasons in order.
Comprehension:	Students will define "justice" in their own words.
Application:	Students will use a math formula to solve a problem.
Analysis:	Students will reorder the sentences to form a proper paragraph.
Synthesis:	Students will construct an hypothesis that explains the observed phenomenon.
Evaluation:	Students will criticize a poem using accepted criteria.

Teachers and curriculum writers often use the categories of the cognitive domain to create depth and breadth of instruction as they strive to challenge students at all levels of their intellect.

Table 2.3
THE AFFECTIVE DOMAIN

Receiving	Becoming aware of and open to specific stimuli. Verbs: show awareness, show tolerance, indicate acceptance, indicate alertness, etc.
Responding	The student passively or willingly responds to stimuli. Verbs: comply, obey, show eagerness, volunteer, show pleasure, answer a question, etc.
Valuing	Recognizing a value, preferring a value and committing to a value. Verbs: shows preferences, favors a position, expresses a strong judgement, shows loyalty to, etc.
Organization	Identification of values and development of a value system. Verbs: criticizes, judges, weighs alternatives, adopts a course of action, chooses a position, etc.
A Value Complex	A philosophy of life by which one behaves.

By using appropriate verbs one may write informal objectives for each of the levels of the Affective Domain. Illustrations are below:

Receiving:	The student will show awareness of class proceedings.
Responding:	The student will willingly answer questions.
Valuing:	The student will express strong opinions on issues under discussion.
Organization:	The student will criticize arguments and positions presented in class.
Value Complex:	The student will demonstrate a philosophy of life by the consistency of his daily actions.

Though less frequently utilized in the daily activities of teachers, the affective domain is a valuable system when considerations of student attitude, feeling, and self concept are included in the instructional plan.

The Psychomotor Domain

Table 2.4 illustrates the Psychomotor Domain as it was defined by Anita Harrow. The levels of movement in the domain are hierarchical starting with the simple reflexive movement of a newborn infant. Examine the levels of the domain and consider how objectives may be written for each.

Table 2.4
THE PSYCHOMOTOR DOMAIN

Reflex Movements	Reflex movements such as grasp. Verbs: grasp, follow a light with the eyes, turn to a sound, etc.
Basic-Fundamental Movement	An extension of the reflex level, locomotor and non-locomotor, walk, stoop, crawl, etc.
Perceptual Abilities	The ability to discriminate visually, kinesthetically, auditorily and tactility and demonstrate coordination abilities. Verbs: hop, skip, jump, catch, etc.
Physical Ability	Abilities such as endurance, strength, flexibility, agility, dexterity and reaction-response time. Verbs: run, dance, dodge, walk three miles, etc.
Skilled Movement	Simple, compound and complex movements. Verbs: punt, hit a ball, dive, perform tumbling stunts, etc.
Non-Discursive Communication	Posture, gestures and facial expression and aesthetic and creative movement. Verbs: express emotions, gesture, pantomime, etc.

Examples of objectives written at each of the levels of the psychomotor domain are:

Reflex Movement	The child will turn his head toward a loud sound.
Basic-Fundamental Movement	The child will crawl on hands and knees.
Perceptual Abilities	The child will walk a balance beam.
Physical Abilities	The learner will catch a volleyball that is thrown.
Skilled Movement	The learner will dance a demonstrated routine.
Non-Discursive Communication	The learner will pantomime a work given to him by the teacher.

The most frequent uses in education of the levels of the psychomotor domain are made in physical education instruction and the development of perceptual and motor skills of young children.

SELF CHECK FOR OBJECTIVES FIVE AND SIX

CAN YOU: list and describe the three taxonomic domains with all subparts? write informal objectives in a variety of levels for each taxonomy?

SUMMARY

This chapter has presented a rationale and method for the use of objectives when planning. Although educational goals are a necessary part of the planning process, they are general statements which describe expected student behavior. Therefore, goals should be restated more specifically as objectives. And, objectives can be written in a formal style with four components or informally with a verb phrase only. We also described three types of student behavior called domains. Each of the three domains was subdivided so that expected student behavior could be more specifically described.

We believe that effective unit and lesson planning depends on clear thinking by teachers. Properly written objectives express clear teacher thinking. The next chapter describes effective unit and daily lesson planning using properly written objectives.

ACTIVITIES

1. Discuss the effects of the following forces on educational policies and school programs: television, microcomputers, religion, teacher unions, sex education, and instruction in basic skills.

    Name and discuss how any forces not mentioned in Item 1 or elsewhere in the chapter are influencing school programs.

2. Try to trace to its antecedent events in educational history: open space school building (where several classes of children occupy a single large room or pod), the middle school movement, work-study programs in the high schools, graduation robes and other trappings, grades (A, B, C, etc.), spelling contests, etc.

3. Using any level of a student literature textbook write one objective at each cognitive domain level.

4. Write an objective for each level of the affective domain using the content of history.

5. Write an objective for each of the upper five levels of the psychomotor domain. Use any content area.

BIBLIOGRAPHY

Bloom, B., Engelhart, M., Hill, W., Furst, G. & Krathwohl, D. (1968). *Taxonomy of educational objective, the classification of educational objectives handbook I: cognitive domain.* New York: David McKay.

Emmer, E.T. (1986). Academic activities and tasks in first year teachers' classes. *Teaching and Teacher Education, 2*(3), 229-244.

Harrow, A.J. (1971). *A Taxonomy of the psychomotor domain.* New York: David McKay.

Henderson, J.G. (1989). Positioned positive practice: a curriculum discussion. *Journal of Teacher Education, 40*(2), 10-14.

Knoop, R. (1986). Setting and achieving objectives. *Education Canada, 26*(4), 15.

Krathwohl, D., Bloom, B., & Masia, B. (1967). *Taxonomy of educational objectives, the classification of educational goals - handbook II: Affective domain.* New York: David McKay.

Mager, R. (1962). *Preparing instructional objectives.* Palo Alto: Fearon.

Marlowe, J. (1983). Before retooling your curriculum, determine what your kids must do. *American School Board Journal, 170*(12), 49.

Schug, M.C. (1989). Why teach social studies? Interviews with elementary teachers. *Social Studies, 80*(2), 73-77.

Yatvin, J. (1984). Two muddled recommendations from a nation at risk. *Principal, 63*(4), 41-43.

CHAPTER THREE

INTRODUCTORY CASE STUDY

CASE STUDY 3.1

HELP ME, PLEASE

Suzanna Frake is a friend and a fellow student teacher at Young Elementary School. She is in trouble with her university coordinator and the school principal who are not happy with the job she is doing in the classroom. A note from the school principal reads "You need to improve your discipline! Your organization and planning for instruction could be more creative." Suzanna is very upset as the two of you review her plan book in an attempt to help her improve her instruction. She has been assigned to teach Social Studies to four third grade classes in a departmentalized grade level.

Suzanna's Plan Book:

THIRD GRADE SOCIAL STUDIES
Topic: The People and Places of Mexico, Our Neighbor to the South.

Monday
Introduction. Show pictures, a sombrero and leather purse from Mexico. Take turns reading the chapter. Homework: Answer questions one through five at the end of the chapter.

Tuesday
Finish taking turns reading the chapter. Seatwork: complete a puzzle which requires knowledge of facts from the chapter. Homework: questions six through twelve at the end of the chapter.

Wednesday
Library day. Assign a report, 250 words on Mexico. Students will use classtime to locate information.

Thursday:
Students will read their reports in class. They will be graded on their oral presentations. Review for a test to be taken tomorrow.

Friday:
Test, 20 fill-in-the-blank items. Film: Acapulco, A Vacation Paradise

WHAT IS YOUR DECISION?

What do you suggest to help Suzanna do a better job?
Is planning a factor in creating her dilemma?
Make specific suggestions.

CHAPTER THREE
PLANNING FOR EFFECTIVE TEACHING

"A human being is not in any proper sense a human being until he is educated."

-H. Mann

GOALS

After reading this chapter the student will understand and appreciate planning for teaching.

OBJECTIVES

After reading this chapter students will
1. discuss the importance of planning for instruction,
2. list and describe the parts of a resource unit,
3. write a resource unit,
4. describe the nature of a unit plan,
5. create a unit plan,
6. list and describe the parts of a daily lesson plan,
7. write an acceptable daily lesson plan,
8. describe the nature and purpose of an integrated curriculum resource unit, and unit plan,
9. create an integrated curriculum resource unit and unit plan and
10. using examples, describe an interdisciplinary plan.

Now that you know how to write instructional objectives at the various levels of the cognitive, affective, and psychomotor domains, it is time to examine procedures for constructing unit and daily lesson plans.

PLANNING AND THE TEACHER

"Teaching is fun. It's writing the lesson plans that I hate."

"Teachers don't really write detailed lesson plans; they just write page numbers of the textbook."

"It takes more time to write plans than it does to teach."

School principals and college instructors of preservice teachers have heard laments such as these a great number of times. It seems that many people like to teach, but few enjoy the planning that is necessary for effective teaching.

When considering the issue of planning for teaching let's accept a few frequently made statements. Planning is for most people not as much fun as teaching, although many teachers like the interaction of cooperative planning with colleagues. Some teachers appear to teach effectively in the classroom without much apparent lesson planning. And some teachers do not write detailed, extensive lesson plans. However, the research on effective teaching is clear; careful planning for instruction is highly correlated with the success of students in classrooms. Do you wonder how much more effective non-planning teachers could be if they planned their lessons?

Elementary and middle schools have programs that do not require the type of planning that is common to other programs. A complete management system for reading predetermines all skill objectives that are to be taught, supplies all the materials both primary and remedial that are necessary for instruction, and provides for evaluation of the learning of each student. This requires that a teacher perform as a technician. A technician implements a curriculum exactly as it is written, managing the grouping of students, sequencing of learning activities and implementing testing. Operating effectively as a technician in a highly individualized curriculum is no easy task. This role requires the teacher to be highly skilled in such areas as classroom management, control of discipline, handling materials, maintaining an academic focus, and maintaining a warm atmosphere in the classroom. The planning of the teacher-technician centers on the small details of managing an intact system. This type of teaching requires no less attention to planning than the most open of curricula.

Many school program curricula are less structured than a formal management system, but do specify the topics, concepts and skills to be taught and textbooks and other materials to be used. Teachers in these situations are free to modify, add to, and in some instances delete small parts of the program. They may be considered manipulators of the curriculum. The teacher-manipulator is required to do more creative planning than the technician while total planning time may not be greater.

In some curriculum areas of most schools and in all curriculum areas of other schools, a teacher is free to create a program, to plan it from beginning to end, from formulating goals to evaluating the learning outcomes. The teacher who creates a unique program may be thought to be operating as a teacher-synthesizer of the curriculum. Teachers operating at all three levels of planning—technician, manipulator, and synthesizer—must take time to plan if they are to maximize their teaching effectiveness. In this chapter we will consider curriculum planning at the level of the synthesizer with the belief that all teachers at some time will have the opportunity to synthesize—plan a curriculum.

Teachers find that planning together is a professionally rewarding experience. In addition to the positive feeling that planning together promotes among teachers, students benefit from their cooperative efforts. This process helps teachers to meet the needs of a wide variety of students in their classrooms.

SELF CHECK FOR OBJECTIVE ONE

CAN YOU: discuss the importance of planning for instruction?

THE RESOURCE UNIT

The most common type of plan of the teacher operating at the level of synthesizer is the resource unit. The resource unit provides the fabric of the curriculum. The resource unit is the substance from which daily lesson plans may be developed. Some characteristics of a good resource unit are below.

The resource unit should
a) establish and maintain feelings of curiosity and a need to know more about the topic by students,
b) include learning experiences appropriate for all students,
c) provide a variety of learning which is cognitive, affective and psycho-motor,
d) help students to grow intellectually and to develop habits of indepen-dent learning and problem solving,
e) introduce learners to new resources and methods of learning,
f) provide for closure of the learning experience,
g) be part of an accepted course of study and
h) provide experiences that help students develop positive self concepts and attitudes toward school.

Procedures for Organizing the Resource Unit

A resource unit should encompass a broad range of goals and objectives. The cognitive objectives should range from knowledge to evaluation. The complete resource unit will also include activities aimed at developing students' attitudes and psychomotor skills.

Learning activities present in a unit plan should be designed to aid students to develop desired behaviors. Activities that are suitable for development of low level cognitive skills in knowledge and comprehension levels might appear to be different in structure from those used to develop skills at analysis and synthesis levels. For instance, the learning activity designed to satisfy the goal, "The student will demonstrate a knowledge of the major battles of the War for Independence" might appropriately be lecture, textbook reading assignments and other forms of direct instruction. However, if the teacher wishes to emphasize the affective goal, "Students will demonstrate an appreciation of the heroism of the colonial patriots in the War for Independence," drama groups might be organized to reenact the deeds of Paul Revere or Tom Paine. In most instances a unit plan will use learning activities that address a variety of levels of cognitive objectives as well as the affective and psychomotor domains.

A completed resource unit should include the following:

1. a title,
2. a rationale which states why the unit is to be taught,
3. a list of all goals of the unit,
4. and separately under each activity or activity cluster the following:
   a) appropriate goals,
   b) objectives,
   c) a description of each learning activity,
   d) a list of resources available to teach the units such as books, films, filmstrips, field trips, community resources, etc. and
   e) a statement of evaluation procedures.

SELF CHECK FOR OBJECTIVE TWO

CAN YOU: list and describe the parts of a resource unit?

The following is a brief illustration of a resource unit plan.

Title: An eighth grade resource unit on the American War for Independence.

Rationale: No event is as descriptive of the character of the American nation as its struggle against great odds to achieve its independence. Children should know the circumstances that preceded the War for Independence, and the events and leaders that were part of the struggle of a colonial people to be free. With this knowledge they can take pride in their nation's heritage and develop an appreciation of America as a nation and as a people.

Goals:

1. Students will understand the events and issues that led to the War for Independence.
2. Students will understand major military events that took place during the War for Independence.
3. Students will appreciate the sacrifices and heroism of the leaders of the War for Independence.

Activity cluster one:

Goal One: Students will understand the events and issues that led to the War for Independence.

Objective A: Students will list 15 events and five issues that preceded the War for Independence.

Objective B: Students will write a short paragraph about the pre-war lives of Thomas Paine, Patrick Henry, John Adams and John Hancock.

Learning activities:

1. Read chapters ten and eleven in the textbook, *The Story of America.*
2. View film: "The Boston Tea Party" and "The Bold Signature of John Hancock."
3. View sound filmstrips in the series, "The Men of the Continental Congress."
4. Invite a visiting teacher from the historical society to share pertinent materials.
5. Organize group dramatizations of events in the lives of Patrick Henry, Thomas Paine, John Adams, and John Hancock.
6. Write a 250-500 word paper on a subject of the student's choosing using learning resource center materials.

Resources:

Textbook: *The Story of America.*
Library bibliography (see librarian).
Films: "The Boston Tea Party," "Colonial Williamsburg," "The Bold Signature of John Hancock."
Filmstrips: "The Men of the Continental Congress," "The Declaration of Independence."

Methods of evaluation:

1) One thirty item objective test covering the information from the textbook and media presentations.
2) One 250-500 word report on a topic to be selected by the student.
3) Observation of group dramatization of an important pre-revolutionary leader or hero.

Activity cluster two:
Goal Two: Students will understand major military events that took place
during the War for Independence.
Objective A: Students will list the names of ten men and ten events that took
place during the revolutionary war.
Objective B: Students will compare military forces and tactics of the colonial
and British forces in the American War for Independence while
writing a 250 word essay.
Goal Three: Students will appreciate the sacrifices and heroism of the leaders
in the War.
Objective A: Students will write a paragraph describing the personal sacrifices and acts of heroism of three American patriots during the
War for Independence.

Learning activities:
1. Read chapters twelve, thirteen and fourteen in the textbook, *The Story
of America.*
2. Construct a topographical salt or soap map of the battlefield at one of:
Breed's Hill (Bunker Hill), Yorktown, or Trenton. Write a 500 word
report of events that took place before, during, and immediately following the battle.
3. View the films, "The Whites of Their Eyes," "Surrender at Yorktown,"
and "Washington at Valley Forge."
4. Take a field trip to the Revere museum to see the Revolutionary War
collection of military and civilian artifacts.

Resources:
Textbook: *The Story of America.*
Bibliography (See Librarian).
Films: "The Whites of Their Eyes," "Surrender at Yorktown," "Washington
at Valley Forge."
Museum, Colonial Period

Methods of Evaluation:
1. One thirty item objective test covering the information related to the
military campaigns of the War for Independence.
2. One essay test covering specific acts of heroism and sacrifice of American patriots.
3. Teacher's evaluation of one salt or soap map of a Revolutionary War
battleground with a 500 word account of the events before, during, and
immediately following the battle.

SELF CHECK FOR OBJECTIVE THREE

CAN YOU: construct a resource unit?

THE UNIT PLAN

A unit plan is an outline of the day to day activities that a teacher wishes to conduct over a given period of time. Once a resource unit has been created, the task of developing a unit plan is primarily one of selecting goals, objectives, activities, and appropriate teaching methods from the resource unit and fitting them into the daily schedule. Although this step in the long-range planning process appears to be simple, it is very demanding in terms of making judgements about allowing reasonable time allocations for the planned learning activities. It is at this stage in the planning process when you must decide the proper sequence of the learning activities and the number of class periods necessary to achieve the desired objective. Like the taste of fine wine and good cheese your ability to estimate reasonable timeframes for instructional experiences will improve with time. Some insights of those who have undergone the instructional planning process may be of some help.

It is a common tendency of many teachers to plan more learning activities for a given time period than may be accomplished. This is sometimes called overplanning. While teaching a planned unit you will be constantly faced with the decision whether to speed up or slow down the rate of instruction. At times you may be required to decide what activities must be deleted or added. The dilemma of determining the proper coverage of a topic will be one that will face you nearly every school day. In addition to the problems inherent in establishing the proper instructional schedule, classroom teachers are faced with interruptions in instruction that are outside of their control. Public address announcements may negatively affect instruction on any given day and unscheduled assembly activities often impact long range plans. Inclement weather and epidemics may also wreak havoc with teachers' plans.

But even in the face of all these factors that negatively impact a schedule, it is still necessary to create viable long-range plans and attempt to follow through with them. The necessary bywords of creating and executing instructional plans in the school setting are flexibility and good judgment.

A well conceived instructional plan, modified and restructured as adjustments are required by the events that are part of normal school operation, will produce far superior instruction and student performance than the "hit-or-miss" of unplanned classroom activities. One of the most important attributes a teacher may possess is the ability to adjust and modify instructional plans, always striving to create the best possible learning environment and experiences each day.

SELF CHECK FOR OBJECTIVE FOUR

CAN YOU: describe the nature of a unit plan?

Procedures for Organizing The Unit Plan

As stated earlier, a unit plan for classroom instruction is a day by day outline of goals, objectives and activities which are largely drawn from a previously constructed resource unit. Daily lesson plans are then constructed using the unit plan as a guide. The daily lesson plan, as demonstrated on the following pages, contains specific information concerning teaching methods, materials and procedures required for teaching one day's lesson. Following is an example of one week of a three week long unit on the Revolutionary war. You may wish to join your classmates in constructing the remaining two weeks of the unit. You might note that some assignments made during the first week are to be concluded and brought to closure during the two remaining weeks. Also notice that activities found in the resource unit may be altered as the teacher desires and new activities may be added that are not included in the resource unit.

UNIT PLAN
EIGHTH GRADE AMERICAN HISTORY

Topic: The American War for Independence

Instructional period: Three weeks, 10/3 to 10/22.

Rationale: No event is as descriptive of the character of the American nation as its struggle against great odds to achieve its independence. Children should know the circumstances that preceded the War for Independence, and the events and leaders that were part of the struggle of a colonial people to be free. With this knowledge they can take pride in their nation's heritage and develop an appreciation of America as a nation and as a people. (Note: This rationale was copied directly from the resource unit.)

Week One Goals: Students will understand the events and issues that led to the War for Independence.

Objectives:

Objective A: Students will list ten events and five issues that led to the War for Independence.

Objective B: Students will write an acceptable short paragraph about the prewar lives of each of the following: Thomas Paine, Patrick Henry, Samuel Adams, John Adams, John Hancock and George Washington.

Objective C: Students will draw a map and describe the actions of the Minutemen at the battles of Lexington and Concord.

(Note: Teachers often alter objectives [see objective B] and add objectives [see objective C] as they construct the unit plan.

Outline Week One

MONDAY: Goal One, Objective A
Introduction of unit: Show film, "The Boston Tea Party." Lecture on events and men of prewar colonies, textbook materials, chapters ten and eleven.

TUESDAY: Goal One, Objective B
Assign research reports on patriots; introduce library resources, due Friday of second week.

WEDNESDAY: Goal One, Objective C.
Film, "The Ride of Paul Revere"; Lecture on the Boston Massacre and the battles at Lexington and Concord. Media: Large map of Boston and surroundings; film, "The Ride of Paul Revere."

THURSDAY: Goal One, Objectives A, B, and C.
Debate Tories and Patriots; provide study sheet to aid in the review of events and men important in the prewar colonies.

FRIDAY: Goal One, Objectives A, B, and C.
Read and discuss the Declaration of Independence; quiz, chapters ten and eleven, text, and objectives A, B, and C.

The addition of the plan outline for weeks two and three would complete the construction of the unit plan for the topic, "The American War for Independence." Not shown, but also included in a unit plan is an overall plan for evaluating student achievement which lists all of the factors that are to be evaluated and the weighing of each factor. The methods of evaluation listed in the resource unit serve as the basis of the unit evaluation plan, although this too is often modified by many teachers as they finalize their unit planning. Next we will consider the daily lesson plan.

SELF CHECK FOR OBJECTIVE FIVE

CAN YOU: create a unit plan on a topic of your choice?

THE DAILY LESSON PLAN

Daily lesson plans are written to implement unit plan goals and objectives. A unit goal or objective may require several days of instruction to accomplish the desired level of achievement. Daily lesson plans focus on the details of organization and implementation that will make learning activities successful.

A completed daily lesson plan should contain the following:
1. Topic,
2. Goal statement(s),
3. Objective statement(s),
   a. Concept Objective(s) when appropriate,
   b. Skill/attitude Objective(s) when appropriate,
4. Materials required,

5.   Procedures
a.   set,
b.   lecture outline or questions if the expository method is used,
c.   examples (and non-examples) of concepts,
d.   review/closure/bridge to the next lesson and
e.   evaluation procedures

The following is a sample of a daily lesson plan:

Topic: The War for Independence (grade five)

Goal statement: Students will understand events and issues that led to the War for Independence.

Objectives:

Concept objective 1: Students will write a short paragraph about the pre-war lives of Patrick Henry, Thomas Paine and John Adams.

Attitude objective 1: Students will discuss acts of defiance by groups of people unjustly treated. Two recent acts of civil disobedience should be included.

Materials:
A map of colonial America; filmstrip, "The Boston Tea Party"; and film clips of recent acts of defiance of government.

Procedure:
1.   Review: Review concepts taught in previous lesson, then "today we will..."
2.   Set: Read from Paine, "These are the times that try men's souls..." while in colonial dress.
3.   Lecture; John Adams and the Boston Tea Party.
     Patrick Henry and his political activities.
     Thomas Paine and "Common Sense" and "The Crisis."
4.   Group discussion questions: "Why did the patriots risk their lives to defy the King?" "What would you have done in their places?"
5.   Examples and non-examples: George Washington, Benjamin Franklin, Thomas Jefferson. (Non-example is Benedict Arnold as a traitor.)
6.   Closure:
     a. Review; Restate the contribution of John Adams, Patrick Henry, and Thomas Paine.
     b. Bridge; "Tomorrow we will..."
7.   Evaluation procedures: Oral questions or short quiz and teacher observation of student participation.

Listing appropriate goals and objectives for each daily lesson provides a sense of the relationship of a single day's lesson and the long range plan. The statements of the concepts and skills/attitudes to be dealt with in the daily plan give a focus to the lesson. Those concepts, skills and attitudes represent immediate objectives of the lesson. Several techniques are listed under the procedures heading. Set is the opening, the attention grabber, the motivator. Sometimes this is merely a statement of what is to follow, the subject of the day's lesson. The teacher may say, "today we are going to discuss the patriots of the pre-revolutionary period." The proper design of the lecture outline and delivery is discussed in chapter six and the use of questions in teaching inquiry lessons is discussed in chapters four, five and seven. The introduction of examples and non-examples of the concepts developed in a lesson has been found to aid student understanding as does a summarizing review. With many activities that can occur in the classroom the procedures section will take on many different appearances. At times the teacher is reviewing and drilling, at times giving directions for projects and activities, at other times supervising seatwork activities, and so on. Regardless of the activity it is always a good idea to give examples of desired learning and to review at the conclusion of the lesson.

SELF CHECK FOR OBJECTIVES SIX AND SEVEN

CAN YOU: list and describe the parts of a daily lesson plan?
           write an acceptable daily lesson plan?

PLANNING FOR INTEGRATED CURRICULA

Attempts have been made at all levels of the public school programs to integrate the curricula of two or more subjects. The most frequently publicized integration of curricula in the secondary schools has probably been the combination of mathematics and science, although attempts have been made in other subjects as well. Some efforts have also been made in the secondary schools to integrate the subjects within the fields of science and mathematics that resulted in courses combining, for instance, chemistry and physics and algebra and trigonometry. While here and there across the country there exist teachers, schools and school systems dedicated to the integrated secondary curricula, there appears to be little general movement to break with the traditional subject matter in the secondary schools of the nation.

In the elementary schools the integration of subjects is somewhat commonplace. Pushed for time to include instruction in all of the separate subjects, the elementary teacher must frequently combine instruction in two or more subjects during a single lesson. Whether in the secondary or elementary school, the secret for successfully integrating instruction in multiple subjects is to define the goals and objectives of each subject employed and work to meet them. As each of the activities of the various subjects contributes to an overall lesson plan the traditional boundaries are broken and the children's learning, concepts, skills and attitudes form a unified whole unfettered by the traditional, compartmentalized thinking of the normal curriculum.

SELF CHECK FOR OBJECTIVE EIGHT

CAN YOU: describe the nature and purpose of an integrated curriculum resource unit plan?

Following is one example of an integrated resource unit and unit plan.

PLANNING AN INTEGRATED READING/SCIENCE RESOURCE UNIT FOR THE PRIMARY GRADES

Teachers at the elementary school level who teach all or most of the subject matter areas in the curriculum are often challenged because of time pressures to plan and teach two or more subject matter areas during the same lesson. They integrate the subject matters of multiple subjects to form a single cohesive topic so that they achieve the goals and objectives of each subject. Following are abbreviated examples of a resource unit, a unit plan and a daily lesson plan that utilize the subjects of reading and science to teach selected goals and objectives of each.

Title: A Primary Grade Resource Unit For Reading and Science: "Living Things Around Us."

Rationale: Young children are very curious about the things that are about them in nature. This unit will capitalize on this interest by providing direct experiences with nature to build understandings of the science, concepts and skills while using the vocabulary derived from the experiences along with other materials to build skills in reading comprehension, writing and spelling.

Goals:
1. Students will increase their vocabulary power in the topic of "Living Things Around Us."
2. Students will be able to write simple sentences using the vocabulary acquired in the unit.
3. Students will be able to read experience stories generated from their science experiences.
4. Students will demonstrate the skills of observing, classifying, communicating and inferring.
5. Students will demonstrate an understanding of the concepts of living, non-living, stimulus and response and the life processes of eating, breathing and reproducing.

Activity Cluster One

Goal One: Students will increase their vocabulary power in the topic "Living Things Around Us."

Objective A: Students will recognize and write the vocabulary words derived from the science activities.

Goal Four: Students will demonstrate the skills of observing, classifying, communicating and inferring.

Objective A: During discussions following the activities students will demonstrate the skills listed above.

Goal Five: Students will demonstrate an understanding of the concepts of living, non-living, stimulus and response, and the life processes; eating, breathing and reproducing.

Objective A: During discussion students will demonstrate a knowledge of the concepts listed in Goal Five.

Objective B: Students will demonstrate understanding of the concepts listed in Goal Five by correctly responding to the items on an objective worksheet.

Learning Activities:

1. Plant rye grass and observe the effects of water, sunlight and fertilizer.
2. Construct a hydroponic birdseed germinator and observe the germination of the seeds.
3. "Open up" soaked lima beans and observe the "baby plant" inside.
4. Discuss any of the activities, have students describe their observations, make inferences about those things that are necessary for life and how plants reproduce.
5. Write new vocabulary words on the chalkboard, have students copy the new words on paper.
6. Create simple sentences that represent the students' observations and have students read the statements and relate the sentences to the observations.
7. Have students read trade books on the subject of germination and growth of plants.

Resources:

Readily available materials: ryegrass seed, birdseed, plastic baggies, foam cups, potting soil, etc.

Lined paper on which children copy and write vocabulary words and sentences derived from their experiences.

Trade books from the school library or classroom collection.

Methods of Evaluation:

1. Observation of students during science activities and discussions.
2. Observation of students during the development of the science experience sentences and their reading.
3. Grading students' seatwork, vocabulary words and sentences.
4. Grading a quiz or seatwork assignment that evaluates students' understanding of the vocabulary words and sentences.

Activity Cluster Two:

Goals:

Goal One: Students will increase their vocabulary power in the topic of "Living Things Around Us."

Objective A: Students will correctly copy new vocabulary words and use them in a sentence.

Goal Two: Students will be able to write simple sentences using the vocabulary acquired in the unit.

Objective A: Students will write simple sentences which correctly describe their activities, observations and concepts acquired from the activities.

Goal Three: Students will be able to read experience stories generated from their experiences.

Objective A: Students will read selected experience stories written by students and answer questions that demonstrate comprehension.

Goal Four: Students will demonstrate the skills of observing, classifying, communicating and inferring.

Objective A: During class discussion following science activities students will demonstrate the skills of observing, classifying, communicating and inferring.

Objective B: Students will properly respond to demonstrations or hypothetical situations provided by the teacher, demonstrating their ability to utilize the skills listed in Goal Four.

Goal Five: Students will demonstrate an understanding of the concepts of living, non-living, stimulus response and the life processes— eating, breathing and reproducing.

Objective A: Orally and/or an objective quiz; students will correctly respond to questions related to the concepts listed in Goal Five.

Learning Activities:

1. Set up an aquarium with rocks, castles and other inanimate objects as well as a few guppies and goldfish. Following a period of observation and writing exercises guide the children to form conclusions concerning living and non-living things, the life processes and stimulus and response.
2. Construct a terrarium which contains several types of plants, rocks and other inanimate objects, frogs or chameleons, and insects such as crickets. Observe the terrarium for a period of time and discuss the students' observations while building vocabulary and writing skills. Discuss the concepts listed above which are appropriate to the activities.
3. Have the students read trade books that are related to the activities and concepts.
4. Utilize filmstrips, films and other media appropriate to the activities.

Resources:
1. Glass aquaria or large plastic jars.
2. Gravel, ceramic objects, aquatic plants, guppies and goldfish to build the aquarium.
3. Land plants, rocks and other inanimate objects, insects, frogs, toads, or chameleons, and crickets or cockroaches to build the terrarium.
4. Trade books from the library or classroom collection.

Methods of evaluation:
1. Observation of student performance during the science activities and the discussions.
2. Vocabulary word collections and seatwork.
3. Student experience stories.
4. Objective quiz and/or seatwork related to the concepts listed in Goal Five.

SELF CHECK FOR OBJECTIVE NINE

CAN YOU: write a sample resource unit for an integrated curriculum?

AN INTEGRATED READING AND SCIENCE UNIT PLAN FOR THE PRIMARY GRADES

Following is an abbreviated (one week) unit plan which was structured from a resource unit. Remember, all of the activities in the resource unit need not be utilized in the unit plan and new goals, objectives and activities may be added. The unit plan firms up the decisions as to what to teach and in what order.

Topic: Living Things Around Us, an integrated reading and science unit.

Rationale: Young children have a natural curiosity about the world of nature. Hands-on experiences with reproduction and other life processes may provide a rich source of vocabulary, experience stories and related reading and science skills. This integration of reading and science will make maximum use of available class time.

Week One Goals:
1. Students will increase their vocabulary power in the topic of "Living Things Around Us."
2. Students will be able to write single sentences using vocabulary acquired from their experiences.
3. Students will understand the basic concepts of science related to the week's activities.
4. Students will demonstrate the process skills of observing, communicating and inferring.

Objectives:

Objective A: Students will list new vocabulary words and match the words with their meanings.

Objective B: Students will write one sentence for each new vocabulary word which correctly uses the word in context.

Objective C: Students will state orally and/or in writing that "Plants reproduce from seeds" and "Plants require water and sunlight to grow."

Objective D: During activities with materials students will properly observe, communicate and make inferences.

Outline Week One

MONDAY: Goal One, Objective A; Goal Four, Objective D.
Introduction of the unit. Students will observe, classify, communicate and infer using the "bird seed" activity. They will then plant ryegrass seed in soil contained in foam cups. The vocabulary words "seed," "water," "cup," and "soil" will be introduced during discussion following the activity.

TUESDAY: Goal One, Objective A; Goal Four, Objective D.
Students will observe ryegrass germinators. Add "no change" to their vocabulary lists. Examine open lima beans. Add "baby plant" to the vocabulary lists. They will make inferences about what they expect to happen with the ryegrass.

WEDNESDAY: Goal Two, Objective B.
With students review vocabulary words, create simple sentences that describe the activities of Monday and Tuesday. Students copy the sentences on paper. Use oral drill and seatwork to reinforce knowledge and understanding. Students examine the ryegrass germinators and record their observations.

THURSDAY: Goal One, Objective A; Goal Two, Objective B; Goal Four, Objective D.
Students observe the ryegrass germinators and record their observations. The teacher will introduce any new vocabulary words necessary. Some ryegrass plants should be showing through the soil at this time. Discuss observations, make inferences, review student logs; reinforce knowledge and understanding of vocabulary words and sentences. Add water to the students' germinators if necessary.

FRIDAY: Goal Two, Objective B; Goal Three, Objective C.
Have students observe ryegrass germinators and enter observations in their logs. Discuss and read to students the concepts, "plants reproduce from seeds" and "plants need water and sunlight to grow." Collect and examine student logs and have students complete seatwork that reinforces their knowledge of the vocabulary words.

A similar outline of daily activities for weeks two and three would complete a unit plan. Of course, daily lesson plans would provide the details of instructional methods and materials management required to provide guidance for teaching lessons.

AN INTEGRATED READING/SCIENCE DAILY LESSON PLAN FOR THE PRIMARY GRADES

The general form and content of the daily lesson plan for an integrated lesson is generally the same as the lesson plan developed for a single subject. The major differences are in the statements of goals and objectives. The plan for the integrated curriculum will contain goals and objectives from each of the subject matter areas utilized. Also in the elementary school it is common for teachers to list goals and objectives in skill and affective categories as well as for the subject matter. Proper planning permits the successful achievement of all goals and objectives while conducting the daily lesson.

The following is a sample daily lesson plan for a lesson that employs an integrated curriculum from reading and science.

Topic: "Living Things Around Us."

Goal Statement: The students will demonstrate the ability to employ the skills of observing and inferring.

Objective: During discussion of an activity in which they participated the students will appropriately state observations and make acceptable inferences.

Goal Statement: Students will demonstrate a knowledge and understanding of the new vocabulary words employed during the activity.

Objective: Given a worksheet containing the words ryegrass, soil, water, seeds, and sunlight, the students will correctly match them with the pictures depicting each.

Materials: Foam cups, soil, ryegrass seed, water.

Note: This lesson will occur following a five day long observation of ryegrass sprouting and growing from the foam cups where students have planted seeds.

Procedure:

1. Students once again examine the ryegrass specimens and record their observations. Children are permitted to report orally upon their observations. The teacher probes through questioning to extend and expand their understanding of what they have observed. The teacher asks: What things are necessary for the ryegrass to grow? What would happen if no water is added to the cups? What happened to the ryegrass that was covered with foil?
2. The teacher then lists the new vocabulary words on the chalkboard and the children copy them in a notebook. Each word is discussed and the teacher evaluates the children's understanding by asking selected stu-

dents to define and use the word in a sentence.
3.   The students are given a worksheet that contains the vocabulary words
     and matching illustrations. When the children complete the worksheets
     the lesson is concluded.

SELF CHECK FOR OBJECTIVE EIGHT

CAN YOU: describe the nature and purpose of an integrated curriculum
          resource unit and unit plan?

SELF CHECK FOR OBJECTIVE NINE

CAN YOU: create an integrated curriculum resource unit and unit plan?

TEAM PLANNING AND THE
INTERDISCIPLINARY UNIT

In departmentalized elementary schools, middle schools and junior high
schools, teachers often plan together in teams to better integrate the various
subjects in the school curriculum. In some instances schools are organized
into teaching teams that group together an English (reading) teacher, a
mathematics teacher, a social studies teacher and science teacher (with
support from art, music, and physical education teachers). Each team of
subject matter specialists teaches the same small body of 120 to 150 students
who are rotated through their classes. In such schools there may exist several
teams, each operating independently of one another while planning and
teaching. Such an organizational structure is sometimes called "a school
within a school." Where team planning of any type exists, the resulting
multidisciplinary approach helps students to relate what in many schools are
isolated learning environments, and helps teachers to support one another
with their own special skills and knowledge.

To illustrate the nature of an interdisciplinary unit let us use the social
studies unit described earlier as the major theme.

The English Teacher:
Report Writing: The English teacher might use special knowledge of library
          research and report writing to help students write their research
          reports on the topic, the War for Independence.

Dramatization: An English teacher trained in drama may help students to
          write and produce a dramatization of events related to the War for
          Independence.

The Science Teacher: The science teacher might organize a unit on
          meteorology and climatology to study the effect of the weather and
          terrain on battles to be fought.

The Mathematics Teacher: A unit on the history of measurement
          featuring the British and Colonial American system of measurement.

The Music Teacher: Old English ballads and American frontier music would be a natural area of support of the unit on the American War for Independence.

The Art Teacher: The art teacher might introduce students to the paintings that depicted the Revolutionary Period; or examine the crafts of the period; and, assigning a project involving a craft, painting, drawing, collage or other medium related to the period .

The variety of activities that can be incorporated into an interdisciplinary unit on any topic is only limited by the imagination of the teachers involved. Some topics more than others lend themselves to cooperative planning. But the broad based experiences of students who are the beneficiaries of such cooperative planning and teaching would appear to make such efforts worthwhile. Team planning, where it takes place, also appears to have a positive effect on the morale and self concept of the teachers who are working together.

SELF CHECK FOR OBJECTIVE TEN

CAN YOU: using examples describe an interdisciplinary plan?

SUMMARY

Planning for instruction is a time consuming and demanding part of teaching. Yet no other part of the teacher's role is more important than formulating good lesson plans. Teachers who teach in classrooms where basic skills management systems are in use generally plan at the technician level, focusing on the details of classroom management, materials handling, control of discipline, and other such activities. The teacher who operates at the level of the manipulator uses a textbook or school program as a basis for his curriculum and changes it to better meet the needs of his students. The teacher who operates at the synthesis level creates a program, sets goals and objectives, locates materials and plans the substance of the instruction. Most teachers at some time act in each level of curriculum planning.

Planning the resource unit allows the teacher maximum opportunity to use planning skills. A complete unit plan should: meet the felt needs of the students, include learning experiences appropriate for all students, provide for a variety of cognitive levels from knowledge to evaluation, promote student growth and habits of independent learning and problem solving, introduce students to a variety of resources and new learning methods, provide for closure of the learning experiences, and should be an integral part of an approved course of study. The resource unit includes a title, rationale, and a list of goal and objective statements. Under the heading of each learning activity should be found a statement of the pertinent goals and objectives, description of the activity, list of resources, and a statement of evaluation procedures.

In creating a unit plan a teacher uses the goals, objectives and activities found in the resource unit to create the schedule of daily activities for a predetermined period of time. The teacher may not use all of the activities created in the resource unit and may modify those he chooses to utilize. Of course, the teacher may create and use activities not found in the resource unit. A real challenge for the teacher in maintaining the flow of instruction described in a unit plan is to modify the schedule of activities as various factors impact on the long range plan.

The daily lesson plan is specific concerning the content and methodology to be introduced during a single class period. The daily lesson plan contains the following parts: goal statements, objective statements, skill and attitude statements, concept statements, list of materials, and a description of the procedures to be followed. The procedures include considerations of set, concept development (lecture outline or discussion questions), examples and non examples of the concepts, and provision for a review of the concepts.

There currently exist in the secondary schools of our country examples of curricula that integrate the curricula of two subjects. Integrated mathematics and science is the most often cited example, although many other combinations are also found. In the elementary school the teacher is often faced with the necessity of making maximum use of class time by integrating two or more subjects into a single lesson. The integrity of each subject may be preserved in an integrated lesson plan by recognizing the goals and objectives of each subject and attempting to teach them all. Integration of subject matter can also serve to demonstrate the relationships of the concepts and skills often taught in isolation.

The variety of activities that can be incorporated into an interdisciplinary unit on any topic is only limited by the imagination of the teachers involved. Some topics more than others lend themselves to cooperative planning. But the broad based experiences of students who are the beneficiaries of such cooperative planning and teaching would appear to make such efforts worthwhile. Team planning, where it takes place, also appears to have a positive effect on the morale and self concept of the teachers who are working together.

ACTIVITIES

1. Create a sample resource unit on a topic of your choice. Be sure to include at least one cognitive goal and one affective goal in the unit.
2. Create a sample five day unit plan.
3. Construct a daily lesson plan on a topic of your choice. If time permits separate daily lesson plans may be constructed for two lessons, one of which being primarily fact or information oriented, and a second which deals with the higher level cognitive skills and attitudes.
4. Create a brief integrated curricular resource unit and unit plan.

BIBLIOGRAPHY

Arnold, V.D. (1989). Teaching for effective instruction. *Teacher—Educator 24*(3), 10-12.

Brissenden, T. (1985). Children's language and mathematics, rewriting the lesson script. *Mathematics In School, 14*(4), 2-7.

Crahay, M. (1988). Stability and variability of teaching behavior: a case study. *Teaching and Teacher Education, 4*(4), 289-303.

Donnellan, K.M., & Roberts, G.J. (1985). What research says: Activity based elementary science — A double bonus. *Science and Children, 22,* 119-121.

Frudden, S. J. (1984). Lesson plans can make a difference in evaluating teachers. *Education, 104,* 351-353.

Hunter, M. (1982). *Teaching.* (Videotape Series, Los Angeles: University of California.

Jacobsen, D., Eggen, P., Kauchak, D., & Dulaney, C. (1985). *Methods for teaching.* Columbus: Charles E. Merrill.

Martin, R.J. (1988). Research into practice. *Reading Psychology, 9*(2), 163-167.

Mosston, M. (1972). *Teaching: From command to discovery.* Belmont, CA: Wadsworth Publishing.

Smith, L.R. (1985). A low-inference indicator of lesson organization. *Journal of Classroom Interaction, 21*(1), 25-30.

Swank, P.R. (1989). Sensitivity of classroom observation systems: measuring teacher effectiveness. *Journal of Experimental Education, 57*(2), 171-186.

Tephly, J.B. (1989). A rare collection of teaching ideas. *Science and Children, 26*(5), 16-19.

CHAPTER FOUR

INTRODUCTORY CASE STUDY

CASE STUDY 4-1

QUESTIONS ABOUT QUESTIONS

Littlefield Junior High School was given a grant by the school district to develop materials that would help teachers develop skills and understanding related to the proper use of classroom questions. Anson Adams, the eighth grade science teacher put in charge of the project decided to help himself and other teachers learn something about classroom questions by making video tapes of teachers' lessons and analyzing them with small teams of some of the teachers involved in the project. Following are the transcripts of two seventh grade science teachers teaching the same concept, soil erosion.

Sandy Storms' Class

Ms. Storms: "All right, you have read the chapter on soil erosion, so can anyone tell me the four main agents of soil erosion?" "Jim."

Jim: "Aah. Aah."

Ms. Storms: "Carlotta, can you help him? Tell me just one agent of erosion."

Carlotta: "Wind is one. Wind blows soil around."

Ms. Storms: "Very good, Carlotta." And turning quickly to the class, "Another one anyone? Paul."

Luther: "Water, rain and rivers carry away soil."

Ms. Storms: "Good, Luther, water is usually the most important agent of erosion. "Another one, anybody?"

Brief silence.

Ms. Storms: "Quickly anyone." And after a slight pause. "What happens in the winter time when it is cold?"

Joseph: "Freezing and thawing cause rocks to chip and break apart."

Ms. Storms: "Good thinking, Joseph. Now there is one more. Anybody? It begins with a C."

Silence.

Ms. Storms: "Remember in your book, the pictures of the caves?"
Silence.
Ms. Storms: "Come on class, think. What science will you take in high school after Biology? It begins with a C."
Kirstin: "Chemistry."
Ms. Storms: "Chemical weathering, of course. The acids in the water react with the minerals in the ground, especially limestone, and form caves."

Elijah Stone's Class

To begin the activity, Mr. Stone, in quick succession shows the class a cracked and broken glass jar filled with frozen water, a small pile of talcum powder placed in front of a fan and blown away, an Alka Seltzer® dropped into a weak vinegar solution, and a jar of water poured over an inclined plastic tray which contains a layer of sand.

Mr. Stone: "The topic is soil erosion. Can anyone tell me how anything we just saw is related to soil erosion?"
Jack: "Well when you poured the water over the sand it washed away. That is erosion."
Mr. Stone: "Can anyone think of any examples in nature of what Jack just said?"
Ashley: "Rivers like the Mississippi carry soil and dump it where they enter the ocean."
Silence.   Mr. Stone waits patiently.
Jennifer: "Every time it rains, mud from the hill next to the bus ramp washes down on the drive."
Mr. Stone: "It looks as though we agree that water is an agent of erosion. What about one of the other demonstrations you saw?"
Sharon: "Well, the fan blew away the powder. That is just like the wind blowing sand and dust. That is erosion.
Mr. Stone: "What else did we see?"
Bill: "The jar broken by the freezing water. Is freezing water one?"
Mr. Stone remains silent and looks around the room.
Jacqueline: "Well, freezing water breaks up roads in the winter time."
Juan: "Some rocks are soft and hold water. They might break up when the water freezes."
Mr. Stone: "You folks are too smart. I can't stump you! What about the Alka Seltzer® in the vinegar solution?"
Prolonged silence.
Mr. Stone: "Remember when we soaked the chicken bones in vinegar? What happened to the bones?"
Alonzo: "They got soft. The vinegar ate away the calcium from the bones."
Carmen: "Maybe it's like acid rain. In Art class, Mrs. Fusia said acid rain is destroying the limestone and marble sculptures and buildings all over the world. Is that it? Is there acid in water that eats away rocks?"
Mr. Stone: "You've got it. That is called chemical weathering. Now can we name the four primary agents of erosion?"

What Is Your Analysis?

1. What is the difference in the way Sandy Storms and Elijah Stone used questions?
2. Were there differences in the way each teacher responded to student answers and statements?
3. Did the students in both classes come away from their respective learning activities with the same concepts, skills and attitudes?
4. How would the fact that Mr. Stone appeared to permit longer periods of silence between questions and responses affect the learning activity and learning outcomes?
5. Summarize what Anson Adams and his teachers could learn from this type of analysis.

CHAPTER FOUR
VERBAL QUESTIONS, A PRIMARY TOOL OF TEACHING

"Judge of a man by his questions rather than by his answers."
-*Voltaire*

GOALS

After reading the chapter the student will understand:

1. techniques and types of verbal questions,
2. the impact of various types of questions on students,
3. the impact of pacing on classroom verbal interaction and
4. the impact of verbal praise and other reinforcement on students.

OBJECTIVES

After studying this chapter the student will:
1. describe the Socratic method of questioning,
2. describe the Suchman procedure of questioning,
3. define convergent and divergent questions and illustrate the result that each type of question will have on verbal interaction,
4. describe wait-time and its use in oral questioning and
5. list eight of nine positive effects that are derived from the proper use of wait time coupled with the minimal use of verbal praise in problem solving discussions.

Teaching has been defined as the art of asking questions. Although demands made on teachers are too complex to be simply defined, the science and art of asking questions and responding to students are skills essential for successful teaching.

Classroom questioning is a science to the extent that its use causes predictable responses from the learner. Experienced teachers skilled in the use of questioning techniques will testify that in a given set of circumstances specific questions will cause predictable actions by students. Armed with proper knowledge and skill teachers may use oral questions in the classroom to reproduce similar results. This suggests that classroom questioning is at least in part a science.

If oral questioning by teachers was entirely a science, and the process comprised only of selecting the proper questions to ask and asking them, the use of questions in teaching would be a simple, uncluttered procedure. It is not simple or uncluttered. Oral questioning is an interaction among human beings that contributes greatly to the fundamental relationship that a teacher establishes with a class. The effective use of oral questioning in the classroom requires the selection of proper questions, creation of an open classroom atmosphere, listening and responding to students and pacing the interaction to achieve maximum student contribution. The art of oral questioning requires the teacher to judge when it is proper to accept student responses and when to challenge them, when to stop to clarify an idea and when to proceed, and when to solicit more ideas and when to seek closure of a discussion. Just as the science of oral questioning may be learned, the art may be developed by most individuals. The teacher who takes the time to acquire the skills necessary to conduct interesting classroom questioning activities with a class adds variety to the learning experiences. Oral questioning is a tool worth adding to your repertoire of behaviors.

MODELS OF CLASSROOM QUESTIONING

The use of oral questions in teaching does not follow a single pattern or format. Questions may be mixed with lecture or may flow from an informal discussion. Oral questions may be precisely structured to elicit specific responses from students, or as in one model of questioning students become the questioners and the teacher the responder. Questions may be used in any learning activity and for a variety of purposes.

The Socratic Questioning Method

The Greek philosopher Socrates, one of the world's great teachers, walked the garden pathways of ancient Athens with a small group of students following at his heels, listening to his every word. Their discourse might have gone something like this:

Socrates: What might be the requirements for a perfect state?

Student: Perfect leaders.

Socrates: In addition to perfect leaders what must be true to create a perfect state?

Student: There must be perfect citizens.

Socrates: Any man who believes the creation of a perfect state is a desirable ideal must do what in his personal life?

Asking the right question is the teacher's most powerful tool. Through questioning, students' thinking can be facilitated and their minds kept actively involved in the problem-solving processes. This develops the skills of critical thinking and decision making.

Student:	He must become a perfect citizen.
Socrates:	And if the man's beliefs come into conflict with the state what must be done?
Student:	He must change his beliefs.
Socrates:	And if he cannot change his beliefs?
Student:	Then he must remove himself from the state.
Socrates:	To what does such a man owe his loyalty?
Student:	The man's first loyalty is to the state.

This hypothetical interchange demonstrates the questioning method of Socrates. He asked questions that carried the student step by step through a reasoning process to form a conclusion that would be acceptable in its logic.

A contemporary social studies teacher might use the Socratic method when teaching issues such as the environment. For example:

Teacher: A company wishes to build a chemical plant on the river above the city. How might that affect people?

Student: It would cause pollution.

Teacher: Is it ever worth it to tolerate pollution?

Student: Yes. People need jobs.

Teacher: Are there other benefits from the chemical plant?

Student: The company would pay taxes.

Teacher: Are there any other benefits?

Student: We may need what they manufacture, say fertilizer or plastic.

Teacher: Under what conditions should the city agree to permit the plant to be built?

Student: When the benefits are greater than the problem of pollution.

By leading students through a discussion using questions, Socrates believed he would teach them the process of logical thought. Some contemporary learning theorists agree with Socrates. They believe that to develop logical thinking ability learners should experience problem solving procedures. By repeating this process in a variety of situations learners will begin to assimilate both the information and the process and develop their own ability to think logically.

SELF CHECK FOR OBJECTIVE ONE

CAN YOU: describe the Socratic method of questioning?

The Suchman Questioning Method

Another procedure for using questions in the classroom reverses the roles of the teacher and the students. This method, popularized by Richard Suchman, uses the format of the game of Twenty Questions. Students ask questions in an effort to solve a problem while the teacher answers them. Student questions are asked so that a teacher can answer with a response of "yes" or "no." An example of such an inquiry episode might be:

Teacher: Class, I have a problem for you to solve. You may ask me questions so that I will be able to answer them by saying yes or no. I will not provide you with any additional information.

              Looking at the map of the world you see the Sahara Desert in Northern Africa. Your problem is to determine what

	causes the Sahara to exist there. You may begin asking questions.
Jimmy:	Is it because there is not enough rain?
Teacher:	(laughing) Yes, Jimmy, the desert is there because there is not enough rain. Your job is to determine why there is not enough rain. Remember, from now on I'll only answer yes or no.
Suzie:	I see the Mediterranean Sea next to Africa. Is it because all the rain falls in the sea?
Teacher:	No.
Silence.	
Jimmy:	What causes rain anyhow?
Teacher:	You must ask questions that I can answer yes or no.
Jimmy:	Uh, let's see. Is rain caused by clouds coming off the water?
Teacher:	Yes. I must break a rule since we are just starting this game and answer Jimmy's questions by saying, 'sometimes, but not always.'
Joanie:	Does the wind usually blow onto North Africa from the Mediterranean Sea?
Teacher:	No.
Suzie:	Is rain sometimes caused by air that gets water from the land?
Teacher:	Yes.
Suzie:	Does rain always come from air that picks up water?
Teacher:	Yes.
Louis:	What makes the water fall from the air?
Teacher:	Yes or no, please.
Louis:	Ah. (silence) Does rain fall when the air has too much to hold?
Teacher:	Yes.
Jimmy:	I know! I know! It was on the television. Rain falls when air gets cold. Does rain fall when air gets cold?
Teacher:	Yes.

Suzie:	I know in Washington and Oregon there is a lot of rain because the air off the ocean gets cold as it goes over the mountains. Does that happen with the Sahara Desert? Then there is no water left in the air when it gets to the desert?
Teacher:	Yes.
Louis:	(Looking at the map) There are a lot of mountains in the middle of Africa. Does the wind blow from the middle toward the desert?
Teacher:	No.
Joanie:	There are lots of mountains in Turkey and Russia along there. Does the wind blow from that direction to the Sahara Desert?
Teacher:	Yes.
Joanie:	Then, is that it? The wind loses its moisture when it blows over the mountains and there is none left to fall as rain on the land.
Teacher:	Yes. You have it. Look at the map and you will see that all countries southwest of the mountains are arid. By the time the air gets to North Africa it is dry.

This questioning procedure is designed to enhance students' abilities to ask questions that are thoughtful and meaningful in order to solve a problem at hand. If the art of problem solving is related to the art of asking the right questions, an inquiry activity should aid students to develop this important ability. Teachers who have used this technique have found the game-like format of the activity to be highly motivating. Students participate with enthusiasm.

SELF CHECK FOR OBJECTIVE TWO

CAN YOU: describe the Suchman procedure of questioning?

DISCUSSION AND CLASSROOM QUESTIONS

The Socratic and the yes-and-no techniques of Suchman are special models of questioning that are used by a small percentage of teachers. Most teachers who use oral questions in their teaching use a variety of questions that suit the needs of their students and the purpose of the lessons. A teacher's purpose in asking questions may range from a review of information from previous lessons to conducting an open ended problem solving discussion. The teacher may wish to lead the class to form generalizations or conclusions, or perhaps to formulate a procedure for investigating an issue. Teachers who develop an array of questioning skills will have a kit of instructional tools that will permit them to introduce variety into their day to day teaching, and to challenge students at several intellectual levels.

QUESTIONS DETERMINE TEACHING STYLE

Nothing characterizes a teacher's style of teaching more than the type of questions asked and teacher reaction to student responses. The following brief dialogues may illustrate this point.

Ms. Smith:	We are studying about drugs, and I hope you have read the booklets that I passed to you yesterday. Can anyone tell me what the booklet was about?
Sue:	It was about drugs.
Ms. Smith:	Uh, huh, and what drugs were described in the booklet, Jack?
Jack:	Marijuana and heroin, I think, and speed.
Ms. Smith:	What is another name for speed? Dick?
Dick:	I think they are called amphetamines.
Ms. Smith:	That's right. What are some bad effects of drugs? Anyone?
Sue:	The book said they can affect babies.
Ms. Smith:	How?
Sue:	Make them born crippled or mentally retarded.
Ms. Smith:	Anything else?
Sam:	They can warp your personality; make you blow your mind.
Ms. Smith:	What else did the book say could happen to people who took drugs?
Jack:	It said something about how much the drugs cost. That it takes a lot of money to buy heroin.
Ms. Smith:	How much does the average addict spend per day for drugs?

And so it goes. How do you rate Ms. Smith's class? Was Ms. Smith getting to the students? Were they deeply involved with the topic? Let us see how Mr. Jones handles the same topic.

Mr. Jones:	You read the booklets I handed out yesterday. What do you think we are going to talk about today?
Class:	Drugs.
Mr. Jones:	Is this a real problem here at Nameless High School? Is it worth discussing?

Jack:	There is a lot of it around, but I don't know what could be done to stop it.
Sue:	It's hard to use the restrooms with so many kids smoking in them.
Mr. Jones:	Can it be stopped or at least reduced?
Sue:	Well, adults drink alcohol and nobody stops them.
Mr. Jones:	Would anyone like to comment on this? Adults drink and yet they don't want young people to use drugs.
Sam:	It is not the same. Two wrongs don't make a right. Just because some adults drink doesn't make it right for kids to use drugs.
John:	Why not? Why should they try to tell us what to do when they do things just as bad?
Sue:	But that is just some adults, not all of them. Someone has to set the standards.
Mr. Jones:	That is a good point, Sue, but what is so bad about drugs?
Dick:	Well, they can ruin your health. When they really get the habit bad, addicts don't eat or take care of themselves.
Mr. Jones:	Remains silent, his face showing neither approval or disapproval.
Sue:	Drugs can affect the babies of drug addicts.
Mr. Jones:	Uh. Huh. What about the money angle? How much does a cocaine addict pay per day for drugs?
John:	Three hundred or more dollars per day, I have read someplace.
Mr. Jones:	O.K. Suppose you had to come up with $300 every day. How might you get it?

And the discussion continues in this manner. Is there a difference in the two lessons? Was one group more intellectually involved than the other? If you said the students in Mr. Jones' class were more involved than those in Ms. Smith's class you are probably right. The students in Mr. Jones' class were more deeply involved in the discussion because they also were permitted greater leeway in responding to most of the questions. Do you see the reason for the difference between the two classes? Do you see that the tone of the interaction of the two classes differed because questions that each teacher asked were different? The type of questions that a teacher uses is probably the single most important determiner of the interaction that takes place in a classroom.

As a student what would you do to prepare for Ms. Smith's class, Mr. Jones? Would there be a difference in the manner in which you did your assignment? Would the serious student tend to memorize facts presented in the booklet to prepare for Ms.Smith? Would he concern himself more with issues to prepare for Mr. Jones? So there is more than the nature of classroom interaction at stake here. The form of that which is learned by students is determined by the style of the classroom interaction, and therefore by questions that are asked by the teacher.

Convergent and Divergent Questions

Oral questions are frequently categorized as convergent and divergent because of the results they have on the learner's thought processes. Questions that call for specific answers that have been committed to memory cause the student's thoughts to focus on that part of his memory where that fact has been stored, excluding all others. "Who is the author of 'Evangeline'?" and "What were the causes of the Vietnam War?" are illustrations of convergent questions.

Divergent questions on the other hand solicit opinion, judgment and inference from the learner, rather than recall of specific facts. They tend to cause student thoughts to range about searching for relationships, forming inferences and conclusions. "What options did Evangeline's people have open to them?" and "Can you think of causes of the Vietnam War that the author of your textbook overlooked?" are examples of divergent questions. Divergent questions tend to ask students to respond with what they think while convergent questions with what they know.

As we observed earlier in the dialogues that took place in the classrooms of Ms. Smith and Mr. Jones, the use of one type of question to the exclusion of the other produces different performances. Convergent questions are used in instruction when recall of memorized facts is the goal of the teacher. Divergent questions are used when teaching goals are associated with problem solving, higher level thinking skills, and the development of principles or relationships.

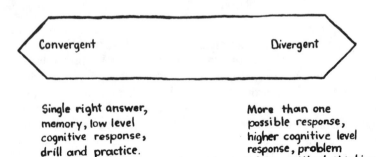

FIGURE 4.1
A DICHOTOMY OF CLASSROOM QUESTIONS

Using convergent and divergent questions in the classroom.

A middle school English teacher, Mrs. Santini, asks her class the following questions: "Who was the author of the story?" "In what city did it take place?" and "What was the name of the boy about whom the story was centered?" What will be the result on the amount of verbal interaction that is likely to take place in the classroom?

Who can answer the questions posed by the teacher? How lengthy will the responses be? Convergent questions asked by a teacher tend to limit verbal interaction in a classroom to those who have read the story and committed the facts of the story to memory. All other students will be shut out of verbal interaction that is taking place. Convergent questions asked by the teacher are likely to result in diminishing the number of students who take part in the verbal interchange that takes place in the classroom. Fact oriented questions tend to close off and restrict the participation of many students.

After lunch Mrs. Santini approached teaching her literature lesson differently. She asked the questions, "What is this story about?" and "Should Gary stay on the football team although he is no longer getting to play quarterback?"

These divergent questions tend to open the discussion to most of the students in the class. Those students who are a little less able academically, and those who did not make the effort to study the story enough to commit it to memory may still participate. Responses depend less on recall of facts and more on interpretation and inference. The goal of the teacher, to help students to develop higher level intellectual skills, may still be realized although there are differences in the students' knowledge of the story.

It should be noted that we have been discussing the effects of convergent and divergent questions on classroom verbal interaction; no value judgment was made about the general merit of types of questions. Whether to use one or the other depends on the instructional goals of the teacher. While open-ended, divergent questions have great value in creating a positive atmosphere for discussion and problem solving, closed ended, convergent questions, when properly used, aid the learner in memorizing and retaining information. Where raising students' scores on standardized or fact focused teacher made tests is a goal, convergent questions have been found to be more efficient. Figure 4.1 illustrates the results of using convergent and divergent questions.

SELF CHECK FOR OBJECTIVE THREE

CAN YOU: define convergent and divergent questions and illustrate the effect of each type on classroom verbal interaction?

PACE

Nearly all teachers have used oral questions in their classrooms, either as drill to reinforce an array of information or in the more open-ended mode of problem solving and discussion. When lessons fail we sometimes comment to a colleague, "My class sure is tired today," in an attempt to explain the lethargy and lack of participation. When lessons that center on oral questions of the teacher fail, the reason is often pace.

Certain types of lessons, chiefly those that are drill activities, require a quick tempo and a sense of energy and excitement. However, lessons that are designed to solicit student participation in class discussion and group problem solving have pacing requirements that are different. Nothing is more important to the success of inquiry lessons than the proper pacing of verbal interaction.

In a well known study it was discovered that on the average teachers asked about two or three questions each minute. Thus, students were subjected to a steady diet of inquiries to which they were expected to respond. Perhaps the more startling fact discovered was that *typically teachers waited less than one second for students to respond to questions before moving on* to rephrase the question, call on another student, or to some other action. Therefore, many students are given too little time to think of an answer they do not immediately know. This finding raises many implications for teaching.

Many students have learned by the third or fourth grade that they may never again be forced to answer an oral question asked by a teacher. All they must do is wait a second or two and the teacher will call on someone else or answer the question himself. A sizable percentage of students have discovered that they can outwait and outwit teachers. They have effectively opted out of most of the verbal interaction that takes place in the classroom. Most questions asked by teachers appear to be answered by a small group of students who are usually high achievers and are motivated. This disproportionate opportunity for verbal responses by a few students can be changed to allow time for other students to think and to respond.

Wait Time

One researcher, Mary Budd Rowe, describes two places where it is important that the teacher attempt, during questioning, to increase the pause or wait-time. The first is after the teacher asks a question. Giving students time to think before rephrasing a question or calling on another student will have positive effects on the quality and amount of student response. The second point in the interaction at which teachers should attempt to allow adequate wait-time is following a student response. In a study where a group of teachers attempted to allow at least three seconds at each of these points and to limit the amount of reinforcement they gave for students' responses, Rowe reports the following interesting results. They are:

1. The length of student responses increased. The completeness and com-

plexity of responses increased. The pause that followed student responses contributed to this result.

2. The number of spontaneous and appropriate student responses increased.
3. Failure to respond decreased. This result was affected by the pause following a teacher question.
4. Student confidence increased. This phenomenon was noted in the lower incidence of hesitance and inflected student responses.
5. The incidence of speculative thinking increased. This was influenced by both wait-times.
6. Teacher-centered talk decreased and student-student interaction increased. Students tend to listen to one another and react to peer statements more often.
7. The number of questions asked by students increased. The number of experiments they proposed increased. This factor was affected by both wait-times.
8. Contributions by low achieving students increased. When group problem solving discussions were introduced with proper wait-times and a low schedule of reinforcement, teachers observed a shift in the star performers of their classes. Many students considered average or low achieving under the old strategy become leaders in the new activity.
9. Disciplinary problems decreased. Many teachers are surprised to discover that when classroom interaction becomes more open and students are involved with problem solving activities, discipline problems decrease and children who previously had been discipline problems became productive members of the class.

SELF CHECK FOR OBJECTIVE FOUR

CAN YOU: describe wait-time and its use in oral questioning?

SELF CHECK FOR OBJECTIVE FIVE

CAN YOU: list eight of the nine positive effects that are derived from the proper use of wait-time coupled with minimal use of verbal praise in problem solving discussions?

REINFORCEMENT

Humans respond in predictable ways to rewards. Most of us feel good when rewards are bestowed on us and bad when rewards are withheld. We tend to work to achieve rewards that appear to be within our grasp and compete with others to win them. Behaviors of children and adolescents may be greatly affected by systems of rewards in classrooms. It has been noted in the literature that many teachers spend nearly twenty-five percent of their verbal interaction in the classroom rewarding and blaming students.

Teachers use a wide array of rewards. Some give students candy or toys to reward desirable behaviors. Others use films, free time, extra outdoor periods, permitting a child to be first in the lunch line and other such positive actions as rewards to reinforce desirable behaviors. Frequently tokens, or paper "chips" are given to students that may later be redeemed for physical rewards or favors. The practice of issuing rewards to elicit optimum behavior of students is useful for many teachers, although it is deplored by some parents and educators as making children dependent on and motivated by physical reward systems or bribes.

The most frequent reinforcement used by classroom teachers during questioning activities is verbal praise. Some teachers follow nearly every student statement with a comment, "very good," "that's fine," or something similar. Verbal praise has been found to be very effective in many situations when modifying student behavior, especially that of young children. Verbal praise increases the student's perception of safety when answering a teacher's question. Acts of reinforcement tend to create a warm atmosphere in the classroom and generally increase student willingness to respond to teacher questions. This means there will be more hands raised to respond to questions a teacher asks. But constant reinforcement of student response also has adverse results that are worth noting.

Constant and overt praise by a teacher increases the dependence of students on the teacher as a guide for their behaviors, academic and social. Overpraise tends to create an environment in which student actions are largely designed to please the teacher, and are less likely to be products of student judgment. Students who are given a high level of overt praise are less adventurous in their thinking, choosing the safe answer to the creative one. A pattern of frequent overt teacher praise also reduces subject matter related interactions among students. Students tend to guard their responses so they can acquire the praise. In a high praise classroom, students listen less to one another and seldom react to another student's statement except to disagree. The use of overt praise can result in discipline problems as students compete to be called on by the teacher.

A pattern of frequent overt praise can have desirable effects in situations where a teacher is attempting to improve social behavior and work habits or to aid the memorization of information. Undesirable effects are caused by frequent overt praise when the purpose of a lesson is to enhance student problem solving skills and independence.

Teacher Behavior During Problem Solving Discussions

If overt praise has undesirable effects on the problem solving process, how does a teacher react to students' verbal responses during this kind of lesson? First, there are few times when an occasional praising statement by a teacher will do great harm to such lessons; there are few lessons where teachers will completely refrain from its use. However, to achieve an optimal level of verbal interaction during problem solving activities, a teacher may use open-ended questions and maintain a neutral and noncommittal posture to student responses. Such a lesson might sound like this:

After reading an account of a man who returned a very large amount of money ($50,000) that he found on the street and received a very small reward ($20), a teacher asked, "What do you think? What is your reaction to this story?"

Ivan: I think he was a dope to give the money back.

Teacher: (A neutral look on the face, remains silent for several seconds.)

Priscilla: He sure got cheated. (teacher pause)

Andy: (laughing) Maybe he could steal it back. (teacher pause)

Teacher: How much should the man have been rewarded? What would have been fair? (teacher pause)

Andy: At least a thousand dollars. Fifty thousand dollars is a lot of money.

           (long pause)

Priscilla: That's only two percent. Real estate salesmen get seven percent.

           (teacher remains silent showing no signs of approval or disapproval)

Joseph: I don't know. It wasn't his money. The owner didn't have to give him anything.

Ivan: Yeh! The guy is a cheapskate. (teacher silence)

Teacher: Why should the man give the money back? Why not just keep it?

           (pause)

Joseph: It didn't say who the money belonged to. Maybe it was the life savings of some old people. Maybe they needed it to pay a doctor or something.

           (after a pause of about five seconds)

Teacher: Does it make a difference to whom the money belongs? Should the man return it?

The lesson proceeds with the teacher asking divergent, probing questions, waiting several seconds after both the question and student responses while offering no positive or negative reinforcement of student statements. The combination of extended wait-time and neutral response will often result in maximum student involvement in the discussion. Both factors, extended wait-time and neutral reinforcement, are vital to the optimum progress of the problems solving activity.

SUMMARY

Oral questioning by teachers is both a science and an art. The science of questioning lies in the selection of appropriate questions coupled with proper handling of student responses; this causes predictable results. The art of questioning is found in the teacher's feel for the needs of students and the setting the pace of the lesson. Two special forms of questioning are associated with Socrates who carefully guided his students through a problem to a logical conclusion, and Suchman who had students ask questions posed in a form to which the teacher could respond with yes or no.

Questions asked by a teacher determine the teacher's style of teaching and set the tone of learning activities. Convergent questions are those that require answers that are specific; they are fact oriented. Divergent questions allow the student to have more than one answer; they require inference, judgment and opinion from the student. A teacher who uses mostly convergent questions will emphasize memory and knowledge of the subject matter. Verbal interaction will be rapidly paced with brief questions and short responses. In a classroom where divergent questions are generally used, problem solving discussions and a greater amount of pupil-pupil and pupil-teacher interactions will result. The quality of problem solving discussions in a classroom will be enhanced when the teacher uses a wait-time of at least three seconds before and after the question and follows the student response with a minimum of reinforcement or verbal praise.

ACTIVITIES

1. Develop a brief script that would depict the interaction of a teacher and student where the teacher is using the Socratic method of questioning.

   Possible problems:
   a. The obligation of the government to provide social services.
   b. Why the sun and stars rise in the east and set in the west.
   c. The obligation of man to preserve dying species, i.e. the humpback whale.

2. Develop a brief script that would depict the interaction of a teacher and a class where the teacher is employing the Suchman procedure of questioning.

   Possible problems:
   a. A metal can covered with moisture is displayed to the class. (The can is filled with ice water.) The class is to find out why the moisture is on the can without knowing what is inside.
   b. The teacher thinks of one state of the United States and the students try to determine which one it is. A map of the U.S.A. may be seen by the students.

3. The following list of questions contains both convergent and divergent questions. Identify the different questions by placing a "C" before a convergent question and a "D" before a divergent question.

_____a.   Who invented the telephone?

_____b.   Can you tell me a story about a boy, a duck, and a boat?

_____c.   What procedure must you follow to obtain a fishing license?

_____d.   Which drawing do you like the best?

_____e.   What would be some consequences of the United States refusing to offer any foreign aid to other countries?

_____f.   What possible endings could have been written for the *Cat in the Hat.*

_____g.   What do the following phrases mean? "Je suis," "Bonjour," "Etudiez-vous?"

_____h.   What are five main causes of air pollution, as discussed in the text?

4. Practice extending wait-time by teaching a brief lesson to three or four of your peers.

    Possible lessons
    a. Should there be a draft of eighteen year-olds in the U.S.A.?
    b. How does a siphon work? (Look it up in a science book.)
    c. Should girls have varsity sports the same as boys?

BIBLIOGRAPHY

Conley, M.W. (1986). The influence of three teachers' comprehension questions during content area lessons. *Elementary School Journal, 87*(1), 17-28.

Davey, B. (1989). Active responding in content classrooms. *Journal of Reading, 33*(1), 44-46.

Kelly, T.E. (1989). Leading class discussion of controversial issues. *Social Education, 53*(6), 368-370.

Los Angeles County School District. (1980). *Teacher expectations and student achievement.* Bloomington: Phi Delta Kappa.

Necca, E. (1989). Stimulating curiosity. *Gifted Education International, 6*(1), 25-27.

Rowe, M.B. (1973). *Teaching science by continuous inquiry.* New York: McGraw-Hill.

Shaffer, J.C. (1989). Improving discussion questions: is anyone out there listening? *English Journal, 78*(4), 40-42.

Suchman, J.R. (1958). *The elementary school training program.* Illinois Studies of Inquiry Training, NDEA.

Swift, J.N., & Gooding, C.T. (1983). Interaction of wait time feedback and questioning instruction on middle school science teaching. *Journal of Research in Science Teaching, 20*(8), 721-730.

Wixton, K.K. (1983). What you ask about is what children learn. *Reading Teacher, 37*(3), 287-293.

CHAPTER FIVE

INTRODUCTORY CASE STUDY

CASE STUDY 5-1
IMPROVING THE ART OF QUESTIONING

Arthur Form and Anne Surmee, both Middle School social studies teachers, had joined forces to become a cooperative learning team that observed, videotaped and discussed each other's teaching in order to improve their classroom skills. Anne and Art's current project is the improvement of classroom questioning abilities. Art and Anne decided to approach the self-improvement project by listing all of the various purposes or applications they made of oral questions in their teaching. They listed the general instructional uses of oral questions in two categories, convergent, fact oriented questions and divergent, problem solving questions. Their initial lists look like this:

Applications for Oral Questions in The Classroom
Convergent, Factual Questions:
Use   Examples

drill
review
pre-instruction assessment of student knowledge
post-instruction assessment of student knowledge

Divergent, Problem Solving:
Use   Examples

encouraging participation of students
seeking and discussing ideas
guiding students to form conclusions

WHAT WOULD YOUR CHART OF ORAL QUESTIONS LOOK LIKE?

Create a chart of your own that lists all of the uses of oral questions employed in the classroom by teachers and all possible examples of each use. Add or delete any of the materials created by Art Form and Anne Surmee and change it as you see fit. Compare your chart with your classmates.

CHAPTER FIVE

QUESTIONING, THE SCIENCE OF THE ART OF TEACHING

"In some small field each child should . . . attain the power to draw
. . . inferences from observed facts."

-Charles W. Eliot

GOAL

After reading this chapter the student will understand how categorizing verbal questions helps teachers use them in the classroom.

OBJECTIVES

After studying this chapter the student will

1. list explanations of why teachers ask eliciting, probing, closure seeking and information seeking questions and
2. write one illustration of each question type.

While watching a skilled teacher conducting a problem solving discussion we are impressed with the teacher's ability to keep academic order. Events appear to be open-ended and to lack structure. Unstructured learning activities cause many teachers to avoid using discussion and problem solving activity. The following discussion will help you to gain insight into the process of conducting open-ended, problem solving discussions and to gain confidence in your ability to use this valuable strategy for teaching.

STAGES OF PROBLEM SOLVING DISCUSSION

Classroom questions are used in a particular order when they are a part of a problem solving discussion. First, the teacher presents a problem question and elicits student response. As the discussion begins and ideas flow the teacher probes for new ideas and relationships. When the quality of student ideas begins to diminish and responses become redundant, the teacher directs the class to begin to seek closure to the discussion or problem. Closure could be a generalization or conclusion. Sometimes the most appropriate conclusion is that no conclusion can be made. Or closure might be a plan to continue to study the problem. To conduct problem solving discussions a teacher must know how to use questions which elicit responses from students, probe for ideas, and direct the discussion to closure.

Educational literature has articles and books which concern classroom questioning that focuses on levels of learners' intellect that are required to respond to questions. These discussions use various taxonomies of cognitive activity to write objectives and create evaluation procedures. Knowledge of the learner's cognitive levels that are engaged by questions adds little to a teacher's ability to conduct lessons that use oral questioning in the class-room. The skills of oral questioning center on the intent or purpose of each question, and not the intellectual level of the response.

CATEGORIES (BY USE) OF CLASSROOM QUESTIONS

In this chapter we are concerned with developing and maintaining verbal interaction in the classroom with questions. The most practical approach to developing the necessary skills for promoting classroom discussion is to ask the question, "What are the various purposes a classroom teacher may have for asking questions?" There are few purposes. They fit into four categories according to the purpose for which they are used. Besides purposes related to problem solving discussions, eliciting responses from the class, probing for ideas, and seeking closure to a discussion or problem, a teacher may use questions to seek information.

Eliciting Questions

Eliciting questions are asked to: 1) encourage the initial response of a class, 2) expand participation to include a larger percentage of the class, 3) elicit responses from reluctant students and 4) rekindle a discussion that is losing momentum, is lagging or dissolving. Eliciting is taking place any time a teacher is trying to extract responses from students who were not responding.

Encouraging Initial Response

When initiating a class discussion or problem solving lesson, questions directed to the entire class usually provide opportunity for more students to respond than questions directed to specific students. When a teacher pre-identifies the student who is to answer a question, other students feel no obligation to become involved. To elicit responses from a group, it is best to address questions to the class as a whole than start the question with a student's name.

Questions can be classified as open or closed-ended. As previously de-scribed, open-ended or divergent questions are those questions which have several possible answers. They are general in nature. Such questions provide an opportunity for the unsure student to take a risk and respond. Examples of open-ended questions are:

"Watch this (chemical) reaction. What do you see?"
"What do you see in the picture?"
"Who can make up a sentence using any two of our spelling words?"

The second type of whole-class oriented eliciting questions can be described as closed-ended, or convergent. Convergent questions are designed to elicit one correct answer. If inappropriately used, closed-ended questions can cause a discussion to end before it begins. When they require specific replies, closed-ended questions can limit the quantity of response to only the secure, knowledgeable student. Examples of closed-ended questions that would probably produce a limited number of responses are:

"Who was the President of the Confederate States of America?"
"What is the formula which will help us find the answer to this problem?"
"What is the definition of a sentence?"

Although convergent questions result in closing off a discussion, there is one procedure which uses closed-ended questions to elicit student responses. As it is more fully described in the section titled "Information Seeking Questions," convergent questions may be used as background for a discussion and a bridge from the familiar for students. To serve the purpose of opening a discussion or an inquiry lesson and to enhance the likelihood of student responses, convergent questions must be stated so that most students in the class are familiar with the desired response. Examples of convergent questions that might be used to elicit student responses are:

"Name one way that ocean water is different from fresh water."
"What happens to trees in winter?"

Divergent and convergent questions can be used to encourage an initial response from students during a discussion. An important consideration when choosing questions that elicit responses for this purpose is that most students in the class have the opportunity to give an acceptable response. Questions that are of interest to the group with whom the teacher is working, which allow students an opportunity to respond, will tend to maximize the number of initial responses and provide the greatest opportunity for success of the lesson.

Expanding Participation

A desirable characteristic of a good discussion or problem solving lesson is that a large percentage of students participate. To gain maximum participation you must make only two decisions. You must decide, "Will I ask a divergent question or convergent question?" and "Will I address the questions to the individual or the whole class?"

Divergent questions used to expand participation in a classroom discussion may be similar to those used to initiate interaction. Example: "What is one reason the South decided to fight the North?" At times to ensure that the same few students do not dominate the interaction, the teacher may say, "Can anyone else think of another reason?" Divergent questions which are intended to expand participation to additional students usually include a direct phrase or statement which clearly elicits responses from unresponsive members of the class.

Convergent questions can be used to expand participation in a discussion. An inventive teacher may ask a convergent question that "traps" a reluctant participant into responding. Once the ice of lethargy or uncertainty is broken, many students will find themselves more willing to participate in divergent questions. This type of interaction may take something of the following forms:

"How many different kinds of ice cream can you name?" and
"Which kind do you prefer?"

The class then becomes involved in a discussion of basic food groups. The student was drawn into the discussion with a convergent question that could be answered, a question that was designed to generate personal interest.

Eliciting Responses From Reluctant Students

At times, you may find it expedient to direct your energy to individual students in an attempt to expand the amount of verbal participation. In doing this you might use divergent questions preceded by a reinforcing statement. "John, you have had good ideas in the past. Why do you think the South found it necessary to fight the North?" You may find it helps to repeat and reconfirm the idea that what is desired is the student's best answers and all responses will be respected although some are more desirable than others. At times, reluctant students may be cajoled into responding to a question by such soliciting statements as: "Give us your best guess, even if it seems wild." Or "There is no right answer; we want your answer."

Teachers have been known to solicit responses from reluctant students by appealing to their emotional biases, hitting them where they live. In an attempt to get students involved in a discussion of the rise of trade unions, a teacher might direct the following remarks to a student: "I am offering you a job at $.15 per hour, twelve hours a day, loading boxcars with one-hundred pound sacks of coal. What do you say to that?" Or, attempting to evolve some feeling for the position of Pre-World War II Germany, "What would you do, Jack, if Joe and Jim told you they were going to take half of everything you earned this week?" When put on a more personal basis most students will respond to international politics, philosophy or the price of coffee beans in Brazil. Once students are involved you may attempt to move the issue to a more rational basis with such questions as: "What could coal miners do who worked under dangerous conditions and from dawn to dark every day?" or, "What alternatives did Pre-World War II Germans have? They were burdened with forced payments to foreign nations and suffering from an economic depression." To be of value students must generalize issues beyond their own personal emotions and biases.

Regaining Momentum

Classroom discussion loses momentum for two major reasons. One reason is that students fail to introduce fresh ideas for a time while rehashing the same ideas. A second reason for discussions losing their momentum is that students lack information which is vital to advancing their arguments. In both instances the teacher must supply leadership to help the faltering interaction regain impetus. This is the fourth purpose for the eliciting question.

Teachers should not allow a discussion to degenerate too far before injecting necessary remedial measures. However, even the best teachers at times find themselves immersed in student talk that is repetitive and based largely on emotion and opinion. At some point, when the teacher thinks it is necessary to redeem the quality of the discussion, questions should be asked that attempt to summarize arguments up to that time. Illustrations are "Let's list on the board arguments for each point of view." "Can anyone state an argument which favors the position for increasing the voting age." To induce students to accept a new vantage point from which to view their previous discussions, the teacher might say, "Suppose you were a senator up for reelection, how would you view this issue?" Thus, one method of regaining momentum in a discussion is to summarize and redirect the arguments of the class.

Problem solving lessons and discussions sometimes lose momentum because of a lack of information on which to base reasonable arguments. In discussion of the desertion rate of Union soldiers during the Civil War, the

---

TABLE 5.1
Purpose and Examples of Eliciting Questions

Purpose	Examples
1. Encouraging Initial Response	Can someone put the following data into sequence? (convergent)
	How many different ways do you think...? (divergent)
2. Expanding Participation	Can anyone else...
	John, you have good ideas; what do you think?
	In your opinion, what is the best ice cream?
3. Eliciting Responses from Reluctant Students	How would you feel if...?
4. Regaining Momentum	Can we summarize the arguments for both sides?
	If I told you that... would you say?

class states all the obvious arguments such as the futility of war and fear. As the discussion begins to lag, the teacher might say, "Do you know that 30 percent of those drafted by the Union Army bought off their enlistments? How could this have affected the desertion rate?" The teacher might also elicit information from the class with "Can anyone tell me what it means to buy your way out of the army?" or, "In what ways, other than desertion, could a Union Army draftee avoid service?" With the addition of new information a discussion might regain lost vitality and move toward a desired conclusion.

Table 5.1 summarizes four major purposes for which eliciting questions are used. After examining Table 5.1 you may conclude that convergent and divergent questions could be used to pursue each of the four purposes. From the illustrations it may also be apparent that little difference exists among questions of various categories. An identical question might be used for each of the four purposes. In categorizing questions according to purpose, which is the basis of the classification system in this book, you must not look at the form of the question itself, but at the context in which it is used. It is the purpose of a question that has meaning. Examine the purpose, context and words used.

SELF CHECK FOR OBJECTIVE ONE

CAN YOU: list the purposes of eliciting questions?

Probing Questions

Probing questions are questions that try to expand an initial student response. While eliciting questions are concerned with influencing numbers of student responses, probing questions are concerned with the quality of student responses. When using probing questions, the teacher intends to expand or extend ideas or to obtain new ideas from students.

A teacher can probe in a variety of ways. Probing can be directed to the student who initiated the exchange. It can be directed to different students, or directed to the entire class. For example:

"Peter, would you like to restate what you said?"
"Sara, do you agree with John's statement?"
"Can anyone add to what was just said?"
"Does anyone have a different idea?"

Teachers use probing questions for four major purposes: extending ideas, redirecting ideas, justifying ideas, and clarifying ideas.

Extending Ideas

When teachers ask a question such as, "Does anyone have additional information?" or "Paul, would you like to elaborate on that idea?," an attempt is being made to get students to continue with the idea expressed earlier. Or they seek additional ideas on the same general topic. Teachers are not attempting to delve deeply into student answers to determine accuracy or justification for particular responses.

A non-committal posture will sometimes cause students to extend ideas. You might present a problem to the class, elicit discussion, then retire from the discussion. As students offer suggestions for discussion, wait silently for additional information. You may at times nod, or utter an occasional "Hmm" to let the students know you are aware of what is happening. To help students to organize their responses, ask divergent questions such as: "Have we considered all aspects of the question?", or "Can we suggest other ways to view this?"

Redirecting Ideas

You may find yourself facilitating a discussion which is headed in an undesired direction. To refocus the attention of the class to the desired goal you may find it necessary to ask questions such as:

"That's a good point. What was the essence of Cheryl's statement?"

"Yes, we could do it that way, but is there a more efficient means of solving the problem?"

At times teachers want to direct the attention of the class to a previous idea in order to redirect their thinking. "Remember what Jean said?" or "What was the point Susan made a while ago?" This may succeed in moving the discussion in a desired direction.

Justifying Ideas

When teachers ask students to justify answers, they usually ask students to support responses by citing examples, sources, data, etc. Often, the teacher is asking the students to form opinions, state values, or search for feelings or attitudes within himself or society. The following are examples of justifying questions:

"Can you explain your reasons for this opinion?"
"What led you to that idea?"
"Is that statement in contradiction to our basic value system?"

Clarifying Ideas

Many times student responses are not easily understood. The student may be unsure of the answer, has only part of the answer, or simply finds it difficult to express ideas. It is up to you, a teacher, to seek clarity. You may ask the student to define terms or use different words. You may ask a different student to clarify ideas suggested by classmates. Questions such as "Would you rephrase what you said," or "What did you mean when you said 'de facto segregation'?" or "Sally, can you explain what Peter meant by ...?" would be classified as questions designed to clarify ideas.

Care must be taken with unsophisticated students so that questions which require justifying and clarifying do not threaten or reduce student self-concept. Supportive statements such as "I think you have the idea" and "You seem to know what you are talking about, but...," should precede requests for clarification and justification to guard against defensive reactions by students. These reactions tend to reduce verbal interaction.

TABLE 5.2
PURPOSES AND EXAMPLES OF PROBING QUESTIONS

Purpose	Examples
1. Extending Ideas	"Can we add anything to this?"
	"Have we mentioned all points of view?"
2. Redirecting Ideas	"Is there a better way?"
	"Does anyone have another idea?"
	"What is some information we need?"
3. Justifying Ideas	"Why do you think this way?"
	"Your idea appears to be sound; how did you arrive at that conclusion?"
4. Clarifying Ideas	"That sounds good, could you re-state it so everyone will understand?"
	"I don't understand. Could you...?"

SELF CHECK FOR OBJECTIVE ONE

CAN YOU: list the purposes of probing questions?

Closure Seeking Questions

Closure seeking questions are those questions used to help students to begin to form conclusions, generalizations or solutions to problems generated by open-ended discussion.

Most people have taken part in lively discussions that went nowhere. Through skillful use of eliciting and probing the teacher may have generated interest and participation. They may have enthusiastically explored many facets of the topic under consideration. Certainly, students appeared motivated by the interaction, and perhaps continued their discussion into the corridor at the end of class. The main outcome of the discussion may have been that it served to clarify an issue and solidify participants' positions. Students formed judgments and orally defended them. If the two teaching objectives were motivation and developing the speaking skills of students, the discussion was a success. However, open discussions do little to help students to develop problem solving skills or positive attitudes about investigation. Closure seeking questions must be used. They help students to form conclusions and generalizations.

Closure seeking questions are used for several purposes. They may 1) invite students to begin seeking a conclusion or pattern based on established information, 2) seek clarification of issues, 3) ask for suggested procedures to resolve a problem and 4) influence students to suggest conclusions based on known data.

Invite Students to Begin Seeking a Conclusion

When you have decided during a discussion that all major points pertinent to the topic have been addressed, you should direct students to seek patterns or generalizations from the information, or to form conclusions. As an example, let's suppose that a social studies class has been discussing the shifting population pattern of the United States in the 1900s. Students have mentioned the population explosion and its dangers, that southern blacks moved into large northern cities, that white city dwellers moved to the suburbs, and that large population centers were growing on the Atlantic and Pacific coasts. In the hope of tying together a discussion the teacher asks such closure seeking questions as: "What have we learned today?" "Can we summarize what we learned in one or two statements?" "What could be the future outcome of this situation?" "How might the situation be changed?"

Seek Clarification of Issues

Not all statements made by students during a discussion are of equal value. When seeking closure a teacher may call for clarification of prior information. After asking the question, "What have we learned today?" the teacher may wish to clarify the issue by asking, "What was meant when we said that blacks were gaining political influence?" or, "Can we select from all factors influencing population shifts in the United States those three or four that would appear to be of greatest importance?"

Many times the discussion generated by eliciting and probing is too broad to invite a successful attack on problems and issues which are raised. The teacher may direct the attention of the class to narrower facets of the general discussion by using particular closure seeking questions. A teacher might ask: "What could happen if all white citizens left a city?" or, "Would the migration of people to the coastal areas impact pollution?" or "To which of the problems should we direct our attention?"

Ask for Suggested Procedures for Resolving a Problem

After a classroom problem has been identified and thoroughly discussed using eliciting and probing questions, you could ask for suggestions about investigating the problem. For problems that are able to be researched in a library you might ask, "Do we need more information?," "What shall we do?," "Where can we find out more about...?," "What is the best procedure for conducting this research?," "How can we report our findings to each other?" and other questions that will aid in organization of the problem solving effort.

Often teachers do not want their students to immediately resolve a problem. Activities are sometimes designed to provide students with the opportunity to master organizing or library research skills. Teaching objectives in these instances would relate to students' library activities, organizing information, communicating information to others, and interpreting the information to form conclusions.

At first glance experimental and library research projects appear to be different. In spite of the apparent differences of the two types of learning activities, questions used by teachers in seeking closure are often similar. The purpose in both instances is to have students make decisions on a plan for attacking and resolving a problem.

TABLE 5.3
Purposes and Examples of Closure Seeking Questions

Purpose	Examples
1. Inviting Students to Begin to Seek Conclusions	"What can be concluded from this?"
	"What can we say about how mealworms behave?"
2. Seeking Clarification of Issues	"What information is important when solving this problem?"
	"Can we only consider the impact of the population explosion on the United States?"
3. Soliciting Procedures	"How can we find the information necessary to help solve the problem?"
	"How can we test our best guess?"
4. Directing Students to Interpret Research Data	"Based on our research data, what can be concluded?"
	"What does our information show about the relationship between the British and the American Colonies?"

Influencing students to suggest conclusions based on known data

Influencing students to form conclusions based on data obtained through library research differs only slightly from their beginning to seek a conclusion. In both instances students are forming generalizations, classifications, or

conclusions based on known information. Research data are generally considered to be more reliable than unsupported information that is offered in the
typical classroom discussion. Information gained through library research is
likely to contain less opinion and fewer errors. The basic task of the teacher
remains the same whether conclusions are to be drawn following class
discussion or after a period of library research. Students should form conclusions based on information. The same closure seeking questions can be used
in either situation. Teachers may ask: "Does this statement agree with all we
know about...?" And in cases of reluctant students, the teacher may prompt
with: "We know that..., How is this related to...?"

Forming conclusions from information derived from experiments is different from the library approach usually because of the quantitative nature of
empirical data. Through questioning teachers lead students to discover
relationships that exist. The teacher may at times ask convergent questions
to help students to draw conclusions from data. Examples of convergent
closure seeking questions are: "What is the total?" "What did we say about
the value of...?" To direct students to form their own generalizations and
conclusions concerning data, teachers ask divergent, closure seeking questions, such as: "What does this data tell us?" "Who can see the relationship
between...?"

SELF CHECK FOR OBJECTIVE ONE

CAN YOU: list the purposes of closure seeking questions?

Information Seeking Questions

Information seeking questions are convergent questions which require a
pre-determined answer. They are used for review and drill exercises, and to
establish a background of information in problem solving activities.

Earlier you were introduced to the convergent-divergent model for classifying questions. According to this model convergent questions are defined as
fact oriented, requiring a single response. It was pointed out that when
convergent questions are used as the primary questioning tool, teachers will
cause little student initiated verbal interaction. Convergent questions are
highly efficient when used to teach and reinforce memorized concepts.

Passing on information is a valid function of the educational process; it
requires the use of traditional tools of memorization, drill, and the use of
convergent questions. As was previously stated, convergent questions can
be used in carrying out the processes of inquiry or problem solving. Fact
oriented questions can be used for a variety of purposes and will continue to
be the most common form of questions posed in the classroom. We should
examine their proper use.

The art of questioning by teachers is one of eliciting and encouraging responses to problems, expanding students' ideas by probing questions and assisting students to form solutions.

Convergent questions are used in problem solving or inquiry lessons for two primary purposes. The first is the introduction of a lesson and the second is to clarify or supply information during the lesson.

Opening Procedures

One way to begin an inquiry lesson is to bring students' past experiences to the present lesson. Convergent questions may refer to experiences from the classroom. "What did we learn yesterday about the primary colors?" Or out-of-school experiences may be a referent. "How many have ever gone fishing?" Convergent questions that are used to build bridges to student experiences are considered a form of eliciting. When using convergent questions in this way a teacher is attempting to begin with what is familiar so that each child can be involved. To be successful the teacher must frame questions which are appropriate to the backgrounds of children in the classroom which will lead to the topic being discussed. The ideal background question is one which every child in the room can answer. The questions, "Who has seen a rainbow?," "What colors do you remember?" can be used to begin a lesson on the colors of light. The question, "Who has been to a grocery store?" can be used to introduce a lesson classifying ideas and objects. Convergent questions, when properly selected and presented to a class in a non-threatening manner, can act as an opening procedure which involves all students. From this beginning the teacher can, with the use of more eliciting and probing, move to more open types of questions to expand the discussion and establish the problem. A series of questions that exemplifies this procedure is:

"Who can tell me what their house is made of?"
"Who has lived elsewhere and can tell me what material was used to make your house in that city?"
"What can be said about the location of houses and the material that is used to make them?"
"Why might they be different?"

Such a series of questions provides for the exercise of inductive reasoning by students as they move from specific information to arrive at generalizations based on the specifics.

Clarifying or Supplying Information

Teachers sometimes use convergent questions in group problem solving activities to supply information or clarify information that is vague or misunderstood. At times in an inquiry session students appear to be on their way to a desired generalization only to be held up or diverted by a lack of information, or by attempting to use false information. If you want to maintain ongoing verbal interaction instead of referring the class to resource materials, use convergent questions. "Who knows the population of New York City?" may supply needed information to maintain a discussion. The information supplied in answer to "Who can tell us the approximate population in _____ city?" may help to refocus a discussion that appears headed in the wrong direction due to erroneous data. Therefore, wherever specific facts are required to maintain the momentum of verbal interaction in group problem solving activities, desired information can be obtained from students with the use of convergent questions.

In Review and Drill Activities

Convergent questions assume prior knowledge by students. Thus, the most common function of convergent questions is in review and drill exercises. Drill exercises are those that are involved with specific information such as the multiplication tables or states and their capitals, while review involves more general information.

One of the challenges a teacher faces is to make drill and review activities interesting, to maintain a high level of participation. There are several strategies commonly employed to turn the drill and review activity into an exciting event and thereby maintain a high level of student interest and involvement.

Pacing in Review and Drill

Few ideas in education can be stated as absolutes. One idea that is nearly certain is that you will never generate student enthusiasm for a subject unless you are enthusiastic. To achieve success when administering a review exercise, you must generate an air of interest and show your feelings through a display of physical energy (being alert, moving around the room, etc.). Vocal inflections help too. Students usually remain alert if they are kept off balance by a vigorous teacher with a sense of timing. When asking review questions and reinforcing student responses it is important that you maintain a consistently energetic pace.

USING HIGHER LEVEL QUESTIONS IN DRILL ACTIVITIES

A continual staccato of convergent questions and short student responses that characterize review exercises may be broken by the mixture of questions requiring a higher level response than recall. This form of pacing could maintain students' attention. Questions that require students to translate known facts into a different form are considered to be at the comprehension level on the cognitive scale. After a student states a memorized definition for a term, the teacher could ask another student to state it in his own words. Not only does this evaluate the level of comprehension of student responses, it provides a change of pace in the questioning routine. Application questions can be mixed with convergent questions as a change of pace. For instance, after a student has stated the rule for finding the area of a rectangle, the teacher may provide dimensions and ask a second student to apply the rule to solve a problem. Students may also be asked to analyze facts, laws, or principles they are studying. You may find that mixing fact oriented, convergent questions with others which require the exercise of higher cognitive levels of thinking to be an effective method of pacing a review lesson which will tend to relieve tedium and maintain student interest.

Many teachers enhance memorization and drill activities with games and contests. The use of games and contests for drill and memorization will be discussed later in this book.

PROVIDING REVIEW TO INCREASE PARTICIPATION IN DRILL ACTIVITIES

Nothing is more disheartening when attempting a review session than to have questions meet with prolonged silence. Some teachers permit time for their classes to look over the material to be discussed. These teachers realize that even students who have read the assignment have had many intellectual demands made on them between the time they did the reading and class time. Permitting five or ten minutes for a quick review could provide the mental set that enhances the chances for student response to the teacher's questions.

When conducting a review exercise with few responses from students you may decide to break complex questions into a series of simpler questions. By doing this you tell students that you are persevering. They must produce answers to questions! This procedure also points out that answers can be obtained to questions with simpler mental associations. For example, a teacher asks: "What are the reasons that General Braddock was unsuccessful in the French and Indian War?" Student silence might be followed by such questions as: "What did British soldiers wear?," "How did the British go into battle?" or, "How did the Indians fight?"

A teacher who has established a good relationship with a class can be a success when soliciting responses to convergent questions from students. However, no amount of skill can enable a teacher to make a success of a review lesson with a group of students who do not know a good part of the basic facts with which they are dealing. Good review is dependent on good prior teaching.

TABLE 5.4
Purposes and Examples of Information Seeking Questions

Purpose	Examples
1. Opening Procedures for Inquiry	"What do we find on the ground after it rains?"
	"What color is the sky?"
2. Clarifying or Supplying Information in Inquiry Lessons	"What if I told you that there are 360 degrees in a circle; what would you say about a right angle?"
3. Review and Drill Activities	"Does anyone know how many states were in the Union in 1820?"

SELF CHECK FOR OBJECTIVE ONE

CAN YOU: list uses of information seeking questions?

SUMMARY

It's convenient to categorize questions according to the use the teacher makes of them. One category of verbal questions is eliciting questions. Eliciting questions are commonly used to encourage initial response from students, to expand participation in discussion, and to regain momentum for a discussion that is lagging. A second category of verbal questions is probing questions. Probing questions are used by teachers to extend ideas of students, redirect ideas, justify ideas and to clarify ideas. A classification of questions that is used to bring closure to a verbal interaction is closure seeking questions. Closure seeking questions are used to invite students to begin to seek conclusions, seek clarification of issues, solidify procedures for resolving a problem, and to direct students to interpret research data. A fourth category of questions used by teachers is information seeking questions. Information seeking questions are convergent questions. Responses are factual.

ACTIVITIES

1. Suppose you wanted to have a "discovery lesson" in class today, i.e., you plan to use a series of questions to help students discover a specific idea, principle, procedure, etc. Identify the "idea" to be discovered. What question would you use to elicit the initial response from students?
2. An arithmetic teacher is disappointed in the quantity of interaction in the classroom. Students do not always understand the problems they had for homework and seem reluctant to discuss their difficulties in class. The teacher usually starts the class by asking for volunteers to put their problems on the board and explain them. How can the teacher encourage greater participation in the class?
3. Bobbi Smith is a shy and quiet third grade girl. She is an excellent swimmer and has a pool at home. The class is discussing safety in and around the home. Write a question the teacher could ask to get Bobbi to participate in class discussion.
4. For each of the four purposes of probing questions write three appropriate questions. Be prepared to describe the situations in which the questions would be used.
5. For each of the four purposes of closure seeking questions, write three appropriate questions. Be prepared to describe situations in which the questions might be used.
6. For each of the three categories of information seeking questions write three appropriate questions. Be prepared to describe situations in which the questions might be used.

BIBLIOGRAPHY

Austin, P. (1989). Implications for learning through dialogue. *Language Arts, 66*(2), 184-90.

Cassidy, D.J. (1989). Questioning the young child, process and function. *Childhood Education, 65*(3), 146-149.

Desruisseaux, P. (1984). The p's and q's of q and a. *Currents, 10*(8), 50-52.

Dyeneyin, A.M. (1989). Development and validation of an integrated teaching plant (ITP) for school science lessons. *Research in Science and Technological Education, 7*(1), 51-60.

Gall, M. (1984). Synthesis of research on teachers' questioning. *Educational Leadership, 42*(3), 40-47.

Goor, M.B., & Roe, D.L. (1989). You get what you ask for: assisting and giving feedback. *Academic Therapy, 24*(3), 321-328.

Nessel, D. (1987). Reading comprehension: asking the right questions. *Phi Delta Kappan, 68*(6), 442-445.

Plourde, L. (1989). Teaching with collections. *Young Children, 44*(3), 78-80.

Reding, R.J., & Powell, S.D. (1986). The improvement of thinking skills in young children using computer activities: A replication and extension. *Educational Psychology, 6*(2), 179-183.

Sanders, N. (1966). *Classroom questions.* New York: Harper & Row.

Shake, M.C., & Arlington, R.L. (1985). Where do teacher's questions come from? *Reading Teacher, 38,* 432-438.

Smilanski, J., & Hallberstadt, N. (1986). Inventors versus problem solvers: An empirical investigation. *Journal of Creative Behavior, 20*(3), 183-201.

Swicegood, P.R., & Parsons, J.L. (1989). Better questions and answers equal success. *Teaching Exceptional Children, 21*(3), 4-8.

CHAPTER SIX

INTRODUCTORY CASE STUDY

CASE STUDY 6-1
INCREASING THE FLOW FROM THE FOUNTAINHEAD

Ernest Fountainhead believed that students in his music classes should come to know the history and theory of music, not merely how to sing or play an instrument. Unfortunately, Ernest, a first year teacher, had much more success directing his students in song than he did teaching them about the structure and theory of music and the literature about musicians and composers. Ernest used the time honored methods for imparting information he knew so well from his experiences as a student in the public schools and the university. He had accumulated a collection of pictures and photographs which he employed in his lectures about the lives and times of the great composers. He played excerpts of the compositions of the composers that were the subjects of his lectures. He tried very hard to be serious and business-like to impress his students with the importance of the subject matter. Yet each Friday few of his students were successful in passing the tests he gave over the week's work. Mr. Fountainhead was at a loss as to how he could present the information about the subject he loved so well so that students would learn it successfully.

WHAT DO YOU THINK? DO YOU HAVE ANY SUGGESTIONS FOR MR. FOUNTAINHEAD?

What are some kinds of activities that would help his students learn and recall the information about music?

Perhaps if he spent more time on the subject matter and less on the vocal music?

Perhaps he should try to have the students do seatwork as the reading and mathematics teachers do.

Maybe he could be more firm and make the students stay on task.

Evaluate these suggestions and make a list of your own that would make Ernest Fountainhead more successful in teaching the facts and information about his subject.

CHAPTER SIX

THE DIDACTIC TEACHER: THE EFFICIENT PURVEYOR OF INFORMATION

"Knowledge is power."

Lord Bacon.

GOAL

After reading this chapter the student will understand the relationship between the didactic and inquiry models.

OBJECTIVES

After reading this chapter the student will

1. contrast didactic and inquiry teaching,
2. compare direct and indirect teaching by listing the advantages of each,
3. write a plan for a 20 minute lecture,
4. describe the characteristics of an effective lecture,
5. list three concerns which teachers have when using media in a lecture,
6. list two guidelines which are used when delivering a lecture with demonstration,
7. list and describe the seven principles and guidelines employed in using direct instruction, and
8. describe the mastery learning model that associates traditional didactic and direct instruction.

CONTRASTING DIDACTIC AND INQUIRY MODELS

The most commonly used method of teaching is didactic. It is characterized by a predominance of teacher talk. The didactic teacher lectures, explains, gives directions, answers questions, drills students on facts, and generally uses direct teaching methods to transmit information. Teachers spend more than fifty percent of the day talking and students spend the majority of their day listening, reading, and writing. We conclude that much of the instruction that occurs in schools is of the traditional or didactic variety.

Research indicates that eighty five percent or more of learning that takes place in school is at the knowledge or comprehension levels. We conclude that because of the prevalence of didactic instruction in our classrooms it is important that teachers know how to use it efficiently.

The history of education is filled with debates over the advantages of direct or didactic instruction contrasted to the use of indirect or inquiry methods of teaching. The object teaching of Pestalozzi, the problem solving methods of Dewey, the project methods of instruction prominent in the decade of the 1930s and the emphasis on inquiry teaching in science and social studies in the post Sputnik era are a few examples of efforts of proponents to promote methods of indirect instruction over the course of several decades. The didactic/inquiry debate is not likely to be resolved soon. The following discussion points out various characteristics, advantages and disadvantages of each model of teaching.

Direct or didactic teaching is generally identified as the most efficient method. A well organized lecture delivered by a skilled teacher may range over a wide array of information and cover conceptual structure and applications. Where learning objectives are narrowly defined as facts or skills, research indicates didactic (direct) instruction to be especially efficient. Inquiry or problem solving procedures, on the other hand, tend to address a more limited array of concepts in a given lesson. And, if indirect methods of inquiry are used to investigate a conceptual structure, a great deal of classroom time is consumed. Direct instruction has proved to be best for raising the scores of students on tests of narrowly defined learning objectives. This probably accounts for its increased popularity in the back to basics movement. Remediation procedures used in the basic skills subjects of reading and mathematics depend on drill and practice activities in a well structured and supervised classroom. The research reviews of Peterson and Horwitz as summarized in Table 6.1 illustrate the research base of the didactic and inquiry teaching debate.

The Peterson review of 117 studies indicated that traditional, direct methods of instruction tend to produce the best results in improving scores in total achievement, mathematics achievement, and reading achievement, while non-traditional, indirect methods of instruction were favored to enhance achievement in creativity, problem solving, and a half dozen affective areas. Horwitz, in his review of 306 studies, found ambiguous results when contrasting traditional and open classrooms in their effects on total achievement. He found the open classroom to be more favored when creativity and most of the affective factors studied were considered. In 17 studies Horwitz found that the anxiety factor was higher by eleven percent in the open classroom.

Although there appears to be some uncertainty concerning the results of traditional instruction on achievement in the Horwitz review, the Peterson review, which tended to concentrate on studies that dealt with basic skills, did demonstrate a positive relationship between the two factors. What does appear to be certain from the two reviews is that the two different methods of classroom instruction yield advantages in different clusters of learning. The one conclusion that may be drawn from this data is that both methodologies have a place in classrooms.

SELF CHECK FOR OBJECTIVE ONE

CAN YOU: contrast the didactic and inquiry teaching models?

SELF CHECK FOR OBJECTIVE TWO

CAN YOU: compare direct and indirect teaching by listing the advantages of each?

THE LECTURE

Planning a Lecture

To achieve its greatest impact a classroom lecture must be well planned and skillfully delivered. Unfortunately, in actual practice many teachers consider lecturing to be talking. When not carefully prepared, lectures come off as rambling, lacking organization and therefore failing to produce the desired result of student comprehension. Planning for a lecture is not difficult.

When lecture or lecture-discussion is used the daily lesson plan is an outline of the material to be covered. The outline includes only as much information as required to guide the lecture. Single words or brief phrases serve as cues for information that has been committed to memory. They are preferred to lengthy sentences or phrases. Since lecture outlines are

	Peterson Review		Horwitz Review	
	N	Favors	N	Favors
Cognitive:				
Total Achievement	25	trad.	26	Neither
Math Achievement	18	trad.		
Reading Achievement	20	trad.		
Creativity	11	open	36	open
Problem Solving	1	open		
Affective:				
Self concept	14	open	28	open
School Attitudes	15	open	44	open
Teacher Attitudes	2	open		
Curiosity	3	open	43	open
Anxiety	5	open	47	open
Independence	3	open	82	open

TABLE 6.1
RESEARCH COMPARING OPEN AND TRADITIONAL TEACHING

designed to be organizers of the teacher's thoughts instead of being read verbatim, a general rule is to use the fewest number of words that will enable you to recall information for delivery. It is normal that a beginning teacher tends to develop a lecture outline with more detail than for an outline on a familiar topic. Experienced teachers, when delivering lectures on familiar topics, require a minimum of lecture notes. However, even the most veteran teacher who delivers a lecture "off the cuff" without lecture notes has experienced the post-lecture realization that some part of the lecture has been omitted. The lecture outline is a helpful tool for all who strive for quality when delivering classroom lectures.

A Lecture Outline

Chapter three discussed lesson planning in detail. Planning for a lecture involves the same basic elements as other strategies for teaching: goals, objectives, media or materials, and, if the teacher chooses, a study guide. If a quiz or worksheet is to be used following a lecture, it must be attached to the lesson plan. The sample lesson plan which follows illustrates the lecture lesson plan format.

PAX ROMANA

Topic: 200 years of peace in the Roman Empire

Goals Statement: Students will understand how peace affects a society.

Objectives: 1. List the five most important emperors of this period.
2. Explain the meaning of "Pax Romana."
3. Describe the Birth of Christianity and its relationship to the Roman Empire and
4. Describe the expansion of the Roman Empire during the Pax Romana period.

Materials: fact sheet, Pax Romana film strip

Procedure: 1. Set; Dress in Roman clothing at start of the lecture
2. Lecture Outline
A. Pax Romana means Roman Peace
B. Period began under Emperor Augustus
1. begins 200 years of peace and prosperity
2. Augustus willed that the borders of the Empire would remain the same. Why?
C. Emperor Tiberius (A.D. 14-37)
1. Pontius Pilate governed Judea.
2. Jesus of Nazarath put to death.
D. Emperor Nero (A.D. 54-68)
1. Rome burned—Christians condemned.
2. Jews revolt in 70 A.D. destroying Jerusalem.

        E. The five "good" emperors.
          1. Nerva.
          2. Trajan.
          3. Hadrian.
          4. Antoninus.
          5. Marcus Aurelius.
        F. Review of major items of information.
     3. Review/Bridge to next lesson:
        a. Review lecture high points
        b. Bridge to next class by asking students about what may
           have happened after 200 years of peace.
     4. Evaluation: prepare 10 oral questions to be asked at beginning
       of the next lesson.

This lecture outline might be considered "bare bones" with little detail recorded. It should remind the teacher of details to be covered. It provides the structure for the lecture. The teacher can insert notes as a memory aid on certain points of information. For instance, if the difference in the old Roman calendar and the modern calendar is to be discussed, the words, "Julian Calendar" may be inserted. Or Hadrian's Wall may be noted if the teacher wants to present information on the Roman occupation of England. The amount of detail that appears on a lecture outline varies widely among teachers. As a general rule the outline should remain as simple and uncluttered as possible.

SELF CHECK FOR OBJECTIVE THREE

CAN YOU: construct a plan for a twenty minute lecture and provide a
           rationale for its structure?

Delivery of a Lecture

A lecture is not merely telling. It is an attempt to communicate information and ideas to others. Stating information while standing or sitting before a group does not guarantee the transmission of ideas and that others understand. There are procedural guidelines that will improve a speaker's chances for effective communication.

Effective teachers do not read their lectures. There are several effects caused by a speaker who reads. The speaker loses the respect of the audience who suspect rightly or wrongly the speaker does not know the subject. Second, reading diverts the speaker's attention from individuals in the class, reducing chances for effective communication. Oral reading, to be effective, must have a rhythm and timing seldom generated by the material found in textbooks.

Effective speakers maintain eye contact with individuals in the class. Speech teachers sometimes tell their students to select a student in each part of an audience and alternately speak directly to individuals selected.

Effective speakers use pacing and voice modulation to maintain the audience's interest in the topic and to emphasize important points. Listeners should know when a speaker delivers an important point. An illustration is a summarizing statement in a lecture. The speaker can make the listener aware by raising voice intensity and changing the pace of the delivery, either slowing down or speeding up the flow of words. Effective speakers avoid using a monotone, single pitch, single intensity, regularly paced delivery that quickly causes the listener to lose interest. Besides using voice modulation, effective lecturers emphasize important points by telling their audience, "This is important."

The organization of a lecture

A rule that is often given in public speaking courses that guides the construction of a speech is, "Tell them what you are going to tell them; tell them; then tell them what you have told them." This rule translates into a plan for classroom lecture. It begins with a review of the previous lesson to set the context for new information. Next, a preview of the information (objectives) to be covered is offered. Following the lecture a review of major points of the lesson is stated. To improve the clarity of presentation some teachers provide the class with copies of a study sheet that parallels the lecture for the day. Study guides supply the student with a sense of structure. They also reduce the need for note-taking, freeing students to give more attention to listening to the lecture. An example of a preview of a lecture is:

> Today we are going to move along in our study of the Roman Empire to the period of Pax Romana or Roman Peace. We will consider the rule of Caesar Augustus, a powerful emperor who initiated a 200 year long period that is considered the zenith of Roman influence, the dramatic growth of Christianity and its effect on the Empire, and the efforts of the Empire to protect its expanded borders under what are generally called the "five good emperors." Let us first take a look at Caesar Augustus.

These introductory remarks bridge to the previous lesson and provide an overview of what is to come. With or without a study guide in their hands students listening to a lecture benefit from opening statements.

As was stated earlier, to maximize learning, the lecturer should also end a lecture with a review of important concepts and information that were covered. When a lecture is lengthy it is often advisable to review by summarizing periodically during the class period.

SELF CHECK FOR OBJECTIVE FOUR

CAN YOU: describe the characteristics of an effective lecture?

Using Media With a Lecture

The effectiveness of a lecture is enhanced by media. The most common forms of media employed by lecturers are slides, overhead transparencies, charts, graphs, and pictures. Regardless of the type of media that are being used, there are some guidelines that will enhance the quality of the lecture.

First, an obvious, but sometimes neglected rule is that the visual media must be clearly visible to members of the class. Materials of poor quality or of insufficient size will have a negative effect on the transmission of information.

Second, media should fit the objective that is to be taught. Media that are inappropriate to the objective produce negative results. A filmstrip titled "Our National Parks" may focus on the economics of the National Park System when the teacher is expecting scenes of Old Faithful and the Painted Desert. Previewing media to be used with a lecture is an absolute must if maximum learning is to be achieved.

Third, the medium must not become the focus of the lecturer's attention during a lecture. Media should enhance the communication between the lecturer and the class. But when the lecturer becomes engrossed with the chart, transparency, or other medium and forgets the class, the use of the medium has a negative effect on the level of communication.

SELF CHECK FOR OBJECTIVE FIVE

CAN YOU: list three concerns which teachers have when using media in a lecture?

Using a Demonstration in a Lecture

A geography teacher may use a flashlight and a globe to demonstrate the relationship between the sun and earth that causes daylight and dark. A mathematics teacher may show a class the relationship between cylinders and cones by filling three cones from one cylinder of equal diameter and height. The art teacher may demonstrate to a class how pigments may be mixed to produce complementary colors. Physical education teachers demonstrate the proper method for shooting a basketball. And music teachers use demonstrations to show students the proper way to hold a musical instrument. At some time most teachers have occasions to use the lecture-demonstration method of teaching. A lecture with a demonstration involves manipulative materials that a teacher uses to present a technique or principle. To use the lecture-demonstration method of instruction, a teacher must develop the ability to manipulate the environment and use the results to demonstrate and clarify a concept.

There is an old vaudeville routine in which a stranger to New York City accosts a man on the street and asks, "Could you tell me how to get to Carnegie Hall?" The New Yorker answers, "Practice, man, practice." The advice offered to the visitor to New York is equally valid for the question, "How does a teacher become skilled at giving lecture-demonstrations?"

Before teaching a demonstration lesson the activity should be practiced at least once and several times if possible.

It is important to select the right demonstration for each lesson to be taught. A demonstration that is not directly related to the desired concept causes student confusion. A teacher who lectures on the properties of right triangles while using equilateral triangles causes lasting misconceptions. So does the science teacher who discusses the dynamics of volcanic action and uses a chemical reaction that yields smoke and sparks but misrepresents the nature of volcanic activity. A demonstration used with a lecture must clearly illustrate the exact nature of the concept under investigation.

Demonstrations must be easily seen by all members of the class to be effective. Demonstrations that are too small, hidden from view, or for any reason not easily observed will not serve the desired purpose of illustrating a principle or concept.

A classroom demonstration must also be safe for all those present in the classroom. If an open flame or potentially dangerous chemicals are used, precautions such as goggles or plexiglas screens must be used. Most states have laws that pertain to the safe use of dangerous materials and open flames in classrooms.

In summary, a lecture-demonstration should be appropriate to the objective of the lesson, be capable of being observed by all students in the class, and not jeopardize the safety of the teacher or students to be suitable for classroom use.

The following is a sample lecture-demonstration with comments which relate lecture to discovery and inquiry teaching.

Roland Stone, an earth science teacher, was lecturing on the movement of the earth about the sun and its relationship to the earth day. "Look," Mr. Stone lectured, while holding a lighted flashlight so the beam shone directly on a large globe of the earth. He used his free hand to cause the globe to slowly spin from west to east. "Notice how the east coast of the United States comes into the light while the western part of the country is still unlighted. It is morning in New York while it is still dark in the plains states." He continued, "Nebraska and Texas are still in darkness while New York and the Atlantic coast is in the light. It is morning in New York while not yet morning in Nebraska and the rest of the Midwest." Mr. Stone continued to rotate the globe as he talked, "See how the sun is now directly over New York? It is noon there. Look at the west coast. The states of California, Oregon, and Washington are just inside the lighted area. It would be early morning between the east and west coasts of the United States."

Mr. Stone would continue to use the flashlight and globe to illustrate examples of daylight and dark on the earth. Since he is lecturing and performing the demonstration, he is in complete control of events that occur. He may proceed through his presentation at his own pace, emphasizing points, and reviewing to reinforce prior information as he wishes. You may contrast this with the sample lessons demonstrated in earlier chapters where inquiry or discovery were utilized. In an inquiry or discovery lesson Mr. Stone would show the relationship demonstrated by the globe and light beam and ask the class, "What do you see?" "What does this show?" and other open-ended questions. In the inquiry lesson, Mr. Stone would have much less control over the events of the lesson as he elicited responses from students, waited and guided their responses. The inquiry lesson and the lecture-demonstration would have different appearances while using the same demonstration materials.

SELF CHECK FOR OBJECTIVE SIX

CAN YOU: list two guidelines to follow when using demonstration with lecture?

DIRECT TEACHING — A MORE DETAILED LOOK

Earlier in this chapter we took a brief look at the strategy of direct teaching in order to compare the advantages of traditional/direct instruction with inquiry/indirect instruction. Because of its widespread use in all levels of the public schools, direct teaching bears a more detailed discussion and understanding. The direct teaching methods are commonly used whenever the subject matter to be learned is of a highly structured nature, especially in the study of mathematics and reading. Direct teaching methods are employed at the introductory levels of the elementary and to remediate the weak skills of low achieving or so-called "at risk" students at the middle, junior high and senior high school levels. The principles of the direct teaching method are effective when applied to the memorization of factual materials in any subject matter, and their use is highly appropriate in subjects such as teaching the rules of grammar, memorization of states and their capitals, and memorization of the Latin names of flora and fauna. Since much of the instruction that is presented in the low achieving classes at the secondary levels is aimed at the memorization and comprehension levels of cognition, direct teaching methods are effective in a wide variety of subjects of this type. Let's take a more comprehensive look at the guiding principles and practices of direct instructional techniques.

Direct instruction is one of the most highly researched areas in education. As the result of the many studies, a number of guidelines and practices of the strategy are accepted with confidence by experts in the field. Some of the most common are:

1. Instructional objectives must be clearly stated. The teacher and the students must know exactly what they are trying to accomplish at all times.
2. Learning activities must match the desired objective. Inappropriate activities waste time of both teachers and students, cause confusion and result in a lack of purpose and direction.
3. Learning activities must be appropriate for each learner. The learner

must have a reasonably good chance of being successful. The curriculum should be "success oriented."

4. The teacher should do everything possible to ensure maximizing "time on task," the time students are engaged in active learning during a class period. This includes:
   (a) beginning instruction promptly at the start of a class period,
   (b) making a smooth transition from one subject or activity to another,
   (c) handling materials efficiently such as passing out and collecting homework or manipulative materials, etc.

5. Maintain an academic focus during learning activities. That is, not get sidetracked from the purpose of the lesson or activity by permitting discussions to drift or allowing interruptions to distract the students.

6. Provide academic feedback during seat work. This is best accomplished by walking among students monitoring seat work assignments and by promptly correcting homework and tests and returning them to students.

7. Handle discipline problems promptly with as few distractions as possible to the learning process.

The teacher who applies these guidelines and principles in an appropriate subject matter setting will maximize the achievement of students in basic skills and general achievement areas according to the impressive research base which has accumulated over the past several decades.

SELF CHECK FOR OBJECTIVE SEVEN

CAN YOU: list and describe the seven principles and guidelines employed in using direct instruction?

Mastery Learning

The term "mastery learning" has been applied to a variety of teaching methods in the past twenty years. The first perhaps were the highly energetic primary grade reading and mathematics programs, Distar, wherein the teacher "drilled" the whole class by rapidly asking fact oriented questions and expected choral responses from the students. Some research indicated this procedure was somewhat successful in raising achievement scores of students in these subjects. Currently, mastery learning is being applied to a number of varieties of direct instructional techniques as they are applied to subjects such as reading and mathematics (the basic skills) which have a theoretical hierarchy of sequential skills. Mastery learning basically implies that each learner will master each subordinate skill before he or she progresses to the next skill in the hierarchy. In practice mastery learning resembles the management system strategy presented in Chapter Eight with some attention given to the classroom behaviors of the teachers involved. The model of mastery learning which has special application to today's school setting is one that permits the assimilation of direct instructional techniques into the didactic classroom.

In this model of mastery learning the teacher begins a unit of study by employing the traditional didactic methods of lecture, lecture-demonstration, lecture-discussion, review and drill. At appropriate intervals (often about three to five days) the teacher deviates from the normal didactic procedures and administers a test or some other form of evaluation to assess the understanding of the students. This test is formative in nature, that is, its purpose is strictly diagnostic and is not used in assigning grades to students. At this point the successful students, those who met the standards set on the formative evaluation instrument will undertake assignments which might be considered as enrichment activities. For instance, in mathematics the successful students might work word problems on calculators or in reading may read the textbook or trade books that are appropriate. While the successful group works on their enrichment activities, the students who did not meet the standards on the formative instrument will perform remedial activities designed to teach the skills in which they were deficient. These remedial activities will continue for these students until a second (or third or fourth) formative evaluation procedure reveals they have mastered the required skills and information. At this point all students, remedial group and successful group take a test that does count in determining a grade. This test is called a summative evaluation of the material studied during the three to five day period. (See Chapter Thirteen for a more complete discussion of summative and formative evaluation procedures.) Following the successful experience

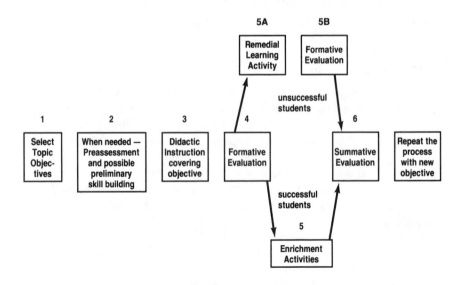

Figure 6.1
MASTERY LEARNING MODEL
Didactic/Direct Instruction

on the summative test the class will move on to the next set of learning objectives and the related learning experiences. By employing this mix of the traditional didactic teaching methods and the remediation and drill activities of direct teaching, all of the students in the class should be successful on the summative evaluation procedure.

A Few Observations on Mastery Learning

Preassessment

Some applications of mastery learning stress the use of a preassessment instrument to determine whether the students have the prerequisite skills to handle the planned learning activities. In practice the use of a formal preassessment test is rarely necessary. Most mastery learning occurs in conjunction with one of the basic skill areas or the memorization of facts in a non-basic skills area. Normally the basic skills programs have a well defined continuous progress format and the progression of the learning objectives is well defined. In the non-basic skills subjects the memorization of factual information has few specific or easily definable prerequisites. In practice the use of preassessment testing is necessary only when the instruction is to begin in the middle of a continuum and the skill levels of the students are not generally known to the teacher. It appears the concept of preassessment is more important than its general application.

Managing the Varied Groups

Managing the groupings of students that are formed after a formative evaluation has revealed that some require remediation and some do not is a somewhat unique challenge to teachers whose primary experience with grouping is managing groups who are at different places on a skills continuum. In the latter case all of the groups are generally engaged in the same sort of activity, performing seatwork assignments related to their own skill level. In the mastery learning scheme which combines traditional didactic teaching with direct instruction techniques some students are engaged in remedial type seatwork while other students are undertaking enrichment activities. In these circumstances, wherein some students may spend a major portion of class time on remedial activities of a drill and practice nature while others are engaged in more unstructured and varied assignments, care must be taken to maintain the motivation of the remediation groups. This can be accomplished with contests, rewards and other behavioral reinforcers. The teacher must also strive to make sure the enrichment activities of the non-remedial students are interesting and challenging. Otherwise enrichment becomes "killing time" and the interest of these students will wane. With the variety of learning activities that take place in the didactic-direct mastery learning model, a greater stress must be placed upon planning and management of the curriculum. Despite these challenges posed here, teachers experienced with this model of teaching find the strong points of the model, mastery of basic skills and variety in classroom learning activities, to be worth the extra effort required.

SELF CHECK FOR OBJECTIVE EIGHT

CAN YOU: describe the mastery learning models that associate traditional didactic and direct instruction?

SUMMARY

Didactic and inquiry teaching models provide advantages when learning. Didactic teaching is better for providing the greatest content coverage, teaching basic skills, and raising scores on tests. Inquiry teaching is best for teaching problem solving skills, developing creativity and positive attitudes among learners. When lecture is to be used as an instructional strategy it must be well planned with a concise outline. Lecture should be structured to relate to previous lessons, to provide a preview of the content, to deliver the content, and to review the content at the conclusion of the lecture. The common skills of public speaking should be used in the proper delivery of a quality lecture. Lectures are often enhanced by media when properly employed. The lecture-demonstration is a specialized form of lecture that requires teachers to manipulate materials or equipment while presenting a concept. Lecture-demonstrations should be appropriate to illustrate the desired concept, capable of being observed by the students, and safe. During seatwork and drill activities the didactic teacher should attempt to maximize the time students spend on meaningful learning tasks by starting class promptly, reducing the time to a minimum for transition between one learning activity and the next one and maintaining an academic focus on learning.

The most common use for direct teaching is in teaching the basic skills at all levels of the K-12 curriculum. The principles and guidelines used while using direct teaching are (paraphrased) 1. Use clearly stated instructional objectives, 2. Learning activities should match the objectives, 3. Use appropriate learning activities that permit each learner to be successful, 4. Maximize student "time on task," 5. Maintain academic focus during learning activities, 6. Provide academic feedback during seatwork activities, and 7. Handle discipline problems efficiently as they arise.

One model of mastery learning efficiently combines the procedures of traditional didactic teaching with those of direct teaching. After employing didactic procedures to teach one or more objectives, the teacher employs some form of formative measurement to assess the progress of each student. Those students who "passed" the formative criteria undertake enrichment activities while those who require remediation proceed under the procedures of direct instruction. Following the completion of the remediation and enrichment activities the whole class undergoes a summative test on which all have a good chance of being successful. The mastery learning teacher must have the skills and knowledge to employ the techniques of didactic and direct instruction as well as managing individualized and group learning activities.

ACTIVITIES

1. Plan a brief lesson that might be taught as a lecture or lecture-demonstration and as an inquiry lesson.

   Example 1: Show a class that a burning candle goes out when placed under a glass jar and
   a) ask them what they observed and why it occurred (inquiry);
   b) after showing the demonstration describe in detail the reason the candle flame was extinguished.

   Example 2: List the following word pairs on the chalkboard:
   folly—follies and dolly—dollies,
   rally—rallies and holly—hollies
   Ask the class the relationship between the words in each pair. Ask students to establish a rule for forming the plurals of words ending in -lly. (inquiry). Then place the same word pairs on the chalkboard and point out that the y is dropped and -ies is added to form the plural of each word. (lecture-demonstration). Following each lesson the teacher may ask for additional examples (inquiry) or offer additional examples (lecture-demonstration).

2. Select a topic of interest and create a lesson plan using the technique of lecture or lecture-demonstration. Be sure to include an introductory overview of each day's lecture and an ending review. Where appropriate include examples and non-examples of concepts presented and brief summaries to emphasize important points of information.

3. Form a group and plan a brief (one objective) lesson to be taught using the mastery learning techniques outlined in the chapter.

BIBLIOGRAPHY

Berliner, D.C., & Rosenshine, B. (1976). *The acquisition of knowledge in the classroom, technical report IV-1*. San Francisco: Far West Laboratory for Educational Research and Development.

Cooper, J.M. (Ed.). (1986). *Classroom teaching skills (3rd ed.)*. Lexington: Heath.

de Bono, E. (1983). The direct teaching of skills. *Phi Delta Kappa*. *64*(10), 703-8.

Hanning, R.W. (1984). The classroom as theatre of self. *ADE Bulletin, 77* (Spring), 33-37.

Good, T.L., & Brophy, J.E. (1984). *Looking in classrooms*. New York: Harper & Row.

Jackson, R. (1986). Thumbs up for direct teaching of thinking skills. *Educational Leadership*. *43*(8), 32-6.

Jacobsen, D., Eggen, P., & Kauchak, D. (1989). *Methods for teaching, 3rd ed.* Columbus: Merrill.

Keller, C.W. (1988). Enhancing the expository approach for teaching history. *Social Studies*. *79*(3), 92-96.

Killen, L.R. (1989). Reflecting on reflective teaching: a response. *Journal of Teacher Education*. *40*(2), 49-52.

Levin, T., & Long, R. (1981). *Effective Instruction*. Washington: Association for Supervision and Curriculum Development.

Sykes, G. (1988). Inspired teaching: the missing element in "effective schools." *Educational Administration Quarterly*. *24*(4), 461-469.

CHAPTER SEVEN

INTRODUCTORY CASE STUDY

CASE STUDY 7-1
WHY TELL WHEN YOU CAN ASK?

The teachers of the sixth grade team at New Era Middle School had agreed to increase the use of problem solving in all of their classes by restructuring the usual learning activities using the guideline, "Why tell when you can ask." The team was meeting to discuss how they might accomplish this goal. Mrs. Painter, the art teacher, suggested, "Instead of telling and showing the formation of complementary colors I will have the children mix primary color paints together and discover the complementary colors." Mr. Severn, the mathematics teacher, added, "I think the students could discover how to construct identical angles if I provide rulers and protractors and a bit of direction." Ms. Tory Novel, who taught language arts asked, "Do you think the children could analyze a well constructed paragraph and a poorly constructed paragraph and form some conclusions about writing a good paragraph?" Thus, each teacher on the team added ideas and helped others generate ideas for increasing the use of problem solving in the sixth grade curriculum.

CAN YOU HELP?

Consider your own chosen subject matter or interest area. Describe one activity where students may be asked to discover a rule, pattern, relationship or concept rather than learning the concept directly from reading or being told about it.

Now help a teacher in another subject matter area. Describe an activity in any subject other than your own special interest that permits students to use problem solving skills to discover a rule, pattern, relationship or concept.

CHAPTER SEVEN
TEACHING PROBLEM SOLVING AND CRITICAL THINKING SKILLS

"The development of general ability for thinking and judgment should always be foremost, not the acquisition of special knowledge."

-Albert Einstein

GOALS

After reading this chapter the student will understand

1. The general nature of the problem solving teaching strategy,
2. The advantages and disadvantages related to instruction and learning of the problem solving strategy,
3. The general nature of the three types of problem solving as defined in the chapter.

OBJECTIVES

After studying this chapter the student will:

1. orally or in writing discuss the advantages of teaching problem solving in the context of the normal curriculum.
2. list four of the five skills associated with Type I problem solving.
3. create an outline that describes one Type I, Rational Inquiry lesson, one Type II, Discovery Inquiry lesson, and one Type III, Empirical Problem Solving lesson (either experimental or using stored data) to be taught in a content area.
4. list five of the six skills associated with Type II, discovery problem solving.
5. list five of the six skills associated with Type III, Empirical/Experimental problem solving.
6. list seven of eight skills associated with Type III, Empirical/using Stored Data problem solving.
7. orally or in writing discuss the practice of incorporating problem

solving into the content areas of the normal curriculum, focusing upon the appropriate use of the three types of problem solving activities.

8. list and describe the four guidelines presented for incorporating problem solving into an ongoing curriculum.

THE NATURE AND ADVANTAGES OF INQUIRY LEARNING/PROBLEM SOLVING LEARNING ACTIVITIES

Inquiry or problem solving is a comprehensive model of instruction which is characterized by students' active participation in the learning process. When participating in inquiry learning strategies, students may manipulate materials and equipment, participate in problem solving discussion groups, respond to open ended questions posed by the teacher and collect data from the library or from direct observations. While the array of activities identified as inquiry or problem solving appear to be diverse, they share one thing in common. The learner is involved with higher level cognitive activities such as applying rules, analyzing, organizing information and inferring and generalizing from data. In each instance the learner is intellectually required to go beyond the given or observed data to make an intuitive leap to form an individually derived conclusion. The great variety of activities that are called inquiry is exemplified by two models of teaching, the discovery method and the research or empirical method.

Some Advantages of Inquiry/Problem Solving Learning

Research and experience have provided educators with a list of advantages to be derived from using inquiry teaching techniques in the classroom. Some of these are:

1. Higher level cognitive skills are used and developed.
2. Retention of learned concepts is greater.
3. Students learn how to solve problems.
4. Inquiry learning increases the internally derived motivation of students as opposed to the more external motivational base associated with didactic learning.
5. Children who take part in inquiry learning have improved attitudes toward the subject matter, teachers, and schools.
6. Many students who have not been successful in didactic instruction gain self-confidence. They are successful in inquiry learning.

Other positive results are increases in language concepts, mathematics concepts, social studies concepts, and listening skills. Therefore, part of the instructional time in each day should be devoted to acquiring knowledge by inquiry. Learners have a right to participate in at least some activities that will more fully develop their intellects.

SELF CHECK FOR OBJECTIVE ONE

CAN YOU: orally or in writing discuss the advantages of learning problem solving in the context of the normal curriculum?

TEACHING PROBLEM SOLVING AND CRITICAL THINKING SKILLS

Across the country in recent years there has been a growing concern that those who graduate from school do not know how to think, or solve problems encountered in the home and on the job. The first wave of solutions to this perceived problem consisted of a vast array of quick-fix packaged programs. Authors of these programs usually were educators (or those interested in the education of youth) who had some experience with some custom-made materials which they felt were successful in helping children to improve their critical thinking skills and problem solving abilities. Each author and program in stage one of the "Let's teach critical thinking" movement tended to have his or her own definition of problem solving and original list of critical thinking skills. As school supervisors and teachers reviewed the many programmatic solutions for the problem solving dilemma, confusion reigned, for the "solutions" were quite diverse and often, at least on the surface, narrow and unrelated to one another.

There were programs that required students to solve brain teasers (i.e.: How can we measure one quart of water if we have only a three quart pan and a five quart pan?), and others that stressed mathematics word problems. Others taught a children's version of deductive logic, the solution of number analogies, word analogies, or listing all the uses for common objects such as a brick, or stating all possible solutions to a social dilemma. While each program may demonstrate its effectiveness in terms of its own objectives, none could demonstrate what children learned transferred readily to other classroom learning or to real life situations. The problems of scope and transferability inherent in the specialized problem solving programs are now causing curriculum designers to search for new solutions that lie within the ongoing school programs.

The content based problem solving/critical thinking method presented in this chapter is designed to operate in all areas of the school program. It is based upon the practice of establishing open-ended problems in a content area and guiding students as they structure and carry out processes that result in solutions to the problems. The major tool of the teacher in guiding students through the problem solving activities is the proper use of purposive questioning. By applying a wide range of thinking processes and skills within the ongoing curriculum, students greatly broaden their range of cognitive experiences and develop a repertoire of problem solving and critical thinking skills. The teacher who directs this type of learning activity is said to be teaching by the inquiry strategy or method.

THREE TYPES OF THINKING SKILL DEVELOPMENT ACTIVITIES

For convenience it is possible to classify many, if not all, thinking skill development activities into three major categories, Rational Inquiry, Discovery and Empirical Inquiry. Following is a description of each, a statement of the skills developed and some insights as to where each is employed.

Type I Thinking Skills Development Activity: Rational Inquiry

To begin a rational inquiry lesson the teacher presents a problem through the use of media, verbal descriptions, manipulative materials, or by asking questions and guides students through a problem solving process to form a conclusion or solution. The teacher does this primarily through the use of verbal questions and the proper use of reinforcement of student responses. She asks open-ended questions to elicit student responses, probes for student ideas, and guides them to closure which is generally in the form of a generalization that explains the experiences or data presented — the conclusion to the problem under discussion. (See Chapter Five for a detailed presentation of the use of purposive questioning in teaching inquiry activities.)

Following is a list of the major skills developed through the use of Type I Thinking Skill Development Activities:

The ability to:
1. exercise flexibility in thinking, to consider all possible solutions to a problem.
2. make inferences, create ideas.
3. evaluate ideas in relation to problem solutions.
4. evaluate inferences and change inferences when appropriate.
5. formulate conclusions to problems or generalizations that explain a phenomenon.

SELF CHECK FOR OBJECTIVE TWO

CAN YOU: list four of the five skills associated with Type I problem solving?

Illustrations of the Rational Inquiry Method

Social Studies. Waldo Turner teaches American history to a ninth grade class in Middletown Junior High School. A concept in the curriculum which is to be taught addresses factors that led to the creation and development of cities. The textbook which he uses lists factors such as location at a river junction, natural harbors and the presence of transportation systems such as railroads, highways, and navigable rivers. Other factors such as climate, land forms, availability of raw materials for manufacturing, and water supplies are also mentioned. Mr. Turner decides to teach this content using a discovery lesson.

Since they live in Ohio, the class is introduced to the discovery lesson by pinning a large map of the state on the front wall. Mr. Turner said, "Can we see from the map where most of the people of our state live?" The students responded one after another, "Mostly in the cities," as he practiced wait-time techniques. "Cleveland and Akron have a lot of people." "Cincinnati looks like it covers a lot of territory. It's pretty big." "Look at Columbus. It's really big but I drove through there with my family and much of it is undeveloped."

After the class had offered many comments that helped to locate cities in the state Mr. Turner asked, "Did you ever wonder why cities are located where they are?"

He waited as students made suggestions: "Cleveland started where the Cuyahoga River empties into Lake Erie." "Cincinnati is on the Ohio River and on the map it looks as if another river goes through it." "Look at all the roads and railroads that meet in Columbus. It is located right in the middle of the state." Mr. Turner began to list on the chalkboard student comments under the names of the cities mentioned.

CLEVELAND: At the mouth of the Cuyahoga River.
Rolling terrain, not real hilly.
A shipping center for Great Lakes ships.
Canals connect the Cuyahoga River to form a trans-
portation system.

CINCINNATI: On Ohio River.
Had a fort to protect it from the Indians.
Served as a gateway to settle the land given to Revolu-
tionary War veterans.
High rolling terrain.
Had trees to build houses and a fort.
A good place for industry with coal and other goods
along the river.

COLUMBUS: Has two rivers running through it.
In the center of the state.
Became the capital.
Two rivers flow through the city.
Roads and railroads that connected other big cities go
through the city.

After the class had offered many suggestions and he had listed them on the chalkboard, Mr. Turner asked, "Can we summarize what we have said here? Have we discovered anything?"

Various students offered suggestions. "We learned that rivers were important in the location of cities." "Yes, especially when they were navigable and connected to other rivers." "Raw materials for manufacturing were important," "And trees and stones to build shelter." As students made generalized statements Mr. Turner made a new list. To extend their understanding he asked each of them to examine the map and write a one page essay listing one location where it appears a population center may have developed. He also asked them to speculate why the establishment of a city did not occur.

It is important to note that Mr. Turner could have taught the same concepts by lecturing, listing the factors that contribute to the establishment of cities and summarizing major concepts. He chose to teach this lesson by the discovery method partially because of the benefits associated with student learning, but also because he and the class enjoy the experience of learning by discovery.

Science: Mrs. Thomas filled a glass aquarium with water and placed the aquarium atop a wooden box that was turned upside down on her desk. She then placed a second glass container on her desktop. As her class watched Mrs. Thomas said, "I want you to observe what is going to happen very carefully. I am going to ask you to tell me what you saw, so observe it well." Mrs. Thomas then submerged a short, about two foot long, piece of surgical tubing in the water of the aquarium, permitted it to fill with water, then pinched each end of the tubing with her fingers and, leaving the end of the tubing in her left hand submerged under water in the aquarium, took the pinched end in her right hand from the water and moved it to the empty glass container. She then released both ends of the tubing at once. She began her questioning.

"What did you see?" "What happened?" "Why did the water flow from the aquarium to the glass jar?" "Where did the push come from that caused the water to climb up the tubing to the top of the aquarium?" "What can we say about how a siphon works?" In this way Mrs. Thomas guided the students to the conclusion that a siphon works because as the water begins to drain from the tubing into the empty container there is a low pressure created in the tubing. The stronger atmospheric pressure pushes down on the water in the aquarium forcing it up the tubing. During the activity the students had ample opportunity to observe, make inferences, evaluate inferences, and form conclusions.

English/Language Arts: As a means to interest his students, Mr. Kaslow read to them from a synopsis of Jack London's "Call Of the Wild" . . . the story of how a gentle dog in the Alaskan wilderness gradually reverted to the ways of his ancestors. Part way through the story Mr. Kaslow asked, "What is happening to our gentle dog?" "Where did he learn how to fight?" "If he were to return again to civilization, would he again be gentle or is he forever changed?" And at the end of the story where the call of his ancestors is complete, Mr. Kaslow asks, "Are there any lessons in this story for humans?" "How would they behave if thrust into the wilderness?" Through his questions, Mr. Kaslow has involved the students with making inferences, evaluating inferences, and forming conclusions!

Mathematics: In her middle school math classes Sandi Rivers frequently uses analogies and asks students to make inferences. When dealing with simple equations she may ask, "What do you have to do with a teeter totter to keep it balanced? If you take one child off an end what happens?" "What must you do to make it balanced again?" "If we take three away from this side of the equation, what must we do to make the equation balanced?" Or displaying a stack of cubes, "If I separate the stack of cubes into four piles, what operations have I performed?" "Now if I take the four piles and put them together again, what operation have I performed?" "Now what about the total number of blocks?" "What can we say about the operations of multiplication and division?" The students should have inferred multiplication and division are opposite operations. Rather than directly telling this fact, Mrs. Rivers has chosen to permit the students to make inferences and form conclusions. This is what teaching by inquiry is all about, inserting opportunities for student problem solving into the ongoing curriculum.

With but a little thought teachers of art, music, physical education, and the vocational subjects can find opportunities within their curricula to permit students to employ the skills of problem solving. Can you think of any examples in your field of study?

SELF CHECK FOR OBJECTIVE THREE (Rational Inquiry)

CAN YOU: create an outline that describes one Type I, Rational Inquiry problem solving lesson?

Type II Thinking Skill Development Activity—Discovery

In the Discovery problem solving strategy the teacher presents, or assists students in developing a data set that contains elements that demonstrate a rule or relationship. Through questioning, the teacher guides the students to examine the data set and formulate the rule or relationship. Discovery differs from Rational Inquiry only by the amount of emphasis that is placed on the creation and evaluation of data sets. Discovery may be considered a special case of Rational Inquiry.

Because of the emphasis placed upon interpretation of data, the Discovery problem solving strategy provides students experiences that result in a somewhat different set of problem solving skills.

Problem Solving/Critical Thinking Skills Developed by Type II, Discovery Learning Activities. They are: the ability to:
1.   create data by manipulating objects or ideas,
2.   organize data to more easily discover relationships,
3.   separate relevant from irrelevant data,
4.   scan data for relationships,
5.   determine cause and effect relationships,
6.   formulate rules or describe relationships.

SELF CHECK FOR OBJECTIVE FOUR

CAN YOU: list five of the six skills associated with Discovery problem solving?

Illustrations of the Discovery Method

Mathematics. Many relationships exist among the parts of geometric figures and numerals that comprise the study of mathematics. Those relationships make this subject matter easily adaptable to discovery teaching. For example the relationship between the diameter and circumference of a circle, pi, is a well known constant, 3.1416. A teacher may announce this constant to the class and demonstrate and assign problems. Students then use the constant to determine unknown diameters or circumferences of circles. The approximate relationship may also be demonstrated by actually measuring the circumference and diameter of a circle and comparing their lengths.

Mathematics teacher Suzy Klimmer passed out cylindrically shaped cans to her eighth grade class. The cans, although all cylindrical in shape, varied greatly in size. Each pair of students received one can, a string, and a ruler. She then gave directions for using the materials.

"Each pair of students is to use the string and ruler to carefully measure the distance across the bottom of the can and the distance around the bottom of the can." She held a can in her hand and marked the lengths which were to be measured. "To make sure we are accurate, how many times should we measure each diameter and circumference? If our measurements are slightly different how can we find the best measurement?" The students agreed that it would increase the accuracy of their work if they would make each measurement three times and average the results.

As students wrapped their strings around the cans and stretched them along a ruler Ms. Klimmer made a chart on the chalkboard.

TRIALS (in centimeters)

GROUP					
1.	Circumference	15.3	15.5	15.2	15.3
	Diameter	5.1	5.1	5.0	5.1
2.	Circumference	52.0	51.5	51.2	51.3
	Diameter	17.3	17.3	17.4	17.3
3.	Circumference	45.5	45.4	44.9	45.6
	Diameter	15.1	15.0	15.0	15.1
4.	Circumference	42.2	42.0	42.4	42.3
	Diameter	13.7	13.8	13.7	13.7

As each pair of students completed their measurements and computations of the average circumferences and diameters of their cans, Ms. Klimmer entered their data in the data table. When all groups had reported their findings she asked, "Does anyone see anything about the relationship between the circumferences and diameters that is a pattern?"

The class studied the data table intently, but no one responded.

She then prompted them, "Was one measurement always larger than the other?" Johnnie said, "The circumference is always longer than the diameter." "It's farther around the can than across it," Marge added. Ms.Klimmer waited a full ten seconds while the class was silently thinking. Then she asked, "How many times as far?" "For our can it was about three times as far around as across," Johnnie responded.

Ms. Klimmer wrote the number 3 on the data table alongside Johnnie's group data. The rest of the class began to compute the ratio of the circumference and diameter of their cans. She entered their answers in the appropriate space on the data table. "They're all about three," several students said. "What does that tell us?" Ms. Klimmer asked. "The circumference is always about three times as long as the diameter," Mark said. "What shape is the bottom of the can?" she asked, holding up a can. "It's a circle," a student offered. "Can someone make a statement that tells us what we discovered about a circle?" Marge began to speak slowly, hesitantly, "It is about three times as far around a circle as it is across it." "Good, Marge." "Can anyone say the same thing using the words circumference and diameter?" Johnnie then said, "The circumference of a circle is about three times as long as the diameter." "Very good Johnnie."   If we would measure carefully, repeating our measurements many times we would find that the ratio of the circumference and diameter is 3.14. This is called pi." Ms. Klimmer went on to explain that "pi" is a constant and how it may be used to determine either the circumference or diameter of a circle when the other one is known. She could then proceed to demonstrate procedures for solving the unknown dimension of a circle when one of them is known.

Language Arts. Certain relationships and patterns exist among parts of speech, verb tenses, word spellings, the formation of plural forms of words, and many other areas of the language arts curriculum. Wherever patterns are found the discovery method of teaching can be used to teach a concept.

Patsy Pace, a fifth grade teacher, wrote the word, "piece" on the chalkboard and said to her class, "Notice this word, 'piece' has the letters i and e in it. Try to think of other words that contain these two letters. I'll write them on the board as you say them."

She wrote the following words on the chalkboard as they were called out by students.

niece	field	relief
receive	sieve	believe
perceive	ceiling	deceive
die	diesel	thief

Ms. Pace asked, "Do you notice anything about the i's and e's in these words?" Sarah (a student) said, "Sometimes the i is first and sometimes the e is first." Ms. Pace said nothing and waited. Then one student said, "Every time there is a c in a word the e comes before the i." "That's good, Justine. Does everyone see that? Is there anything else that we can say from looking at our list?" After a long silence a second student said, "Except for the c's all the

Learning through inquiry activities is found in a wide variety of subject matters. What could these social studies students discover through examination of the globe of the earth?

other times the i's come first." "That's a good observation, Tony. Can we put this into one statement, a rule for spelling words which contain 'i' and 'e'?" Sarah slowly and thoughtfully stated, "Always put the i before the e except when it follows a c. Then the e comes before the i." "That's good, class. You have done a fine job in developing this rule." She then had several students state the rule.

Ms. Pace erased the board and wrote the words, eight, either, height, and heifer. "What do you notice?" she said. "The e comes before the i," several students said, "and it's not after a c." "That's right." "You have made a good rule, but here are some exceptions, times when the rule does not apply. What are the exceptions that you notice here?" The students agreed that their rule does not apply when the e and i begin the word and when they follow an h. She let the class list other words that were exceptions to their rule and then asked them to summarize all that they had discovered about spelling words that contain i's and e's.

Science. Discovery lessons in science are usually associated with the use of manipulative materials. A discovery activity may be the unstructured play of a kindergarten child who manipulates geometric shapes of various sizes and colors, places the figures of similar colors in separate piles and discovers the primary colors. Or the students may discover the life cycle of certain insects by observing the hatching of fruit fly eggs over a period of time. In both illustrations the learner manipulated the environment to find a relationship that existed among its elements. To initiate a discovery lesson at any level a teacher needs to introduce students to materials and permit them to manipulate the objects as long as required to achieve conceptualization of the desired relationship. With learners above the primary grades manipulations normally take on a more structured form than with the young learner. With more mature students the teacher guides manipulations by asking questions. Through guidance the learner explores materials in such a way that the chance of making the desired discovery is increased. The following is an example of a discovery lesson Laura Fahrenheit taught to her science class.

After her students were seated Laura Fahrenheit presented each group of five students with an ice cube which she placed on a paper towel. Ms. Fahrenheit asked, "What causes the ice cube to melt?" "Heat," several students volunteered, "the heat from the air caused the ice cube to melt." She then said, "Let's find out what happens when heat is added to ice cubes. She placed a pyrex beaker on a metal stand, inserted a thermometer into the beaker, and lit a propane burner and put it under the beaker. She said, "Let's take the temperature of the beaker each three minutes and record our findings. When each group has completed its work we will examine our data and see what we can discover about how the addition of heat affects melting ice."

When each group of students had completed its observations and recorded the temperature of its ice-water mixture Ms. Fahrenheit had one group fill in a chart she had drawn on the board using the data from its observations. When this was done she asked, "Can you say anything from what you see here? Do you notice anything that happened?"

Students timidly offered several uninspired observations concerning the data in the chart. "Well, let's make a graph of the data," she said, and began to label a set of axes previously sketched on the chalkboard. As she drew the line that connected the points on the graph a student named Sue said, "It's not straight. It goes up steeply and then for a while it is flat, and then is steep again."

Ms. Fahrenheit asked, "At first, what was in the beaker?" "Ice," several students said. "And then, what was in the beaker as we heated it?" "The ice turned to water. There was a mixture of water and ice in the beaker," Sue said. "And finally what was in the beaker after it had been heated a fairly long time?" "Then it was all water," Eddie offered. Ms. Fahrenheit labeled the parts of the line on the graph. The first steeply rising line segment she labeled "ice," on the flat part she wrote "ice and water," and on the third part of the graph where the line again began to rise steeply she wrote "water."

"Can anyone see anything of interest in our graph?" Eddie, now waving his hand and arm in the air in a wide arc shouted out, "The temperature went up fast when it was just water or ice, but did not go up when it was a mixture." "I wonder why?" the teacher asked. "Where did the heat go?" "I guess it takes heat to change ice to water. Maybe the ice took it up." The comment came from Eva. "That's good, Eva." "Does everyone understand what Eva is saying?"

Her students discussed the phenomenon further as they agreed that it appeared the melting of the ice absorbed the heat from the torch. When she decided that most students understood the concept she explained that they had discovered what scientists called the "heat of fusion."

SELF CHECK FOR OBJECTIVE THREE (Discovery)

CAN YOU: Create an outline that describes one Type II, Discovery Inquiry lesson?

Type III Thinking Skills Development Activity— Empirical Problem Solving

In its broadest context empirical problem solving has to do with developing and carrying out a plan for investigating and forming conclusions concerning a defined problem. In practice, there exist two basic types of empirical problem solving, experimental problem solving and problem solving using stored data.

Problem Solving Type IIIA—Empirical/Experimental

Experimental problem solving is the classical model of inquiry most often associated with the study and practice of science. In conducting experimental problem solving students develop the following problem solving skills:
1. Defining the problem.
2. Formulating an hypothesis or posing a problem question.
3. Naming variables that affect the experimental outcomes.
4. Making operational definitions of the experimental variables.
5. Experimenting while properly manipulating and controlling experimental variables.
6. Organizing and interpreting data.

SELF CHECK FOR OBJECTIVE FIVE

CAN YOU: list five of the six skills associated with Type III, Empirical/ Experimental problem solving?

A simple illustration of experimental problem solving in a middle school science class might take place where the problem question is: "What happens to the total amount of electricity which flows through a series circuit when the resistance of the circuit is changed?" The students would then set out to name the variables that affect the experiment, size and number of light bulbs (resistance), how connected (series), source of electric power ("D" cell batteries), and any others that come to mind. After formulating a plan on how they are to actually conduct the manipulation of the materials, the students carry out their plan, gathering data as they work. Then they organize the data into data tables and/or graphs. Then students interpret the data and form a conclusion about what the effects are of increasing the amount of resistance in a series circuit.

The experimentation problem solving format may also be applied to social attitudes or other subjects where surveys, either opinion or informational in nature, supply the data for interpretation rather than experimental evidence. Examples of opinion or information polling as experimental research might be a straw vote on a coming election, students' opinions on changing to year-round school, or determining the study habits of the student body, such as, how many hours are spent on homework, how much time is spent watching television, etc. A well conducted experiment using the survey as a data gathering instrument utilizes the same basic steps as the more traditional science activity. The students will formulate a problem question or hypothesis, define the problem's parameters, create the questions to be asked during the survey (this determines the experimental variables), the manner and times when the survey will be conducted, who the respondents are to be, and others. The survey should be conducted according to the developed guidelines and the survey data organized and interpreted. Very often the results of problem solving experiments that employ surveys is communicated to others.

Problem Solving Type IIIB—Utilizing Stored Data

Often the best source of information or data for solving a problem is found, not by generating them through direct experimentation or survey, but by searching out and retrieving them from existing sources. These sources may be written materials such as books, newspapers, magazines, letters or, perhaps at times, personal interviews of knowledgeable people. Some problem solving skills that are developed by students when they engage in Type IIIB Empirical Problem Solving Using Stored Data are:
The ability to:
1.   Define problems.
2.   Formulate problem questions or hypotheses.
3.   Define the nature of the information required to investigate a problem.
4.   Describe possible sources of information required to investigate a problem.
5.   Gather information (includes library, note taking and related skills.)
6.   Organize information into coherent form (includes creating data tables, graphing, summarizing skills.)
7.   Interpret information; form conclusions and/or a course of action.
8.   Communicate findings or pursue a course of action.
An example of an empirical problem solving episode using stored data might be the one taught by Jean Cross in her health class. The curriculum in her school included a unit on sex education and Mrs. Cross's class was

expressing doubts that teenage pregnancy was a problem in middle school grades in communities such as theirs. Mrs. Cross said, "O.K., let's find out if this is a problem in your age group." Taking a piece of chalk she asked, "Where do we start? Let's treat this as a problem we will attempt to solve. How can we state the problem?" The students, as a result of Mrs. Cross's questioning subsequently agreed on a problem question. "Is pregnancy a problem in the pre-teenaged years?" and Mrs. Cross reminded the class that as they sought out information the students should also be considering some possible solutions to the problem if one does prove to exist. (Note: the problem question might also have been written, "How can the problem of teenaged pregnancies be solved?") In the next several days Mrs. Cross guided the class through the process of empirical problem solving using stored data emphasizing the skills listed above. When the problem definition and procedures for gathering data were completed, she divided the data gathering tasks among the problem solving groups she had formed. The children sought out information from the library, several films and filmstrips, and a nurse from the County Health Department. When sufficient information was gathered, the problem solving groups each began to summarize their findings which were presented during class discussion. Mrs. Cross then guided the children to discuss the possible solutions for the problem and to list any actions that might be taken by the class to aid in its resolution.

Many issues of social significance, related to the environment, the school environment, home and community are fair game for this problem solving process. The process undergone during these activities not only provides the students with information, but also helps them to develop skills for investigating and solving problems in their own lives.

SELF CHECK FOR OBJECTIVE SIX

CAN YOU: list seven of the eight skills associated with Type III, Empirical/ Using Stored Data problem solving?

SELF CHECK FOR OBJECTIVE THREE
(Empirical Inquiry)

CAN YOU: Create an outline that describes one Type II, Empirical Inquiry lesson, for either Experimentation or Using Stored Data?

INCORPORATING PROBLEM SOLVING INTO THE DAILY CURRICULUM

After reading the previous pages it may be obvious, because of their possible brevity Type I, Rational Problem Solving and Type II, Discovery Problem Solving may quite easily be interjected into many daily learning activities taught in nearly all subject matter areas. To cause this to happen you will but need to adopt an attitude of "searching for targets of opportunity" as you plan your lessons. That is you may ask, "Instead of telling this concept to the students, how can I have them find it out for themselves and tell it to me?" As you review a lesson in your mind and look for the opportunities, you will find that in many instances it is possible to present a problem using materials, anecdotes, or pictures and guide student responses with open-ended questions as has been demonstrated in Types I and II problem solving. In this way your goal can be accomplished, the students will learn the concept and gain much more from the experience. Becoming a teacher who employs problem solving in an ongoing curriculum is primarily a question of attitude, having the desire to expose children to the processes and skills which they may learn only by taking part in problem solving experiences.

Although it is possible to devise Type III, Empirical Problem Solving activities that are of short duration, this type of problem solving generally is taught as projects that take place over a span of several days or longer. Opportunities for utilizing Type III problem solving may be found in issues that center on the school or classroom (developing conduct codes, safety, cleanliness of the environment of the building, etc.), the environment of the community, social issues (politics, student preferences for curricula or activities), and others. Some teachers feel they might attempt to guide their students through one Type III Problem Solving project during each grading period.

It is possible to teach problem solving in your classroom if you acquire a basic knowledge of the general processes of teaching using these strategies and some skill in classroom questioning. In the end, the mix of the various types of problem solving is not important; each allows students to use higher cognitive processes and acquire skills and attitudes that will permit them to transfer these things to their everyday lives.

SELF CHECK FOR OBJECTIVE SEVEN

CAN YOU: orally or in writing discuss the practice of incorporating problem solving into the content areas of the normal curriculum, focusing upon the three types of problem solving activities?

SOME GUIDELINES FOR IMPLEMENTING PROBLEM SOLVING IN THE REGULAR CLASSROOM

1. When using problem solving activities in conjunction with regular, didactic instruction always start with the problem solving activities.

   With many teachers there is a tendency to provide information on a topic just prior to introducing a problem solving lesson. This should not be done. Providing a minilecture on the topic just prior to starting the problem solving causes the students to focus on the fresh information, closing off new ideas and narrowing the range of ideas which the students will use. The focus of the information provided reduces substantially the achievement of the objectives of problem solving such as fluency and originality of thinking and forming inferences and conclusions. The minilecture prior to problem solving activities changes the problem solving exercise into a demonstration, a reinforcement of the known. When teaching problem solving, you must structure the inquiry in such a way that the students may undertake it successfully without the benefit of additional information. (This, of course does not preclude the occasional interjection of bits of information to remove an obstacle to the progress of the lesson. See Chapter Five.)

2. Use concrete experiences whenever possible regardless of the ages of the students when teaching problem solving lessons.

Even those who sometimes criticize the use of problem solving activities agree that concrete experiences are enriching for all learners even though they may learn a concept directly without them. As was stated earlier, there are many devices that may be used to introduce problem solving lessons such as anecdotes, pictures and other media or simply stating a problem directly. These procedures are effective. The use of concrete, manipulative experiences, however, adds additional dimensions to the students' skill development and general understanding of the concepts presented.

3. Refrain from telling, implying or through the extensive use of reinforcement and guidance robbing students of the opportunities for open-ended, inferential thinking. Closure should always come from the students.

4. Once the problem solving activity is over and students have acquired the desired concepts, teach the additional related information using any of the didactic strategies while making frequent references to the problem solving learning experiences. This practice will help students to process the new written and verbal information and develop a coherent conceptual framework.

SELF CHECK FOR OBJECTIVE EIGHT

CAN YOU: list and describe the four guidelines presented for incorporating problem solving into the ongoing curriculum?

SUMMARY

Learning through the techniques of inquiry or problem solving has many advantages for the learner. These activities provide experiences that enable the learner to develop a number of higher level cognitive skills, such as inferring, observing, classifying, organizing data, interpreting data and others. The inquiry/problem solving strategies also contribute to students' growth in the affective area. A longstanding problem for educators has been how best to incorporate inquiry and problem solving learning activities into the school curriculum.

To achieve maximum relevance to the students' experience and transfer among the various subjects, it has been found it is best to teach problem solving and critical thinking as an integral part of the ongoing school program.

Types I and II problem solving, Rational and Discovery inquiry may easily be introduced as "targets of opportunity" — as brief episodes in the daily lessons of nearly all subject fields in the curriculum. To accomplish this goal, the teacher searches for ways to have the students discover concepts, rules, relationships, and generalizations that occur in the subject rather than being told these things by the teacher or reading about them. In this way students gain the information and also acquire additional skills that enhance their problem solving abilities.

Type III, Empirical problem solving, is comprised of two categories of inquiry, experimentation and using stored data. While the general process of these two categories of problem solving is the same, they differ in the nature sources of the data that are utilized in forming conclusions. Experimental problem solving uses data obtained from direct observation of structured student activities such as science experiments and opinion polls. For category IIIB, Empirical problem solving, students obtain data from libraries, newspapers, and other print and electronic media and through personal interviews of experts. In both kinds of Type III problem solving students learn to define problems, formulate hypotheses or problem questions, name and control variables, carry out data gathering activities, and organize and interpret data. In the kind of Type III problem solving activity that uses stored data, students sometimes carry out follow-up activities to the problem solving as an attempt to rectify the perceived problem. While both of the Type III problem solving strategies aid in the development of a common set of student skills, each also addresses some skills that are unique. For instance, Experimentation emphasizes observation of phenomena and the handling of quantitative data while Using Stored Data emphasizes library research skills and forming "best" solutions to problems.

Some guidelines for use when incorporating problem solving into an ongoing school program are: Always begin with the problem solving and follow up with the direct instruction; use concrete experiences whenever possible; refrain from telling too much and otherwise limiting the students' opportunities to form inferences and conclusions; and after the problem solving activities have been concluded use direct learning strategies to transmit information and concepts to the students.

ACTIVITIES

1.   Develop a lesson plan to teach a lesson by discovery or rational inquiry in the subject matter of your choice. Teach the lesson to a small group of your peers. Critique and discuss the lesson.
2.   Develop a lesson plan to teach a lesson using empirical inquiry. Teach the lesson to a small group of your peers. Critique and discuss the lesson.
3.   Structure a lesson plan for a library research lesson. Discuss the plan with your peers.

BIBLIOGRAPHY

Behr, M.J., & Khoury, H.A. (1986). Children's inferencing behavior. *Journal for Research in Mathematics Education, 17*(5), 369-381.

Birnie, H.H., & Ryan, A. (1984). Inquiry/discovery revisited. *Science and Children, 21*(7), 31-32.

Carr, J., Eppig, P., & Nonether, P. (1986). Learning by solving real problems. *Middle School Journal 2,* 14-16.

Hembrow, V. (1986). A heuristic approach across the curriculum. *Language Arts 63,* 674-679.

Hillkirk, K., & Dupuis, V.L. (1989). Outcomes of a teacher education curriculum module that emphasizes inquiry and reflection. *Teacher—Educator, 24*(3), 20-27.

Hudson-Ross, S. (1989). Student questions: moving naturally into the student-centered classroom. *Social Studies, 80*(3), 10-13.

Kagan, D.M. (1989). Inquiry mode, occupational stress, and preferred leadership style among American elementary school teachers. *Journal of Social Psychology, 129*(3), 297-305.

Marzano, R.J., & Arredondo, D. (1986). A framework for teaching thinking. *Educational Leadership, 43*(8), 20-22.

Ornstein, A. (1990). *Strategies for effective teaching.* New York: Harper and Row.

Perkins, D.N. (1986). Thinking frames. *Educational Leadership, 43*(8), 4-10.

Selin, H. (1989). Turning them loose in the library. *New Directions For Teaching and Learning, 38,* 85-90.

Sharp, A.M. (1987). What is a community of inquiry? *Journal of Moral Education, 16*(1), 37-45.

Sheingold, K. (1987). Keeping children's knowledge alive through inquiry. *School Library Media Quarterly, 15*(2), 80-85.

Sternberg, R.J. (1985). Teaching critical thinking, part I; are we making a critical mistake? *Phi Delta Kappa, 67*(3), 194-198.

Sternberg, R.J. (1985). Teaching critical thinking, part II; possible solutions. *Phi Delta Kappa 67*(3), 227-80.

Swartz, R. (1986). Restructuring curriculum for critical thinking. *Educational Leadership, 43*(8), 43-44.

Tamir, P. (1985). Content analysis focusing on inquiry. *Journal of Curriculum Studies, 17*(1), 87-94.

Turner, T.W. (1984). Following the clues: A group discussion hypothesis making technique. *The Social Studies, 75,* 124-128.

Wedmen, J.M. (1989). Perceptual differences regarding the implementation of an inquiry oriented student teaching curriculum. *Journal of Research and Development in Education, 22*(4), 29-35.

Wilen, W.W., & McKendrick, P. (1989). Individualized inquiry: encouraging able students to investigate. *Social Studies, 80*(2), 51-54.

CHAPTER EIGHT

INTRODUCTORY CASE STUDY

CASE STUDY 8-1
ALL TOGETHER EACH ONE SEPARATE

Linda Vidual decided to reorganize her mathematics class. There were eight students in the class who were high achievers and had high scores in mathematics on the Comprehensive Test of Basic Skills. Miss Vidual moved these students to the rear of the classroom and gave each of them a paper which outlined their written assignments for the next three weeks. She gave them verbal instructions that they were to work independently on the seatwork while they were in mathematics class and complete all assignments in the three week period. The assignments contained some required exercises and some optional ones with directions to "work any three of the five problems." Miss Vidual told this group she would work with them the last ten minutes of each class period.

The remainder of the students, the twenty two individuals not in the "independent" group, worked in the traditional fashion, reviewing the previous night's homework, receiving verbal instruction over each day's new topic and spending the last ten to fifteen minutes of each class working at the chalkboard and at their seats in practice drills. Once or twice a week they would have a short, three problem quiz over their homework assignment.

WHAT IS YOUR ANALYSIS OF MISS VIDUAL'S CLASS STRUCTURE?

Why did she organize the class in this way?

What are some of the advantages of this structure for the "independent" group? The "regular" group?

What are some disadvantages for each group of students?

How might this classroom organization affect student achievement and attitudes?

What is your overall opinion of Linda Vidual's mathematics class?

CHAPTER EIGHT
TECHNIQUES FOR INDIVIDUALIZING INSTRUCTION

"The individual must be free, able to develop the utmost of his abilities... "

-Dwight D. Eisenhower

GOAL

After reading this chapter students will understand individualizing instruction.

OBJECTIVES

After reading this chapter students will describe

1. a management system,
2. a commercial self paced learning program,
3. learning activity packets (LAPS), the systems approach LAP and the LAP with options,
4. an interest center,
5. a drill and practice center,
6. a problem solving center,
7. programmed instruction,
8. contract learning,
9. learning modalities, learning styles, and brain hemisphericity, and
10. individualized instruction for exceptional children.

In the preceding chapters we have discussed a variety of methods for teaching: lecture, lecture-discussion, lecture-demonstration, discovery, inquiry, and empirical investigation. All are designed to instruct a whole class while covering a single set of concepts or facts. While whole class instruction is the most common form of teaching found in the classroom, techniques for individualizing instruction to suit the needs and interests of learners have had a long and valued place in American schools. The "back to the basics" movement has given momentum to the increased use of several forms of instruction designed for the individual student.

MANAGEMENT SYSTEMS

Management systems are usually associated with basic skill subjects of mathematics and reading. However, the procedures of management systems have been applied to other disciplines. "Science, A Process Approach," an elementary school science program, is one illustration. The use of the management system is based on the premise that a body of knowledge or set of skills can be described by a hierarchy of narrowly defined objectives. In mathematics a child begins by recognizing numerals and writing numerals, progresses to skills of counting, then to simple addition and subtraction before going on to more complex skills of multiplication and division. Each skill is defined by a written objective. In some mathematics and reading programs it is common to find 400 or more skills in a program skills continuum. The goal of the program is to have each learner master each of the skills in turn before proceeding to the next skill in the hierarchy. To accomplish this goal, highly structured programs of systematic instruction and evaluation have been developed. The components of a management system are:

1. An individual student profile. Each student will have a chart which lists all learning objectives appropriate for a grade level. By checking off each skill as the student attains mastery, the student and teacher know exactly where the student is in the program continuum.
2. A set of criterion referenced tests. Tests which have items that are identified as being evaluators of specific objectives or skills on the student profile are administered periodically. Student responses to individual test items permit the determination of mastery of the related skill. Typically, correct responses to the majority of all items or three out of five test items indicates mastery of a designated skill.
3. A set of learning activities/materials. Theoretically a child could demonstrate mastery of certain skills by successfully completing items on a pretest. In practice, most reading and mathematics programs in elementary and middle schools require the student to complete a set of learning activities before taking a mastery test. After a learner has completed the required learning activities and taken the appropriate test, skills not mastered will be apparent from the analysis of test results.
4. Remedial learning activities. Most management systems have become sophisticated in the identification of skills not mastered by the learner. They suggest remediation activities. Often, remediation of unmastered skills is accomplished by having the student repeat previously completed lessons associated with the skill. With some programs teachers are supplied alternative activities for remediating skill deficiencies. Some teachers accumulate appropriate remediation materials on their own.

The instructional sequence for classroom use of a management system is teach, test, remediate if necessary, test, repeat as necessary. In practice, instruction is comprised of worksheets that stress drill and practice with skill specific materials. Computer programs are used to supply teachers with individual student profiles and groupings of students with similar profiles and remediation needs.

The use of management systems in the instruction of basic skills subjects recognizes the importance of the learner mastering each step in the staircase of skills. The purpose of the systems approach is to provide a structured and systematic process that facilitates mastery learning by all students, regardless of vagaries of day to day school operations such as student and teacher absences, the lack of consistency in planning instruction, poorly structured programs that omit or treat some skills lightly, decisions that negatively impact the individual as teachers instruct the larger group, and other similar circumstances. If scores on standardized tests are the criterion, the procedures of the management systems approach to teaching basic skills is more effective than traditional approaches taken by many teachers. Children taught by these direct instructional procedures do score higher on such tests. The use of management systems to teach reading and mathematics in the elementary school has critics.

The use of highly structured instructional systems in the classroom reduces the teacher's role to that of a technician. Teachers lose most of the latitude they formerly had to make programatic and instructional decisions. Instead, they are charged with carrying out the automatic and predetermined operations of the system. Teachers using management systems spend less time in direct contact with the learner. Much of their time is spent in managing materials, monitoring seatwork, scoring papers, and maintaining records. This fundamental change in the teacher's role has been observed to adversely impact their morale and job satisfaction. Another adverse effect of management systems that has been observed is that often a student is locked into a skills continuum and may only be permitted to advance through the program in lockstep with others with whom he is grouped. For example, when a child is placed in a reading book along with a group of his peers, and is required to do all the lessons in the program, he may not advance at a rate other than that of the group. Thus, a student once erroneously placed will not be able to escape the lockstep of the system unless the teacher doubles up on instructional time and covers more than the normal pace the curriculum permits. In practice, the theoretical basis of the individualized instruction system is not permitted to operate. That is, the individual is not permitted to progress at his own pace.

Another frequent complaint aimed at the use of management systems in reading and mathematics in the elementary school is related to the time required for instruction. When instructional and clerical requirements of reading and mathematics programs take more than their alloted amount of instructional time, other parts of the learners' school experience suffer. Social Studies, science, art, and music may be neglected. The child's school experiences become skewed, no longer representing a desirable well rounded program. As in all curriculum decisions in school, there are trade offs to be considered. Some benefits are derived and some negative results are introduced by change. It is the task of decision makers to know the nature and extent of benefits and losses from the introduction of any instructional program and decide on a desirable course of action.

COMPUTER MANAGED INSTRUCTION

Several publishers of elementary school reading and mathematics text-books have developed computer programs that relieve teachers of many of the time consuming chores that are associated with the use of instructional management systems. Computer Managed Instructional Systems (CMI) appears to be a reasonable solution to the problem.

While using a CMI reading program the student reads, discusses, and performs learning activities for a small number of lessons in a basal reader. Each lesson is generally associated with development of a single skill. After completing learning activities, the child takes a criterion referenced test over the lesson, marking answers by darkening spaces on a small card. At that time the teacher forwards all student answer cards to an assistant who feeds

Table 8.1
BATCH SUMMARY

TEST ID: 070130
TEACHER: _____
CLASS: 2-02

#OF RESPONSE CARDS	#CARDS SCORED OK	#OF PROBLEM CARDS	#OF STUDENTS IN CLASS	#IN CLASS NOT SCORED
11	11	0	28	17

TEACHER: 2-02   EXCEPTION REPORT
SCHOOL: LEVEL 7/0 SKYLIGHTS   TEST 1 PART 3

NAME		TOTAL SCORE	SCORE ON EACH LESSON
			LESSON 7-10
A	MOSES, SHARON	40% (2/5)	*2/5
	NUNLEY, TARA	20% (1/5)	*1/5
B	POWELL, LESLIE	60% (3/5)	*3/5
B	RUSH, SONIA	40% (2/5)	*2/5

Table 8.2
ITEM ANALYSIS

Teacher _____
School _____
Level 7/G Skylights
Test 1 Part 3
+ = CORRECT RESPONSE
A, B, C, D, E = INCORRECT RESPONSE
? = PROBLEM RESPONSE

ITEMS 1-5	ITEMS 6-10	ITEMS 11-15	ITEMS 16-20
+++++	+++C+	+++++	B+A+?
+++++	CA+C+	+CABC	?++++
++++?	+++++	+?+?+	?++??
+?+++	BAAC+	+++++	B++++
+++++	+++B+	AB+AB	B+A+B
+++++	?++++	+++++	++A++
+++++	+++C+	+++BC	B++++
+++++	++A++	+++++	+++++
+++++	+++++	+++++	+++++
+++++	+B+B+	+++BC	+++++
+++++	+BDB+	A++A+	+++A+
DBECA	ACBAB	BACCA	AABBA

them into an optical scanner which is attached to a computer terminal. Within minutes it is possible for the teacher to receive the following data:

A Batch Summary that shows the number of cards read. It points out any cards that were not marked properly.

An Item Analysis that shows the response of each child on each item of the test. Many systems also indicate which incorrect responses the child made on all missed items.

An Exception Report groups children that failed a subtest for a specific lesson along with their scores on subtests.

A Resource Report that lists suggested remedial, practice, and enrichment activities that are part of the program.

A Scoring Report that lists in alphabetical order all children who took the test, a total score and percentage for the test, and the results of each subtest.

Table 8.3
STUDENT PROGRESS REPORT

TEACHER: 2-02
SCHOOL: LEVEL 7/G SKYLIGHTS
CRITERION: BELOW 80%
TESTS 1 to 4

PROGRESS REPORT FOR: (student name)

LESSON	DATE TESTED	TEST	SCORE	OBJECTIVES
1-1	10-25	TST1,PT1	80%	Noting Important Details
2-2	10-25	TST1,PT1	80%	Vowels and Vowel Sounds
2-3	10-25	TST1,PT1	100%	Ending-es
3-4	11-05	TST1,PT2	80%	Noting Correct Sequence
4-5	11-05	TST1,PT2	80%	Multi-Meaning Words
5-7	11-05	TST1,PT2	100%	Vowel Plus-r
6-9	11-08	TST1,PT3	100%	Following Directions
7-10	11-08	TST1,PT3	80%	Vowel Sounds and Syllables
8-11	11-08	TST1,PT3	80%	Common Syllables ful, ly
8-12	11-08	TST1,PT3	100%	Final "e"
9-50	11-13	TST1,PT1	100%	Recognizing High-Frequency Words
10-13	11-20	TST2,PT1	100%	Cause-Effect Relationships
11-14	11-20	TST2,PT1	100%	Categorizing
12-15	11-20	TST2,PT1	100%	Ending-est
13-16	11-20	TST2,PT1	100%	Sound Associations for ow
14-17	12-06	TST2,PT2	80%	Commas
15-18	12-06	TST2,PT2	100%	Predicting Outcomes
16-1?	12-06	TST2,PT2	100%	Sound Associations for ee, ea
17-20	12-06	TST2,PT2	100%	Cluster str
18-21	01-10	TST2,PT3	100%	Recognizing Base Words
19-22	01-10	TST2,PT3	80%	Main Idea
20-23	01-10	TST2,PT3	100%	Alphabetical Order:First letter
21-24	01-10	TST2,PT3	100%	Sound Associations g/j
21-50	01-10	TST2,PT4	93%	Recognizing High-Frequency Words
22-25	01-17	TST3,PT1	100%	Reviewing Endings
PROGRESS REPORT SUMMARY			95%	PERFORMANCE ON 31 OF THE 31 OBJECTIVES TESTED MET THE CRITERION

Figure 8.4
SOURCES REPORT: ALL

TEST ID: 070130
P = PRACTICE
R = REMEDIATION
E = ENRICHMENT

LESSON	WHERE TAUGHT	RESOURCES
06-09	R063-64;p17	P TEACHER GUIDE 176
		R TEACHER GUIDE 66
		E TEACHER GUIDE 66-67
		P PRACTICE BOOK 63
		P ASSESSMENT TEST 17,18
		E READING BONUS 24
		R READING BONUS 25

SOURCES REPORT: ALL   TEST ID: 070130

LESSON	WHERE TAUGHT	RESOURCES
07-10	TO75; p20	P TEACHER GUIDE 253-254
		R TEACHER GUIDE 77
		E TEACHER GUIDE 77-78
		P PRACTICE BOOK 90
		P ASSESSMENT TEST 19,20
		E READING BONUS 26
		R READING BONUS

SOURCES REPORT: ALL   TEST ID: 070130

LESSON	WHERE TAUGHT	RESOURCES
08-11	R079-81;p25	P TEACHER GUIDE 104, 155
		R TEACHER GUIDE 84
		E TEACHER GUIDE 85
		P PRACTICE BOOK 34
		P ASSESSMENT TEST 21,22
		E READING BONUS 28
		R READING BONUS 29

Figure 8.5
SCORE ON EACH LESSON

TEACHER: 2-02
SCHOOL: LEVEL 7/G
CRITERION: BELOW 80%
TEST 1 PART 3

	NAME	TOTAL SCORE	SCORE ON EACH LESSON			
			LESSON 6-9	LESSON 7-10	LESSON 8-11	LESSON 9-12
14 A	Brown, S.	90% (18/20)	5/5	4/5	5/5	4/5
1 A	Bush, J.	95% (19/20)	5/5	4/5	5/5	5/5
3 A	Conway, J.	90% (18/20)	5/5	4/5	4/5	5/5
4 A	Darwin, B.	90% (18/20)	5/5	4/5	4/5	5/5
18 A	Fouts, B.	95% (19/20)	5/5	5/5	4/5	5/5
19 A	Fullam, C.	90% (18/20)	5/5	4/5	4/5	5/5
6 A	Great, M.	100% (20/20)	5/5	5/5	5/5	5/5
27 A	Jones, B.	95% (19/20)	5/5	5/5	4/5	5/5
21 A	Justin, S.	95% (19/20)	5/5	4/5	5/5	5/5
24 A	Kirsch, C.	90% (18/20)	5/5	5/5	4/5	4/5
11 A	Karnes, J.	95% (19/20)	5/5	4/5	5/5	5/5
12 A	Kern, B.	90% (18/20)	5/5	4/5	5/5	4/5
17 B	Lawson, B.	95% (19/20)	5/5	4/5	5/5	5/5
20 B	Marsh, J.	100% (20/20)	5/5	5/5	5/5	5/5
7 B	Moses, S.	60% (12/20)	5/5	*2/5	*1/5	4/5
9 B	Nunley, T.	70% (14/20)	4/5	*1/5	5/5	4/5
10 B	Owens, J.	60% (12/20)	5/5	4/5	*1/5	*2/5
25 B	Powell, L.	80% (16/20)	5/5	*3/5	*3/5	5/5
26 B	Rush, S.	70% (14/20)	5/5	*2/5	*3/5	4/5
15 C	Smith, M.	80% (16/20)	5/5	4/5	*3/5	4/5
5 C	Towle, S.	80% (16/20)	5/5	4/5	5/5	*2/5
8 C	Walker, T.	70% (14/20)	4/5	5/5	*3/5	*2/5
	AVERAGE	85%	98%	78%	80%	85%

After having a class take the last test associated with a reader, the teacher receives a single sheet Progress Report for each child that shows the date of each test, the results of the subtest for each lesson, and the instructional objective related to each lesson.

With files of remedial, drill, and enrichment materials provided, and armed with the knowledge of which children require remediation and the instructional materials each child requires, the teacher then provides remediation, retests children who failed a lesson and hands each child's response card to the school's computer operator. Using a computer managed instructional system a teacher is never required to grade a test, group children for remediation, or mark a student profile or progress report.

In those schools where CMI reading and mathematics programs are in use, most of the criticisms of the use of the management system as an instructional strategy have been eliminated.

SELF CHECK FOR OBJECTIVE ONE

CAN YOU: describe a Management System?

SELF PACED ACTIVITY

Some individualized learning programs are less structured and have broader goals than management systems. These are self paced, activity based learning.

Commercial programs

Commercial programs and teacher made materials are designed to permit a student to work through a planned set of learning activities. These are commonly called self paced learning activities. If they are well designed, the student follows directions to obtain and use learning materials from a repository in the classroom, evaluate his or her own work and take and score tests when required. When one group of activities is completed the student selects and starts the next set. The student maintains a record of work to be shown to the teacher when requested.

One example of a commercially available self paced program is the reading program of Science Research Associates (SRA). At each grade level the SRA reading laboratory program consists of a set of reading booklets, color coded and numbered within each color set. They are designed to teach reading comprehension skills and build vocabulary. The booklets at each grade level are sequential with difficulty as the criterion. The student enters the series at a place designated by a pretest and progresses one by one through the entire set of booklets. Each booklet contains reading material followed by questions. The student reads the material, answers the questions, checks them, then proceeds to the next booklet in the series. Each student maintains a record of progress. Other programs are available in mathematics from Random House, Addison Wesley and McCormick Mathers. In social studies,

Educational Insights and in science, Imperial Learning Corporation offer self paced material. Self paced, self directed programs are commonly found in elementary and middle school classrooms.

Learning Activity Packets (LAPS)

Learning activity packets are commonly called LAPs or LAP PACs. LAPs are generally teacher made rather than commercially produced and come in two types, those that use the systems approach and those that work with broad topics. We will briefly examine each type.

The Systems Approach LAP

Some learning activity packets use components and procedures of the systems approach to instruction (management system) discussed earlier in this chapter. This type of LAP provides the student with a pretest, a series of learning activities, a series of tests, and a student record. The results of the pretest specify which learning activities are to be completed, omitting those that test results indicate have been mastered. The student then completes all required learning activities and takes the accompanying tests. Some teachers ask the students to score their own tests and record the results while other teachers require students to turn in the completed tests for scoring. A conceptual difference between this type of LAP and the management system earlier described is that learning activities and tests of the LAP are generally less specific or formal in relating the content and tests to specific objectives. Instead, they generally work with recognizable skill or content clusters. For example, a systems approach LAP in mathematics may contain a lesson on converting metric length units (millimeters, centimeters, decimeters, meters, decameters, hectometers, kilometers) which encompass skills of knowing the units, knowing their relationships, and converting among all seven units. The related test would evaluate the student's global ability to evaluate metric length units. It would not be specific to the narrowly defined skills listed above. If the student passed the test on converting metric length units, he may then move to a learning activity that works with converting metric mass units. Thus a LAP titled "The Metric System" would include six or eight learning activities, each of which would take one or two hours to complete. It would also include a test for each activity and a form on which the student would record successful completion of each activity. The essence of this modified systems approach adapted to a self paced learning activity packet is that the student is able to self direct through a series of learning and evaluation activities without help from the teacher (or perhaps only occasional assistance) and is able to work at his own pace. Most teachers using this type of LAP help students set goals for work to be completed.

The LAP with options

Learning activity packets can be used with subject matter that is less structured and sequential than mathematics and reading. Literature and social studies do not require mastery of each objective. They permit a teacher to offer options to students who elect activities they wish to pursue to meet a chosen objective. To structure a LAP with Options the teacher must: 1) select a small number of objectives to be included in the packet, 2) gather material required to complete all activities required in the packet, 3) write a set of directions outlining objectives and optional activities from which students may choose and 4) write a description of the method of student evaluation. An example of a LAP with Options that might be appropriate for an upper middle school literature class is below.

A LEARNING ACTIVITY PACKET
AMERICAN POETS AND POETRY

Directions: This learning activity packet consists of four objectives and activities for meeting each of them. You will be given activity options to meet the requirements of each objective. Examine each activity for an objective and decide which ones you will select. Then complete activities as directed. Your grade on this learning activity packet will be derived from the procedures for evaluation listed with each objective.

Materials: direction sheet, textbook (*Adventures in American Literature*), a set of paperback books, *An Anthology of American Poetry*; a 25 item test for objective one; encyclopedias and books of poetry found in the library.

Complete the following activities as directed:

Objective One: Answer questions related to the lives of the poets Robert Frost, Emily Dickinson, Henry Longfellow, and Carl Sandburg.

Activities (Complete one of three activities):

1.   Read pages 99, 103, 105, and 110 in the textbook, *Adventures In American Literature*, which relate the biographies of the four poets listed in objective one.
2.   Locate the four poets in an encyclopedia and read the information related to each of their lives.
3.   Obtain the filmstrip from the media table that describes the lives of the four poets and view it.

Evaluation: Objective one will be evaluated using a 25 item test found in your packet. Please tell the teacher when you wish to take the test.

Objective Two: You will critique three poems of four of Frost, Dickinson, Longfellow, and Sandburg.

Activities: From your textbook select three of the four poems listed below, read the poem, and write a one page critique. Include considerations of rhyme, meter, and imagery.

1. "After the Apple Picking" by Robert Frost.
2. "Because I Could Not Stop For Death" by Emily Dickinson.
3. "The Village Blacksmith" by Henry Wadsworth Longfellow.
4. "Chicago" by Carl Sandburg.

Evaluation: This objective will be evaluated using the critiques of the three assigned poems.

Objective Three: You will critically examine two additional poems of one of the poets selected for objective two, write a critique of each considering rhyme, meter and imagery.

Activity: From *An Anthology of American Poetry* located in the bookcase or from any other source, select two poems from one of the poets you previously selected when completing objective two. Read the two poems and write a critique of each one. In writing the critiques consider rhyme, meter, and imagery.

Evaluation: Your evaluation on objective three will be based on the critiques of the two selected poems.

Objective Four: You will demonstrate an appreciation of the art form of poetry by evaluating two poems and writing one poem.

Activities (Complete one of two activities):

1. Select any two poems of your choice. In a written report state why each was selected. Write the lines or stanzas that especially appealed to you and tell why you chose them. In a final brief paragraph state why the poems you selected are important for others to read.
2. Write a poem on any topic of your choice. You may use any style you feel is appropriate. The poem should be at least three stanzas in length.

Self paced learning programs, whether commercially produced or teacher made, offer advantages to teachers and students. These programs are self contained. They permit students to work at an individual pace and allow for differences in academic ability. In most instances self paced programs require all students to master all objectives in the program. Students who work in self paced programs often feel less anxiety in carrying out their assignments than in a regular classroom atmosphere. They have the opportunity to experience self direction and some degree of independence. And they are provided the opportunity to develop skills and habits of self actualized learning. In programs which allow options in selecting learning activities students have a small part in shaping learning experiences. This often leads to enhanced motivation and more positive attitudes toward school and learning.

The role of a teacher in self paced learning programs centers on the skills of selecting and creating appropriate learning experiences for students and monitoring their activities. The teacher becomes a consultant as he discusses with individual students decisions they make when choices are available, the quality of their work and their rate of progress in the program. Teachers as well as students enjoy the informal, relaxed nature of the self paced learning program.

There are potential problems with which the teacher in a self paced classroom must be concerned. One is the feeling of competition among students to complete the work. Elementary school children especially, may be found skipping lightly over assignments to stay ahead of or catch up to classmates. Teachers in self paced programs must monitor student behavior and look for evidence of slipshod work that results from competitive behavior. When it is observed, the teacher must attempt to emphasize to the student the importance of working at their own pace and ignoring the work of classmates. Slipshod work can also result when children have tired of the independent, self paced mode of learning. Students at all ages generally require changes in learning activities to maintain a high level of interest in their classwork. It is wise to mix whole class learning activities of various kinds with self paced instructional programs to maintain the optimum motivation of students of all ages.

SELF CHECK FOR OBJECTIVES TWO AND THREE

CAN YOU: describe Commercial self paced Learning Programs?

describe a Systems Approach LAP and the LAP With Options?

Learning Centers

Learning centers are places in a classroom where self paced learning may be carried on by an individual student or groups of students. Some teachers prefer to carry on whole class activities with their students and mix it with independent, self paced learning. They can do this for purposes of drill and practice, to present problem solving activities to students, or provide students the opportunity to participate in independent activities in which they have an interest. Teachers accomplish this mix of whole class and self paced activity by setting aside a counter space or table space as a learning center. Although the general components of a learning center are similar to those of self paced programs such as LAPS discussed earlier, they vary according to their purpose.

The "interest center" is but one method of individualizing instruction. Teachers use individualized instruction to meet a variety of needs students have. Through self directed learning, students acquire the ability to work without direction, accept responsibility for their own learning and finish tasks on their own.

Interest Centers

Picture for a moment a table in the rear of a classroom. It is surrounded with four or five chairs and its top is covered with various books and materials. A sign that hangs from the ceiling proclaims, "Dinosaurs are Gone, But Not Forgotten." Closer examination reveals small models of brontosaurus, tyrannosaurus rex, diplodocus, and other terrible lizards. There is a fossil collection with fern imprints in slate, petrified wood, seashell fossils, and other fossilized evidence of living things. There is also a collection of books, picture books to identify dinosaurs, seashells, rocks and minerals, and story books that tell of life on earth before man. There is a collection of rocks and chemicals with directions for making tests on the rocks to identify them. Another worksheet provides directions inviting students to mold a dinosaur from clay. Although students are invited to show the teacher their completed worksheets and models, no homework is assigned or collected, and no grades are given. This is an interest center.

Interest centers are established to enrich young peoples' lives. They are not a basic part of the curriculum. Sometimes interest centers are used by teachers to motivate students to complete assigned tasks and improve the quality of their work. Participation in the interest center's activity is a reward for a job well done. Other teachers schedule all students into the interest center so that the lowest achiever may benefit from this enriching and anxiety free activity. The materials and topic of an interest center are changed periodically to maintain a high level of motivation and interest among students.

SELF CHECK FOR OBJECTIVE FOUR

CAN YOU: describe an interest center?

Drill and Practice Centers

Some teachers maintain several learning centers in their classrooms to reinforce and extend skills learned in reading, language arts, and mathematics. These centers contain manipulatives such as counters and geometric shapes to teach mathematics concepts. Reading and language arts centers contain paced readers, filmstrips and cassette recorders. Most often learning centers in the basic skill subjects use worksheets or seatwork as a preferred mode of instruction. Often worksheets are designed to be attractive and interesting to the student. They use games, puzzles and art work to entice the learner. Vocabulary building may consist of pages full of rows of letters that invite students to circle words that may be formed in any direction. A mathematics game may have a human-like shape take a step up on a gallows staircase for each wrong answer and move down a step for each right answer. The student is encouraged to save his "friend" by correctly completing a set of addition problems or multiplication problems. Children may count marbles; place twelve marbles in three jars and by counting each jar determine that twelve divided into three parts yields four in each part. They may increase their reading comprehension by reading paragraphs and answering questions. Or they may practice spelling by selecting correctly spelled words and coloring in the object with that name. The variety of tasks found in basic skills drill and practice learning centers is endless, limited only by the imagination and energy of the teacher who creates them or finds them in commercial publications.

Many teachers organize activities for drill and practice centers by color coding all materials related to a particular subject. Red might be math, blue reading, and orange language arts. A box is used to organize materials. File folders are inside the box. Each file folder has an activity in it. Activities include beginning blends and synonyms. In a second box or in the drawer of a file cabinet students find file folders, one for each child. Directions written on the chalkboard list the activity to be completed. When a student finishes a worksheet it is placed in the student's own personal folder. The student then selects the next one on the list. Sometimes children correct their lessons when they are completed. In other classrooms the teacher corrects papers to evaluate the progress of students. Corrective feedback is provided. The math center and the language arts center would be organized in similar ways.

Students are taught to be as self directing as possible and to maintain an academic focus while carrying out activities. Drill and practice centers in basic skills subjects provide valuable reinforcement to previously learned subject matter. Although more popular in the elementary school, drill and practice centers are found in all grade levels including senior high school.

SELF CHECK FOR OBJECTIVE FIVE

CAN YOU: describe Drill and Practice Centers?

Problem Solving Centers

Problem solving centers are generally divided into two types, those that use written problems for students to solve and those that use manipulative materials. Centers that contain written problems are frequently associated

FIGURE 8.1
A PROBLEM SOLVING CENTER

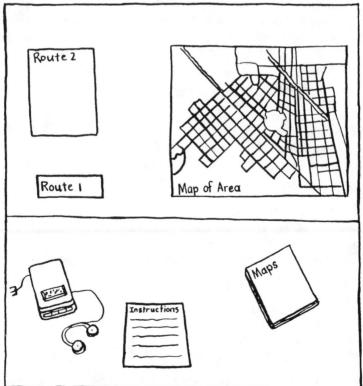

Objective: Students will observe sensory details and chart a course through a city.

with mathematics, social studies or science. They are also identified as problem solving centers.

Problem solving skills include identifying and defining problems, collecting data, differentiation between useful and meaningless information, organizing data, interpreting data and reporting solutions. Also identified as problem solving skills are interpreting spatial relationships (having to do with similarities and differences among various shapes) and using the operation of formal logic such as the syllogism. Several illustrations of activities that teach problem solving skills are below.

Inferential

Eric lives in Switzerland. One winter day while walking along a mountain trail Eric noticed that in the distance a cabin located at the base of a cliff was in great danger. Snow drifts which overhung the cabin appeared ready to form an avalanche that could sweep the cabin away. Eric could see smoke rising above the snow covered roof melting the ice that clung to the wires that ran from the rooftop to a nearby tall pole. Eric could also see that the trail had collapsed making it impossible to approach the cabin to warn those inside. Cupping his hands to his mouth he started to shout, but he stopped short. Eric was afraid the sound would start the avalanche roaring down the mountainside. As he stood on the cold, windy trail, Eric wondered what to do to save the people inside the cabin.

What was Eric's problem? Select one of the following.

1. It was cold and windy.
2. The mountain trail was impassable.
3. An avalanche was about to fall on a cabin.
4. He could not shout for fear of starting the snowslide.

What did the smoke tell Eric?

1. The cabin might be on fire.
2. There probably were people inside the cabin.
3. The snowslide was ready to start.
4. Find a way to notify the cabin's occupants.

How was the sight of the wires that led to a pole important?

1. They might stop the falling snow.
2. The cabin had electric lights.
3. Eric might use the wires to slide down the mountain.
4. There might be a telephone inside.

What should Eric do? Write your solution in the space provided.

Spatial perceptions

Circle the figure on the right that completes each statement.

1. _____ is to _____ as _____ is to _____

2. _____ is to _____ as _____ is to _____

Logic

Analyze the following argument. Tell whether you agree with the statements and why.

> There are twenty boys on the basketball team.
> John is a boy.
> John must be on the basketball team.

These illustrations are a few of the many types of written problems that could appear in a problem solving learning center. The intent of these problems is to help students develop a wide variety of skills such as recognizing and defining problems, demonstrating spatial perception ability, thinking logically, and developing creative and unstructured solutions to problems. Many other types of problems are also found in problem solving centers. These include problems in applied mathematics and situational (real life) problems such as those associated with environmental issues and social values.

Manipulative materials

You may recall that discovery learning depended on a teacher structuring students' experiences with materials in such a way that they perceive relationships and make resulting inferences and generalizations. In mathematics, students discover the volume of a cone to be about one third of a cylinder of the same diameter and height. They do this by pouring sand from the cylinder into the cone. A learning center, perhaps a discovery or inquiry center, is designed by a teacher who places cones and cylinders of several sizes on a table along with a pan of sand, water, or rice. An unstructured or pure discovery center would offer no direction. Students would be expected, with little prompting, to begin to pour the available material from cones to cylinders. After a short time the teacher would ask, "Did you discover anything about the amount of sand the cylinder would hold?" Or perhaps more directly, "Did you discover how many cones of sand it took to fill one cylinder of the same height and diameter?"

A discovery center provides more direction for students. A center might contain a half dozen flashlight cells, some pieces of thin, insulated copper wire, several nails, some magnetic compasses and boxes of carpet tacks and paper clips. A problem card poses the questions:

1. Can you make a magnet that makes the compass needle move?
2. Can you make a magnet that will pick up a carpet tack?
3. How many paper clips can you hang end to end from your magnet?

Students will be expected to discover that holding the bare ends of a piece of copper wire to the bottom and top of a flashlight cell will affect the needle of a compass. And through trial and error they find that wrapping the wire around a nail will allow them to pick up tacks and paper clips. They will have discovered important things about magnetism.

An inquiry center that uses skills of forming hypotheses, naming and controlling variables, making operational definitions, experimenting and interpreting data may also be structured. One example might be: a teacher supplies a six inch long, one inch diameter cardboard tube which has its ends covered. There is a pinhole in one end of the tube and a small square shaped hole in the other. The center has a meter stick and sheets of centimeter graph paper cemented on thin cardboard. The following directions are provided to the student.

1. Look through the tube, holding the end with the small pinhole close to your eye.
2. Look at any flat surface, a map or picture. Move closer and farther away from the picture or map. What happens?
3. Can you hypothesize what describes what you believe to be true about the size of the field of view observed on a surface, and the distance the observer is from the surface?
4. Can you describe a test for your hypothesis which would use the meter stick and the graph paper?
5. Do the experiment that is the test of the hypothesis.
6. Did the test support your hypothesis or not support it?

Discovery and inquiry learning centers provide students with the opportunity to use direct experiences to learn about their environments. Such experiences help them to develop problem solving skills and intellectual skills as well as independence and an inquiring attitude. Problem solving centers, including those that use written and manipulative materials, provide unique and valuable experiences not frequently obtained in the school setting.

SELF CHECK FOR OBJECTIVE SIX

CAN YOU: describe a problem solving center?

Programmed Instruction

Complete the following brief exercise. Cover the right side of the exercise with a blank sheet of paper so that you can't see the answers. Move the paper down one line at a time checking each answer that appears on the far right of each succeeding line.

The Navajo Indians

The Navajo (Nahv a ho) is a tribe of Indians that inhabits the Southwestern United States, residing principally in the states of Arizona and New Mexico.

The Navajo is a tribe of ———————————————— . **Indians**

They live in the ————————————— United States. **Southwestern**

The Navajo live in the states of ———— and ———— . **New Mexico Arizona**

The Navajo Indians built dwellings from dried mud and straw. This material is called adobe. They lived in villages called pueblos by the Spanish.

The Navajo Indians built dwellings from —— and —— . **mud and straw**

This building material is called ————————————— . **adobe**

The Spanish called the Indian villages ————————— . **pueblos**

Some Navajo pueblos were built against tall cliffs. They often had many levels and ladders were required to climb from one to another. This afforded protection against their enemies.

Indian pueblos were sometimes located against ———— . **cliffs**

The Indians moved from one level to another in their

pueblos using ———————————————— . **ladders**

Building against cliffs gave the Indians ————————— . **protection**

This is an illustration of programmed instruction. It is characterized by 1) small increments of learning, 2) a high ratio of learner success in answering questions, 3) immediate feedback or reinforcement to the learner and 4) self pacing as the learner progresses through the program at his or her own pace. Each of these characteristics of programmed learning is a premise of behavioristic learning theory. This kind of instruction, although it has proved to be somewhat effective in providing direct learning experiences to students of all ages, is not commonly used in schools. The strongest criticism of programmed instruction is that it fails to motivate the user over a long period of time. It is most effective when used in small doses. The most common use of this mode of instruction today is in basic mathematics and other subject matter programs in adult and community college education.

Programmed instruction provides the flexibility to start new students at any time regardless of where other students are in the program. It permits them to progress at their own rate. This freedom from entrance and group progress requirements makes it appropriate for individualizing instruction.

SELF CHECK FOR OBJECTIVE SEVEN

CAN YOU: describe programmed instruction?

Contract Learning

Contract learning permits a student to determine a grade and enter an agreement with a teacher to achieve that mark. Contract learning can be adapted to any subject at any grade level. It works best with students who are at least in the upper elementary school. The example that follows is a contract learning package for literature. Please see the LAP illustration in this chapter for another strategy using the same content.

An illustration of an American poetry contract

Directions for the contract: Carefully read the requirements for the four (4) letter grades possible. Decide which letter grade you want to contract for and earn. Write that letter grade at the end of the contract on both copies. Sign and date both copies of the contract. Keep one copy. Return one copy to the teacher. Once you have signed and turned in the contract no changes in the contract will be allowed.

This contract must be completed by the last day of this grading period.

Level One (D=grade)

1. Read pages 99, 103, 105, and 110 in the textbook, *Adventures in American Literature.* Biographies of four poets are on these pages.
2. Go to the Learning Resource Center and read information listed under the names of Robert Frost, Emily Dickinson, Henry Wadsworth Longfellow and Carl Sandburg.
3. Take a test on the content above and pass it with a minimum score of 70%.

Level Two (C=grade)

1. Do everything in level one above and
2. Obtain a filmstrip from the LRC which describes the lives of the four poets. View it.
3. Using the textbook *Adventures in American Literature* read the following poems:
   a. "After the Apple Picking,"
   b. "Because I Could Not Stop for Death" and
   c. "The Village Blacksmith."
4. Take a test on the content of levels one and two and pass it with a minimum score of 70%.

Level Three (B=grade)

1. Do everything in levels one and two and
2. Using the textbook *Adventures in American Literature* read "Chicago" by Carl Sandburg.
3. Choose one of the four poems listed in levels two and three and critique it. The critique must include a comparison to one of the other poems in levels two and three. The critique must include a comparison of the content, rhyme, meter and imagery.
4. Take a test on the content of levels one, two and three and pass it with a minimum score of 80%.
5. The critique will be evaluated using the requirements listed in item three (3) above. Spelling and writing skills will be evaluated too.

Level Four (A=grade)

1. Do everything in levels one, two and three and
2. Write a poem on any topic of your choice. Use any style that is appropriate. There should be at least three stanzas.
3. In a one-two page report state why you chose the topic and style. Identify the lines of your poem which you liked best and tell why you liked them.
4. Take a test on the content of levels one, two and three and pass it with a minimum score of 90%.
5. The poem written for item two (2) above will be judged on length (three stanzas), rhyme, meter and imagery (if these are appropriate).
6. The report will be judged on writing skill, spelling and content (what you say).

Grade _____   Signature _____   Date _____

The concept of contract learning is simple. The teacher stipulates a set of tasks that must be satisfactorily completed for each level and grade. Tasks are cumulative with additional tasks required for each higher grade. Teachers who present contract learning options to students find that it is important to permit the students to take ample time to consider the options and make a decision. Students should be encouraged to aspire to the highest grade they believe they can achieve and not settle for less than their best effort. Contract teaching may help students to set goals and work to achieve them. Many teachers have found that it is best to hold students to the terms of their first contract because if they are permitted to bargain with the teacher later, the lesson to be learned about goal setting and task completion will be lost. Some teachers who have tried contract teaching with students have reported that the most negative result of this strategy is that many students aim for a grade that is less than that to which they should aspire. Sometimes the quality of the work of students who are working on a pass-fail project is not as high as when each project receives a grade.

SELF CHECK FOR OBJECTIVE EIGHT

CAN YOU: describe Contract Learning?

LEARNING STYLES, MODALITIES AND BRAIN HEMISPHERICITY

The construct, learning styles, has to do with how the individual processes the information that comes from his environment. There are two related, but different conceptual bases that underpin the commonly used teaching method. Historically, the first conceptual base for the construct was the human senses.

All of us perceive the world around us with all of our senses, sight, touch, hearing, taste and smell. And common experience tells us that the relative strength of the senses varies among individuals. That is, some have better vision, some hear better, some have a more sensitive sense of smell and so on. Since people are endowed with various sensing abilities, it stands to reason that their perceptions of common experiences are different. Each person perceives his or her world according to the pattern of the strengths of their individual senses. Many educators have come to believe that since learners perceive information according to their individual patterns, they then have varying learning styles.

There are three senses, or modalities, as they are known in education, that contribute most to learning in the school setting. They are the visual modality, which includes mental imaging as well as perception of stimuli; the auditory modality, which includes both listening and speaking; and the kinesthetic modality, which includes sensing muscle movements and positions in space as well as touching objects. We may classify those with pronounced preferences in learning modalities as auditory learners, visual learners, or kinesthetic learners. For these students many teachers attempt to provide instruction which accounts for these perceptual differences. This is often referred to as teaching using learning modalities or learning styles.

Some important observations that have been made concerning learning modalities or styles are:

1. Every one has a dominant modality or combination of modalities (learning style).
2. Dominant modalities or learning styles can change over time. It is possible, through instruction to strengthen and change these attributes.
3. The modality strengths of the general population are estimated as: Visual-30%, mixed-30%, auditory-25%, and kinesthetic-15%.
4. Learners with mixed modality strengths have a better chance to achieve academically than those with any other modality.
5. Shifts in modalities occur naturally over time; primary grade children are more auditory with vision second. By the sixth grade most learners are mostly visual with kinesthetic second; by the onset of adulthood vision is

still dominant, but audition is second.

6. The modalities become more integrated with age.

7. Modality strengths appear to be independent of the factors of sex, left-right handedness and race.

Instruction in the Modalities: A Learning Styles Conscious Classroom

Modalities or learning styles programs take one of two tracks. Teachers either teach to strengthen identified modality weaknesses or to utilize the learners' modality strengths when possible to deliver instruction. To implement either type of program the teacher first identifies the relative strengths of the three modalities of each child. To do this they may employ one of many tests or learning style evaluation kits that are available, such as the Swassing-Barbe Modality Index. Or they may employ observation techniques to assess student modality strengths as advocated by Teaching to Modality Strengths: A Common Sense Approach to Learning of the Zaner-Bloser company. Once the modality strengths have been identified, the teacher may choose to provide learning materials to students which either utilize the identified modality strengths to enable them to learn more easily, or provide learning materials which seek to increase the strength of modalities which appear to be deficient. Most commonly, however, teachers attempt to provide a wide variety of activities which include experiences in all of the modalities for the whole class. They then identify and focus on students who are not achieving well under the normal curriculum and provide special, modality appropriate materials in an effort to help them improve their learning efficiency. Common sense will permit many teachers to attend to modality strengths and deficiencies of students in their classrooms, but a further look at one or more of the special programs available would be helpful to become most proficient in this teaching strategy.

Examples of Learning Modality Specific Activities

SIGHT: This is the modality most commonly employed in the classroom. It includes reading by sight words, seatwork, viewing print media, including the chalkboard, viewing electronic media (with a focus on what is seen as opposed to what is heard), viewing objects and teacher demonstrations, naming objects from their shadows, visualizing objects in different positions in space, and others.

AUDITORY: The speech of the teacher, other adults and students, the sound tracks of electronic media such as tape recorders, video recorders, films, filmstrips, slides, etc., listening stations, which permit a number of students using earphones to listen to a single tape, reading by phonics (sounding out words), active oral communication with teachers and peers, and others.

KINESTHETIC: Feeling and describing objects by shape, texture, size and other attributes, working with "hands-on" materials such as logic blocks, Cuisenaire rods or wooden geometric shapes, doing "hands-on" science, mathematics and art activities, building models, and others.

Learning Styles And Brain Function

In recent years increased knowledge about brain structure and function have provided a second theoretical base for the construct of learning styles. Brain physiologists have now determined that specific areas of the brain are primary centers for the processing and storing of specialized information. For instance, the sensory information from the retina of the eyes is processed in a small, about one inch square, area at the rear of the cerebral cortex, the large outer covering. Other senses and abilities, sight, smell, spatial relationships, speech, hearing and many others also have their own processing units within the cerebral cortex. It has also been noted by researchers that certain functions of the brain, such as those related to spatial ability and creative and spontaneous thought reside primarily in the right side of the brain while structured and logical thinking reside in the left side. This phenomenon has implications for the construct of learning styles since it has been demonstrated that some learners appear to favor the left side and others the right side of their brains while receiving and processing stimuli. This phenomenon has been dubbed brain hemisphericity or brain lateralization. A number of learning style models have been developed in relation to this phenomenon. The 4-MAT program developed by Bernice McCarthy labels right brain users as sensing-feeling and reflective learners and those who favor the left side as thinkers and active learners. In her learning styles model McCarthy utilizes the two continua, sensing-feeling vs. thinking and reflective vs. active as demonstrating the extremes of the processing characteristics of left and right brain learners. She sees the four combinations of these variables as four separate learning styles. See Figure 8.1. Individuals are placed in a learning style through the use of an instrument which may be best described as a personality inventory.

Figure 8.1
FOUR LEARNING STYLES OF THE 4-MAT SYSTEM

Sensing/Feeling

Active/Doing   **Watching/Reflecting**

Thinking

The intent of the 4-MAT and many other similar programs is to have the teacher plan so that activities are provided to service all four learning styles, and therefore both brain hemispheres, during the course of a lesson. In this way all learners will be able to operate in their preferred modes and also be exposed to, and therefore develop some facility to operate with the other learning styles. The definition of learning styles and the utilization of a broad spectrum of learning activities in the classroom to serve the needs of each student are typical of many of the learning style programs that use brain hemisphericity as the foundation of their model.

Some critics viewing the "brain hemisphericity" programs consider the theoretical basis for these applications to be a bit vague, but few argue with the practice of providing a broad spectrum of classroom activities that cut across many cognitive and affective levels. The model for teaching problem solving presented in Chapter Seven advocates beginning instruction for a concept with open-ended activity, employing concrete, "hands-on" materials whenever possible, and following up these activities with good quality direct instruction, with appropriate, monitored seatwork and feedback. It will provide a strong program for children that attends to the issues of using and developing the whole brain and meeting their needs in terms of providing a variety of learning styles. A small percentage of students with special needs will have to be dealt with on an individual basis.

SELF CHECK FOR OBJECTIVE NINE

CAN YOU: describe individualized instruction using modalities, learning styles and brain hemisphericity?

INDIVIDUALIZED INSTRUCTION FOR EXCEPTIONAL CHILDREN

A variety of children with exceptionalities are mainstreamed into the regular classrooms and require special consideration in terms of instructional materials and methods. Exceptionalities are generally classified as mentally handicapped, learning disabled, emotionally handicapped, physically handicapped, hearing impaired, sight impaired and gifted. Those children who have severe forms of one or more of these impairments are usually educated in special centers where they have access to special facilities and equipment and the services of teacher specialists and aides specially trained for the task. Teachers in regular classrooms which contain children with exceptionalities must make provision for meeting their needs by creating and carrying out an individual educational plan (IEP) for each of them.

An IEP for an exceptional child identifies the nature of a child's needs, appropriate learning objectives, strategies that enable the child to learn information and skills specified by the objectives and a means for evaluating a child's progress. The individual educational plans for exceptional children strongly rely upon applications of modality or learning style processes. A child who suffers a deficit in one or more of the learning modalities obviously must learn through the more healthy learning modalities, i.e., a sight impaired child must learn primarily through audition and the tactile senses and the hearing impaired must learn through the senses of sight and touch. The teacher must provide opportunities for exceptional children to use special materials and activities for learning and also integrate these learners into the mainstream of the classroom, maximizing their association with the other students.

Procedures for Mainstreaming Exceptional Children Into the Regular Classroom

Following are some common methods employed by classroom teachers to integrate exceptional children into their classrooms.

1. Seating — In every grouping seat children with exceptionalities where they can see the teacher, the chalkboard, posters or other media and can hear verbal directions clearly.
2. Speaking — When giving directions or introducing important information, the teacher should always say it at least once while looking directly at the child who has a learning disability. In this way the teacher may be sure the child has heard the information and may also assess his or her understanding of it. Of course, the teacher should provide individual instruction when necessary.
3. Companion/tutor — Very often it is a good idea to assign a carefully chosen, normal student to act as the companion and tutor to the exceptional child, at least for a period early in the school year or the child's introduction into the classroom. A capable companion/tutor can offer invaluable aid to the exceptional student both socially and academically.
4. Create a Cooperative Learning Atmosphere in the Classroom — Some teachers encourage group or cooperative learning in their classrooms, where children work together in pairs or small groups during learning activities. The general atmosphere of cooperation in learning is of benefit to the exceptional students who are especially dependent upon the support of their peers.
5. Provide Modality Appropriate Learning Materials — As has been mentioned above, learning materials should permit exceptional students to learn while using their strongest learning modalities. Some educators would state that many students, with and without exceptionalities, can benefit from experiences with a broad spectrum of modalities. Some exceptional learners, such as the mentally handicapped, learning disabled and gifted, particularly derive benefits from the broad spectrum approach to modality selection.
6. Concrete Experiences — There is research evidence that indicates learners with a variety of exceptionalities benefit from activities which include hands-on, concrete activities. Sight impaired students may

"learn" the metric system from handling centimeter cubes, meter sticks and kilogram weights. Mentally handicapped students can understand the concepts and therefore the words connected with handling objects moving up inclined planes, observing the emergence of a butterfly from a cocoon, hearing Mexican music and feeling and seeing a serape or eating a real taco. Young learning disabled children improve perceptual abilities through water play, pouring water among variously shaped containers and placing objects into containers of water to observe whether they sink or float. Concrete experiences provide exceptional learners with multi-modality experiences and an escape from an emphasis upon verbal learning activities that often dominate school curricula.

As you might conclude from this discussion, individualization of instruction for learners with exceptionalities involves considerations of providing both experiences with appropriate learning modalities and the social integration into the mainstream of the classroom activities.

SELF CHECK FOR OBJECTIVE TEN

CAN YOU: describe individualized instruction for exceptional children?

SUMMARY

There are several strategies that can be classified as individualized teaching techniques. Learning activity packets (LAPS) have the characteristics of a systems approach. A LAP contains a set of self directing learning activities which are generally self checking. Some LAPS offer options for the learner to achieve a specific objective.

Learning Centers are found in a variety of forms. The interest center is a collection of motivating manipulative and written materials that usually are associated with a single topic. The activities of the interest center are unstructured and are generally used as a reward for completing tasks or as open-ended learning. The basic skills learning center has worksheets that contain games, puzzles, and other activities designed to reinforce previously learned concepts in mathematics, reading, and language arts. Problem solving learning activities employ manipulative materials that permit students to discover or inquire into concepts and principles of science, mathematics, and social studies. Besides teaching specified concepts, the problem solving center aids in the development of higher level cognitive and manipulative skills.

Programmed instruction consists of small increments of information followed by several questions that are easily answered by the learner who obtains immediate feedback by reading each answer immediately after responding to individual questions. This highly directive teaching strategy is used primarily in situations where it is desirable to transmit a body of information in small increments.

Contract learning permits a student to select the grade to which he will aspire from a series of escalating learning tasks and grades D through A.

Instructional strategies described in this chapter are designed to permit the learner to work individually at his or her own pace. Most strategies described include procedures that permit learners to evaluate their own work and maintain their own record of completed learning tasks. Generally, individualized, self paced instruction must be mixed with other teaching strategies to maintain a high level of student interest.

There are three main modalities by which students learn in the school setting, the visual, auditory and kinesthetic. At any point in her school experience, a student has a favorite modality or combination of modalities by which she learns new information and skills. Thirty percent of learners are classified as visual, thirty percent as mixed, twenty-five percent are considered auditory and fifteen percent kinesthetic. With increased age the modalities become more integrated. Some school programs that utilize modalities or learning styles stress teaching the basic skills employing activities that capitalize on the modality strengths of each learner. Other programs would emphasize using a broad spectrum of modalities to shore up the weaker modalities of each student and hasten the integration of all modalities. The sight modality or learning style has as its basic tool reading by use of sight words or viewing direct experiences. Auditory learning is through spoken words or electronic voice devices such as auditory or video tape recorders. Kinesthetic learning relies upon the sense of touch or body position.

There are modality or learning style programs that have the construct of brain hemisphericity as their theoretical base. Learners whose right brain hemisphere is dominant are considered to be more sensing and feeling as learners while those with left brain dominance are structured and logical thinkers. Left brain dominant learners are considered to be active learners while right brain learners are passive, watching, reflective learners. Once right or left brained tendencies of a learner have been determined by observation of the teacher or by written or oral testing, activities are devised that will cater to the hemispheric strengths of the individual learners' brains or to strengthen the hemisphere of lesser preference. Most learning style programs that are based upon the construct of brain hemisphericity attempt to provide a variety of activities that cause the learner to employ both sides of his or her brain.

ACTIVITIES

1. Critique three learning centers you have seen.
2. Select one or more of the individualized learning strategies described in this chapter and construct a learning unit that uses the chosen strategy. Share and discuss individualized learning units with your peers. Try the units with children if the opportunity presents itself.
3. Create a learning contract for you and one of your instructors.
4. Find a programmed textbook. Use it for 30 minutes.

BIBLIOGRAPHY

Atkinson, E. (1989). Assessing the apprentice approach in the classroom. *Reading, 23*(1), 17-22.

Barbe, W., & Swassing, R. (1979). *Teaching students through their modality strengths.* Columbus: Zaner-Bloser.

Block, J., Gjerde, P.F., & Block, J.H. (1986). More misgivings about the matching familiar figures test as a measure of reflection-impulsivity: absence of construct validity in preadolescence. *Developmental Psychology, 22*(6), 820-831.

Canfield, A., & Canfield, J. (1976). *Learning styles inventory.* Ann Arbor: Humanics Media.

Claxton, C., & Murrell, P. (1987). Learning styles: implications for improving educational practices. Washington: *ASHE-ERIC Higher Education Report 4.*

Copenhauer, R. (1979). Consistency of learning styles. *Teacher Education, 15,* 2-16.

Cornett, C. (1983). *What you should know about teaching and learning styles.* Bloomington: Phi Delta Kappa.

Dalton, D.W. (1989). Effects of individual and cooperative computer assisted instruction on student performance and attitudes. *Educational Technology Research and Development, 37*(2), 15-24.

Deal, C.C. (1984). Big returns from mini centers. *Momentum, 15*(2), 34-35.

Dunn, R., & Dunn, K. (1978). *Teaching Students Through Their Individual Learning Styles: A Practical Approach,* Reston, Va.: Prentice-Hall.

Ferguson, J.W. (1989). A quest for individualization in language teaching. *ADFL Bulletin, 21,* (1), 24-26.

Goldstein, R., Rollins, H., & Miller, S. (1986). Temperament and cognitive style in school age children. *Merrill-Palmer Quarterly, 32,* 263-273.

Gruendike, J.L. (1982). Centering on sea life in the classrooms. *Science and Children, 20*(2), 26-27.

Hopkins, J. (1985-1986). The learning center classroom. *Computing Teacher, 13*(4), 8-12.

Kagan, J. (1965). Matching familiar figures test. In J. Krumboltz (ed.), *Learning and the educational process,* Chicago: Rand McNally.

Kagan, J. (1966). Reflection-impulsivity: the generality and dynamics of conceptual tempo. *Journal of Abnormal Psychology, 71,* 17-24.

Kagan, J., & Messer, S. (1975). A reply to "some misgivings about matching familiar figures test as a measure of reflection-impulsivity." *Perceptual and Motor Skills, 47,* 1247-1253.

Keefe, J. (1979). Learning style: an overview. In J. Keefe (ed.), *Student Learning Styles: Diagnosing and Prescribing programs.* Reston, VA: National Association of Secondary School Principals.

Klingele, W.E. (1987). *Classroom, laboratory and clinical activities for teacher education.* Boston: Allyn and Bacon.

Kontos, G. (1984-1985). Instructional computing: in search of better methods for the production of CAI lessons. *Journal of Educational Technology Systems, 13*(1), 3-14.

Lamwers, L.L., & Jazwinski, C.H. (1989). A comparison of three strategies to reduce student procrastination in PSI. *Teaching of Psychology, 16*(1), 8-12.

McCarthy, B. (1980). *The 4-MAT system.* Arlington Heights, IL: EXCEL Inc.

Messick, S. (1976). *Individuality in learning.* San Francisco: Jossey-Bass.

Milone, M. (1981). *An introduction to modality based teaching.* Columbus: Zaner-Bloser.

Roos, S.M. (1989). Helping at risk children through distance tutoring: Memphis ACOT. *Technological Horizons in Education, 16*(6), 68-71.

Tennebaum, T.J. & Mulkeen, T.A. (1985-1986). Computers as an agent for educational change. *Computers in the Schools, 2*(4), 91-103.

Webber, R.C. (1989). Motivating and teaching disabled students: using variation in adapted pe. *Journal of Physical Education, Recreation and Dance, 60*(2), 85-87.

Weinstock, R. (1984). A title I tale: high reading/math gains at low cost in Kansas City, Kansas. *Phi Delta Kappan, 65*(9), 632-634.

CHAPTER NINE

> # INTRODUCTORY
> # CASE STUDY

CASE STUDY 9-1
WHAT PRICE FREEDOM?

Dave Vergent's Social Studies class operated with a self-paced, independent study format. Dave had organized a series of reading assignments taken from various textbooks, magazines and journals and projects such as research reports, salt maps and dioramas that his students might complete in any order and at each student's own pace. As they completed each reading assignment, students took an objective test that was available in a well marked file folder. As projects were completed they were submitted to Mr. Vergent for evaluation. All tests and projects were evaluated on a pass-fail basis. If a student failed any single assignment, they were to repeat the assignment and achieve a passing mark before starting the next assignment. Each test and project was worth a specified number of points, and those points added together comprised the bulk of a student's grade. Over the four week period allowed for each study unit, each student could work at his or her own pace, and to a large degree select the letter grade to which he or she aspired as a summative evaluation. During class time Mr. Vergent monitored student work, gave feedback, made suggestions and generally assisted students with their projects. He also took time out to grade student tests, evaluate projects, and mark individual progress records.

HOW WOULD YOU ANALYZE DAVE VERGENT'S INSTRUCTIONAL STRATEGY?

What are the positive attitudinal and achievement outcomes?
Are there negative attitudinal or achievement outcomes likely?
What management problems do you see in the strategy? with materials? with student behavior?
What problems would pass-fail grading present for Mr. Vergent?
What is your overall assessment of the teaching strategy used by Mr. Vergent?

CHAPTER NINE
WHOLE CLASS INSTRUCTIONAL STRATEGIES

"The teacher who is attempting to teach without inspiring the pupil with a desire to learn is hammering on cold iron."

-H. Mann

GOALS

After reading this chapter students will understand role playing, games, projects and field trips.

OBJECTIVES

After studying this chapter the student will describe

1. the use of role playing, simulation and games in teaching,
2. how class projects are used as a teaching strategy and
3. how field trips are used as a teaching strategy.

In a previous chapter we examined common teaching strategies such as lecture, inquiry and individualizing techniques. On the premise that it is possible to have too much of a good thing, some teachers search for alternative strategies that provide variety to the curriculum. We will examine some of the instructional strategies which have proven to be effective in stimulating interest while teaching important concepts.

ROLE PLAYING SIMULATION

At times a teacher might wish to have students develop a deeper understanding and appreciation of historical events, social or political problems, or interpersonal relationships among cultures or individuals than may be obtained through traditional strategies of instruction. Many teachers have found role playing simulations to be effective in meeting these goals.

Historical Events

To create a role playing simulation the teacher selects real or imagined characters who represent important current or historical views. Roles are assigned to members of the class. Each role is researched for background information by the person portraying the character so that utterances and actions are as authentic as possible. Through simulation Jesus Christ can debate Julius Caesar on religious and civil issues. Abraham Lincoln can argue issues of slavery and states rights with Jefferson Davis. An industrialist can present to an environmentalist views on industrial pollution. A parent can discuss drug and alcohol abuse with a daughter. When done effectively role playing simulations make issues and historical incidents come alive to participants and members of the class. Through simulated political campaigns and legal trials the process of civil action can be better understood and appreciated. Role playing simulation is a powerful and effective strategy for learning.

Presidential Elections

Two political parties are formed within the class. A primary campaign, primary elections, and party conventions to nominate candidates are conducted. An election campaign and presidential election are held. An electoral college vote is held and the winning candidate announced. The teacher may choose to select parts of this lengthy process rather than simulating the entire procedure. For instance, the political process may begin with an election campaign with each party's candidates and party workers campaigning to win the votes of the other class members.

Courtroom Trials

Simulations of legal proceedings may shed light on issues brought forth in a trial as well as the legal process. Trials may be held that deal with the death penalty, driving while under the influence of alcohol or drugs, child abuse, and many other contemporary issues. Before holding a simulated trial in the classroom a teacher may choose to have the class view a trial in progress in the local courthouse and research both the issues surrounding the charges against the defendant and important and common legal procedures.

Interpersonal Relationship Skills

Parents and children may discuss important issues of family life, a job seeker may interview with a prospective employer, a drug abuser may take part in group therapy, a grandfather and grandson may discuss the values of two generations, a low achieving student may discuss with a peer perceptions of school and how they manage the stress of never being first. Following the simulation the teacher may solicit from the class responses to questions such as, "How would you have responded?" or "What might have been a better way for Paul to have handled Mr. Johnson's accusations?"

SOCIAL PROBLEMS

Society is constantly faced with issues and problems that require discussion and solution. Some formats for the simulation of social issues are:

Television Panels. The panel format has been made popular by national television shows such as "Meet the Press" and "Washington Week in Review" where experts are brought together to discuss issues or to interview others who are viewed as experts on an issue.

Television News Magazines. "60 Minutes" and "20/20" are popular network news magazine shows that offer a format useful for classroom simulations. Newscasters ask hard hitting questions of those involved in a public issue to reveal the truth.

Television and Radio Talk Shows. For this format listeners call in to inform and question the show's host and one or more guest experts. In some instances the talk show host interviews members of the audience, permitting them to state views and ask questions of the experts.

Informal Discussion among Interested Parties. The environmentalist discusses with an industrialist issues related to building a manufacturing plant, or a military leader discusses the use of military force in a third world country with a member of the Peace Movement.

Debates. A formal debate is organized between two persons or panels over an issue. To be a simulation the fictitious identities of the debating parties must be identified while the participants attempt to espouse the views of the characters they represent.

Using one of these formats or others, many issues may be introduced as simulations of real life situations. Medicine offers many problems worthy of classroom role playing simulation.

"Should we transplant animal hearts to humans?"
"Should we sustain humans with artificial hearts?"
"Who should have priority on the kidney dialysis machine?"
"Should embryonic implants to make women pregnant be allowed?"
"Should we use genetic engineering to determine sex and other characteristics of human offspring?"
"Should the federal government be responsible for the medical care of all elderly persons?"
"Should doctors' fees and hospital costs be regulated?"

These are only a few of the possible medically related issues that might be appropriate for simulated discussions among doctors, ministers, scientists, political leaders, and others.

The creative teacher may use a wide variety of whole class instructional strategies such as role playing, drill activities, projects and field trips. By changing the pace of classroom activities, high student interest is maintained which enhances both student attitude and achievement.

Religion offers another arena of powerful issues that might be presented through classroom simulation. Some of the more commonly discussed issues are:

"Should prayer be allowed in schools?"
"Are fundamentalist religious groups acting properly in their opposition to legal abortion?"
"Should politics be discussed from the pulpit?"
"Is the Reverend Moon a criminal?"
"Are religious cults a threat to society?"

The sensitivity of some of these issues is obvious and any teacher who seeks to include role playing simulations should be aware that some groups in some communities might object. It is also important that teachers carefully explain to classes before the activity that the objective of the activity is to discuss the issues with no particular point of view being espoused by the teacher or the class. A simulation for discussion of these issues might use the format of a panel of ministers, lawyers, politicians, educators, and others being interviewed on the television program, "60 Minutes."

There are many social issues related to the environment, immigration, federal welfare programs, and many other areas of social interaction. A few that are currently in the news are:

"Should nuclear power plants be permitted?"
"How can we dispose of industrial wastes and chemicals?"
"Should strict federal controls on industrial emissions be imposed to control acid rain?"
"Should we protect American industry with high import tariffs?"
"Should government workers' pensions be reduced to help balance the federal budget?"
"How much should we spend on the military? Social programs?"

In a simulation it is important that participants play the part of someone else, behaving as that person would behave, saying what that person would say in protecting their interests and making their views known. Role playing simulations offer enormous varieties of opportunities to present issues in the classroom interestingly and effectively.

GAMES

Who has not played the game of Monopoly and felt the pride of owning hotels on Boardwalk and the despair of "going bust" as you handed in your last railroad to pay for landing on another player's square that is loaded with hotels or houses? Buying, selling, trading, investing, paying debts, collecting rents, paying taxes, all important lessons of economics and the free enterprise system are lessons taught by living the game of Monopoly. Monopoly is more than a game of fun; it is a simulation. You are playing a role, making decisions such as might be made in real life. Your solutions to problems use the same processes as are involved in real life economic decision making. Although the act of going bankrupt in Monopoly is not as devastating as if it happened in real life, some of the emotions are as genuine. Other games provide simulations related to other aspects of living in a complex world.

Other board games such as War and Strategy provide players opportunities to maneuver armies and navies, to make and break treaties, and in the end to be a victor or loser of a global war. Other games put players in the role of an industrialist, a politician, or an environmentalist. They play out their hands to create their own type of environment. Complex simulation games are also available for use with computers. Oregon Trail is a computer simulation which requires players to make decisions about provisions for a wagon train trip to Oregon in the mid-nineteenth century and then make decisions daily along the trail. Tools, supplies, and equipment that were carried in the limited storage capacity of the wagon became important factors for survival as the wagon train encountered hostile Indians, breakdowns, and starvation. A winner would arrive in Oregon after an arduous journey, while a loser died of starvation, an Indian arrow, or drowned while crossing a swollen river.

Odell Lake and Odell Woods places players in a decision making role of fish and wild animals in their natural habitats. Correct decisions cause survival and wrong decisions cause the fish or animal to be eaten by a natural enemy as part of the food chain. In computer programs such as these, problem solving and decision making are taught in a dynamic competitive environment where the player is often not competing directly against an opponent but is struggling for survival or at least to promote his or her general welfare. As much as possible a learner is placed in real life situations encountered by others. In this way a player achieves a better understanding of the decision making process and an understanding of the feelings and actions of real people in real life situations.

Verbal games

A mathematics teacher wishes to drill the class on number facts. Instead of passing out drill exercises for students to complete, a baseball game may be used to accomplish the same purpose. The procedure of the game is in the paragraph below.

Divide the class into two teams by rows or brown (color) eyed students and other eye color students. A number problem is presented and a member of Team A is permitted to answer. If correctly answered, Team A places a player on first base. If incorrectly answered a member of Team B is permitted to attempt an answer. If Team B correctly solves the problem missed by Team A one out is recorded for Team A. Players of Team A continue to answer the problems in the order in which they are seated. Misses are challenged by Team B and outs are recorded only when any member of Team B correctly answers a problem Team A missed. As Team A correctly answers problems and places players on base runners are forced to advance around the bases and eventually to score if enough problems are correctly answered. When they make three outs Team A's time at bat is over and Team B has their opportunity to answer problems. After several innings or a period of time the game is over and a winner is declared.

Optional Rules.

Problems of increasing difficulty are placed in boxes marked single, double, triple, or home run. The team in the field could request a "pick off play" at any time whereby they might attempt to answer a question that if correctly answered could remove the runner from first and back up all runners on base. If the fielding team misses the "pick off" question all runners advance two bases. Other typical plays found in the game of baseball may be introduced into the mathematics drill game. However, it is best to keep the game simple and easily understood so little time is spent in explaining the game and keeping track of the players and scores.

It is possible to devise classroom drill games such as Guess What?, Chinese Wall and Dodge Idea (a variation of Dodge Ball). The periodic use of games in conducting drill activities will contribute to relieve the tedium of drill activities. Or, the games or contests may be as simple as choosing teams and keeping score of correct responses. When developing a game to teach drill in the classroom it is wise to build in a provision that causes all members of a team to mentally answer each question. This may be accomplished by randomly assigning turns at answering questions, or at least announcing the option of calling on any member of a team at any time.

Paper and Pencil Drill Games

It is common in school today to find drill activities assigned to students as paper and pencil games. The crossword puzzle devised to cover the vocabulary words of a unit of study is an illustration of such a game. Another is a sheet of paper with apparently random rows and columns of letters; have students search out and draw lines around all the words they can locate that are formed by adjacent letters that run in any direction including diagonally.

In one game a player starts on the bottom step of a six (or some other appropriate number) step staircase that leads to a gallows and a hangman's rope. A missed item moves the player up one step toward the noose. If the exercises on the page are completed before the player reaches the top of the gallows he "beats the hangman" which is the object of the game. A second try at all previously missed items on the drill sheet places the player in double jeopardy as each missed item on the retry costs him two steps upward toward the hangman's noose and each correct answer allows him to descend one step. Ultimately the player is to correctly answer all items on the drill sheet and end up at the bottom of the staircase.

Motivational Psychology

Experience of teachers indicates that a continuous strategy of game activities used with a class over a long period of time begins to lose power to motivate students. Variety in drill activity appears to be an important ingredient in maintaining a high level of student involvement. Practice exercises mixed with paper and pencil games and periodically a competitive game activity provides variety and enhances motivation. Many publishers offer prepared drill activities that are constructed as games.

SELF CHECK FOR OBJECTIVE ONE

CAN YOU: describe the use of role playing, simulation and games in teaching?

PROJECTS

Projects constitute the primary curriculum of such subjects as art, woodcrafting, sheet metal fabrication and agriculture. In each of these areas students use their knowledge and talents to create a product which represents the culmination of cognitive and skill development. Projects are also used for special purposes in other parts of the school curriculum.

Mathematics, science, social studies and English are some of the subjects in which teachers commonly assign projects to students. In these disciplines which are associated with subject matter emphasis, instructional goals are generally related to problem solving skill development. Projects in academic subjects serve the purpose of enriching students' experiences. Some illustrations of project titles are:

Collections of insects, seashells and leaves;
Displays of string art and line and bar graphs;
Diagrams of human anatomy and volcanoes;
Models of geometric shapes, atoms, solar furnaces and human body parts;
Problem solving games and puzzles and written solutions to mathematical problems;
Experiments with physical and biological problems;
Poems, stories, reports, and other written material;
Models of theaters and castles;
Readings, plays, speeches, radio shows, pantomimes and
Social problem solving (ecology, industrial pollution, social behaviors).

Project Development

The development of a project takes place in discrete steps, each requiring direction from the teacher for students to achieve maximum results.

Selecting and Defining the Project

The selection of a topic for a project is often an agonizing experience for students. They have a need to find an original and creative idea. This causes indecision and rejection of many topics. Originality of the topic is of secondary importance to the quality of the effort that goes into executing it. Once selected the topic must be defined; parameters must be set. Generally it is better to set sights low and let the project grow than to tackle a grandiose plan that is found to be overwhelming.

Development of the Project

The least educationally beneficial project is one identified by a teacher who gives little direction for carrying it out. Projects should be defined and constructed so students develop specific skills. If the project requires paper maché, the classroom or art teacher should provide a lesson in the art of creating in this medium. If a written report is an integral part of a project, instruction in writing will aid the development of the project and improve its quality. Projects must be viewed as opportunities for teaching. Students at all levels may benefit from instruction as they exercise their intellectual and manipulative skills in carrying out project activities.

Presentation of the Project

Plays, radio presentations, and other performances may be scheduled to be presented to the class and perhaps other classes in the school. Projects that result in models, charts, diagrams, and displays may also be seen by others in the school community if the teacher desires. The same may be said for problem solving projects in mathematics and science. The culminating activity for many projects may be a fair--the math fair, science fair, or social studies fair.

Evaluation of Projects

Projects should be evaluated on the basis of predetermined objectives and guidelines. Evaluation of a play written by students may hinge on the following factors: originality (10%), quality of the script including grammar and spelling (40%), presentation (40%), and citizenship and cooperation (10%). Students should be aware of evaluation criteria before beginning the project. A science or mathematics problem solving project may have criteria such as: design of the problem (20%), thoroughness of the investigation (50%), originality (20%) and quality of display (10%). The specific nature of evaluation criteria of the completed projects emphasizes the skills that are to be developed.

SELF CHECK FOR OBJECTIVE TWO

CAN YOU: describe how class projects are used in teaching?

FIELD TRIPS

Field trips are educational experiences that take place outside the classroom. Field trips may be taken on the school campus, the immediate neighborhood, or require travel by school bus.

Campus Field Trips

Elementary and middle school teachers take their classes onto school grounds to examine the environment, its plants, animals and signs of erosion. Some classes adopt a tree on the school grounds and return to the same tree each month of the year and draw sketches, write observations and discuss its appearance. Ponds, ditches, and puddles provide organisms for study as do leaves and twigs from plants that grow on the school campus. Campus field trips may provide the most benefit compared to costs since they require the least organization and least dollar expenditure.

Neighborhood Field Trips

Safety may be taught to young children at street intersections. They may learn about the fire department and police department. Middle school children may learn map reading or map construction as they use a map to find their way around the neighborhood and draw a neighborhood map to show the location of important features.

Distant Field Trips

Many distant places provide valuable experiences for students. Young students visit historical sites, dams, power plants, water and sewer processing facilities, dairies, businesses, manufacturing plants and court houses. The only restricting factors are the energy and imagination of the teacher. To take a class on a field trip requires a great deal of planning to obtain maximum benefit for the participants.

A field trip should be part of an ongoing curriculum. Trips taken without prior introduction, preparation and follow up activities will have little educational benefit. Before visiting a dairy children should learn about dairy farms and the pasteurization process. Besides the initial educational experience presented to students several details must be handled, such as: permission slips (required by law in most states), transportation, chaperones (parents, teachers, or aides), and money to defray expenses, lunches, snacks, reststops, and other details. Evidently the successful field trip requires planning. However, experience will make the preparations easier for each succeeding trip and the educational experiences and the motivational benefits that grow out of such excursions make them worth the effort.

SELF CHECK FOR OBJECTIVE THREE

CAN YOU: describe how field trips are used in teaching?

SUMMARY

Role playing simulations are interesting alternative strategies for the classroom. Courtroom trials and presidential election campaigns are illustrations of role playing simulations. Role playing is also used to help students develop an understanding of interpersonal relationships. Role playing in the study of social problems is also found as student-developed radio plays, television panels and radio talk shows. Students may acquire an appreciation for historical events by assuming the roles of historical figures and interacting with their classmates. Simulations may also be found in the playing of situational games such as Monopoly.

Classroom drills may be made more acceptable by using games. Contests between teams of students, often in games that use the basic format of popular sports and game shows, break the tedium of paper and pencil drill activities and are effective in teaching facts and simple skills.

Projects, the major strategy of art and shop classes, are used in mathematics, science, social studies, English and language arts classrooms. They provide an alternative to the more common format of direct instruction. Projects, when properly introduced and conducted, help students to develop problem solving, manipulative, and organizational skills, and to acquire the habit of completing tasks. Projects also tend to enhance motivation and the attitudes of students toward the subject and school. Field trips, educational experiences that take place outside the classroom setting, are similar to projects as a strategy. Planning, conducting, and following-up field trips requires organization, but the rewards are great for students.

ACTIVITIES

1. Form a group and plan one of the following role playing activities. After the plan is complete, the participants will assume the roles as planned and present the simulation to others.
   a. A U.S. senate debate on the issue of abortion.
   b. A trial involving child abuse.
   c. A prison warden discussing capital punishment with a prisoner who is on death row.
   d. A talk show on the topic of prayer in the schools.
2. Write the rules for a game that uses the format of a common sport or game show to reinforce basic skills of spelling, mathematics, or knowledge of any subject.
3. Plan a project or field trip. Indicate in detail the objectives, preliminary learning experiences, steps of project completion, and follow-up. State the method to be used for evaluation of the project or field trip.

BIBLIOGRAPHY

Acker, S.R., & Gordon, J.M. (1987). Designing the group use of video—disc: Socializing communication technology. *Communication Technology, 36*(1), 51-56.

Bloome, D. (1989). Procedural display and classroom lessons. *Curriculum Inquiry, 19*(3), 265-291.

Joyce, B., & Weil, M. (1980). *Models of teaching.* Englewood Cliffs: Prentice-Hall.

Melahan, D. (1989). Putting it in perspective: geography activities for young children. *Journal of Geography, 88*(4), 137-139.

Rubin, L.J. (1985). *Artistry in teaching.* New York: Random House.

Rohrbach, N.F., & Stewart, B.R. (1986). Using microcomputers in teaching. *Journal of the American Association of Teachers in Agriculture, 27*(4), 18-25.

Schmuck, R.A., & Schmuck, P.A. (1979). *Group process in the classroom.* Dubuque: Wm. C. Brown.

Silberman, A. (1989). How your school board can right what's wrong with writing instruction. *American School Board Journal, 176*(10), 29-30.

Tafel, L.S. (1984). Important implications for teacher preparation programs. *Journal of Teacher Education, 35*(1), 6-9.

Villa, R.A., & Thousand, J. (1988). Enhancing success in heterogeneous classrooms and schools: the powers of partnership. *Teacher Education and Special Education, 11*(4), 144-154.

CHAPTER TEN

INTRODUCTORY CASE STUDY

CASE STUDY 10-1
MY CLASS IS FALLING APART

Willie Classon is an education major enrolled in a senior year internship. The school to which Willie is assigned is located in a low middle class area of a suburb near a large city. The class has settled in with their teacher and is comfortable with the relationship although the relationship is apparently not warm. They relate to their teacher at arm's length. The class has a few difficult students assigned to it. This classroom is not a rich environment. Few posters, bulletin boards and displays are present. The sunlight strikes the building in such a way that the classroom would be very hot unless heavy blackout shades are lowered. Consequently, the room is unusually dark. Desks in the room are clustered in the shape of a U. Some students have their backs to the chalk board and overhead projector during instruction.

Willie's current problem is interpersonal. Students are out of control. At first the troublesome students were a problem. Then, other students who normally would follow rules began to challenge them. And, at times would openly challenge Willie Classon. Lesson plan execution is effective for about 20-25 minutes. Then the lesson begins to fall apart. Willie has requested structured observations by the college coordinator and school supervisor. They have made suggestions. You are a senior intern assigned to the same school. You are a college colleague of Willie's although not a close friend. Willie comes to you for help.

WHAT ARE YOUR SUGGESTIONS?

1. How are you willing to help?
2. What should Willie do next?

CHAPTER TEN
PREVENTING DISCIPLINE PROBLEMS: CLASSROOM CLIMATE

"The secret of education lies in respecting the pupil."

-Emerson

GOAL

After reading this chapter and completing the exercises the reader will understand how to prevent discipline problems in the classroom while facilitating student learning.

OBJECTIVES

After reading this chapter and observing teachers and students in classrooms

1. The reader will describe six student factors related to preventing discipline problems. Include violence, motivation and culture.
2. The reader will describe at least five physical and social elements in the environment of a classroom observed. Include cooperative learning.
3. Using the information of a classroom observation the reader will analyze the relationship of two student discipline problems caused by environment and teacher factors. If possible include stress factors present.

Televised increase of violence in society suggests to some students that it's OK to violently negotiate interpersonal differences. The value of deferred gratification is rejected to a greater extent than before. Students want their needs met *immediately*. Often their parents provide a role model for each of these beliefs. In addition, students are frequently insecure in their out-of-school relationships. Single parent families and two working parent families are common, not the exception. Institutional churches have a lessened influence on young persons. Responding to the effects of out-of-school causes of behavior problems results in programs such as suicide counseling and school site before and after care for students. The effect of the cause is treated. The cause continues.

In-school causes of behavior problems can be eliminated to a great extent. Boring classes, confusing lessons, unclear directions and teacher-student interpersonal conflicts motivate students to become less manageable. Few parents and teachers would argue against a school policy which emphasizes discipline problem prevention contrasted to a policy which does not.

Meanwhile, teachers are charged with the management of programs, people and time. In order to make prudent management decisions teachers must consider the background of their students, their students' needs, the environment provided and programs available. If a teacher does not respond to student needs and interests with an appropriate mixture of environment, program and teacher behavior it is likely that student motivation will decline. It is probable that unmotivated students will not master required objectives and possibly cause discipline problems in the classroom. Just consider your own behavior in a class as a student. If you are not comfortable, possibly too warm, don't you become sleepy? If the course is a required one and not very interesting isn't it a bit difficult to stay on task? And if the teacher isn't sympathetic or doesn't have a pleasing sense of humor isn't it more difficult for you to be friendly? Consequently, it is necessary to consider the student, environment, program and teaching methods if learning is to be enhanced and student behavior problems minimized. This chapter will briefly address student, environment and teacher factors.

STUDENT FACTORS

Student Development

For an interesting student program to be designed it is necessary to consider students' social and intellectual stages of development. While students do not develop at the same rate they do develop in stages which proceed in the same order.

Early elementary school

Kindergarten students need to be socialized into their student role. Some students require an additional year or two for the initial socialization process to be completed. During the first few years of school, students are assimilating the school's expectations for them. More specifically, the early elementary school grades are used to orient students to the rules and routine of school. An illustration is the kindergarten teacher who helps a student to assimilate the school rule that he must raise his hand if he wishes to speak in class although that is not necessary in the cafeteria during lunch. Adult models are important to early elementary school students. At the end of this period of time most students have figured out the system called school.

Middle elementary school

Since students who are assigned to grades three and four (and perhaps as early as grade two) have assimilated many of the procedures of schooling, less time needs to be used monitoring compliance with work rules; more time can be scheduled for academic objectives. This is illustrated by the class full of students who raise their hands when a teacher asks a question as well as those students who do not as they call out the answer to a question.

Upper elementary school

Students at this stage are more concerned with peer relationships than ever before. Adult role models no longer have the same power as a few years ago. They identify peers as a referent group. One result of this shift of role model emphasis for the teacher is that greater time must be used to monitor the reluctant learner's compliance with rules and procedures.

Upper Middle school and Junior High school

Many of the characteristics of the upper elementary school student remain at this level in an exaggerated form. Students are in a volatile state. They are rapidly changing, physically and psychologically. So often their behavior seems unexplainable and inconsistent. This is illustrated by the student who wants to be different in the selection of clothing but absolutely needs the same kind of shirt with a pocket patch that friends have. The student is wearing a peer group uniform. Yet, a short while later the student appears aloof from the group, doesn't care about clothing although growing so rapidly that the special shirt bought last month doesn't fit. Did you experience this when you were in school?

High school

Students who remain in school at this stage are more apt to conform to school rules and procedures since they are closer to the goal which they have set for themselves. Frequently students who do not succeed with the school's intellectual goals try to succeed in some other way, perhaps socially or athletically.

Student Needs and Interests

Students are motivated by their needs and interests. Motivation is often cited as the reason why students do or do not learn, are cooperative or uncooperative and disciplined or undisciplined. Teachers and psychologists describe motivation as a set of complex reasons *why* people behave as they behave. Some students are motivated by factors which are external to them while others have internal motivators. Earlier in this book (Chapter One) fate control was introduced. A discussion of high and low fate control identified two extreme positions, the realist and the naturalist. The realist's behavior

Teachers are charged with the management of programs, people and time. A warm classroom climate is the result of the effective interaction of these elements to produce congruence between the learners' needs and the needs of the teacher.

assumes a locus of control which is internal — the person controls his future to a great extent. The naturalist believes his behavior to be controlled by forces external to him. Hence, locus of control is external. The student's value of locus of control impacts his behavior. The student who possesses internal locus of control believes he is responsible for his behavior while the external locus of control student believes someone else is responsible for his problems. Class disruptions, assignments not completed and stealing are common illustrations of scenarios which are treated differently by each type of student.

Both types (internal and external) of control influence a part of the effort students put forth in school. This discretionary effort can be directed to school stated objectives or student substituted objectives such as economic, social and athletic. A commitment gap exists when objectives substitution takes place. If the commitment gap is wide enough a behavior management problem is created.

Behavior management problems stress teachers. Less obviously, students are also subject to stress. Stressors which exist in a student's life include insecure out-of-school relationships and unsuccessful school experiences. Students who do not respond to stress appropriately consider the use of controlled substances (drugs and alcohol), suicide and other methods which give temporary relief. Commonly used positive methods which reduce stress include breathing methods, relaxation exercises and meditation.

Stress

Everyone experiences stress. Teachers and students are not immune from the pressures of life. Some seek short term relief while others commit themselves to methods which have a positive and lasting effect on body and mind. Teachers have discovered methods which relax them. They use these methods in the classroom to reduce their own stress directly and indirectly. The indirect method involves students. Experienced teachers many years ago when faced with a whole class discipline problem asked their students to put their heads on their desks. This method gave the teacher an opportunity to regroup and the students a chance to relax. Some students fell asleep! Contemporary stress reduction methods include breathing and relaxation exercises and meditation.

Breathing. When faced with inappropriate student or adult behavior many teachers become stressed, breathe rapidly and shallowly. Exaggerated hyperventilation occurs. A process which is associated with physical calm is slow, regular abdominal breathing. First, it is necessary to learn how to abdominal breathe. Lie on your back and put two telephone books on your navel. Feel your stomach push against the books when you breathe in. Practice abdominal breathing sitting and standing without the telephone books. When faced with a stressful interpersonal experience try the breathing method. Try to take a few deep, slow breaths before responding to the situation. Try to be inconspicuous.

Some teachers teach this method to their students. When faced with a classwide stressful problem everyone takes a minute to breathe before responding to the situation. The result is a reduction of physical distress and more effective problem solving. This method can even be used when stuck in a traffic jam, during a parent conference and just before an important presentation which may be stressful.

Floor relaxation. Another method which relaxes requires the participant to lie on the floor, untense each part of the body and deep breathe for about ten minutes. This is an exercise which can be done privately at home and by students at school if the class is small enough. Teachers of the emotionally handicapped find this exercise helpful for their students. The exercise anchors students to a place, stops the emotional content of the moment and relaxes the participant. When physical and emotional calm has been restored problems can be solved and decisions made more effectively.

Meditation. It's necessary to make a greater resource commitment to meditation than the first two methods. Meditation is not necessarily associated with a religious belief system. The meditation method described in this book is a relaxation method, not a religious exercise.

First, it is necessary to select a nonsense sound such as "umm" which, if said aloud, sounds like the hum of a fan. Next find a quiet, private place which has a comfortable chair. Do not lie down on a couch. Shut your eyes and begin to repeat the nonsense sound selected. When the meditator becomes experienced the nonsense sound can be thought and not verbalized. The meditator should try to untense muscles and body parts. Try short meditation sessions at first. Twenty minute meditation twice a day should be the goal. With experience, meditation in public transportation and private cars (with others driving) is possible. The result of this exercise is reduced stress and more appropriate problem solving and decision making.

Life span needs

Research suggests that students with special needs such as those who are emotionally handicapped or learning disabled require tasks which are more structured when compared to those students who do not have these characteristics. A student who speaks English hesitatingly requires different treatment than students who use English fluently. A program in bilingual education may be necessary. Or perhaps remedial work for the native speaker of English is appropriate. Volunteer programs staffed by native speakers or those who speak the student's native language may be helpful at all ages.

A student whose security needs have not been satisfied will not be comfortable working in a group. Teachers should consider individual needs; if they do not, student frustration thresholds may be penetrated. The result may be a discipline problem.

Immediate needs

Students often request that immediate needs be satisfied immediately. Classroom procedures can be devised to take care of the restroom, needing a pencil or "I want help with this problem " requests. These needs are immediate, must be attended to immediately and should cause little task disruption if a procedure has been designed and communicated to students. As an illustration, all pencils should be sharpened before class starts or after class ends. Spare pencils should be brought to class to be used if a pencil point breaks.

Culture Integration. Another serious immediate need is culture integration. The migration rate of many school communities requires teachers to be aware of, understand and respond to students who possess a primary culture which is not American anglo, middle class white. Teachers should question themselves about their student group. Is my class culturally diverse? Does a student or a student group appear to be isolated due to language, customs, dress, race and physical appearance or incapacity? Can an environment be created to integrate these students into the mainstream of the class? Students usually avoid situations in which they feel threatened.

Providing positive role models to students will enable students to grow while preventing discipline problems. Students experience fractured home relationships due to single parent family units, two working parent families and trigenerational family units. The single parent family's missing person is probably a father. Therefore, young boys will not have a functional male role model. The two working parent family's disability is lack of leisure time which in earlier years would be family time. Role models for young girls and boys are part-time despite the "quality time" argument. The unexamined life is the result. Introspection and evaluation is not modeled. Positive role models are needed. Perhaps older students of the same gender can be paired with younger students to provide role models. Mentoring provides the opportunity for growth for both persons in the relationship.

Self Concept

A student's self concept influences what will be attempted as well as the level of achievement. If a student believes that the task is impossible the student may not attempt the required task while drifting off to another activity. On the other hand most students believe that most tasks can be accomplished to some degree. Students with a low self concept will choose a lower level of accomplishment than those whose self concept is more developed. "A 'C' is my goal in the math class" is a statement of the anticipated result of self concept. It is necessary for teachers to help students to develop their self concepts through frequent successful interactions with the school's programs, fellow students and teachers. A greater attempt should be made by teachers to fit the task to the student rather than to fit the student to the task. Students should be given opportunities to work within cooperating groups of students and teachers in an effort to assist student development while preventing classroom management problems. A negative self concept often leads a student to conclude that he cannot succeed at school assignments. Each of us has a need to be successful at something. Substitution of tasks may be the student response. When the student attempts to substitute tasks, teachers often interpret the behavior as an authority challenge. A discipline problem has been needlessly created.

SELF CHECK FOR OBJECTIVE ONE

CAN YOU: describe six student factors which are related to preventing discipline problems in schools? Include violence, motivation and culture.

Supply an illustration of each of the six factors which you described above.

ENVIRONMENTAL FACTORS

Teachers are sensitive to the environment's impact on student behavior. Parts of the physical environment are often seen as difficult if not impossible to change.

Most teachers believe that crowding students frequently causes a behavior management problem. Can you imagine a principal's reaction if you wanted a wall in your classroom moved so that your students would not be as crowded as they are now?

Therefore, teachers avoid great physical changes although they make small physical changes by hanging art projects from the ceiling or moving a bookcase. On the other hand teachers believe that they have great control over the social environment. They can and do form work groups and encourage cooperation. Yet, the physical environment is so powerful. How does the physical environment influence students and what can be done?.

Physical environment

Teachers are sensitive to the importance of physical environment elements such as light, windows, room temperature, noise level, wall color and furniture. Certainly each of these has an effect on people in the classroom and consequently on their learning. Have you ever been in a classroom which was too warm or too cold? Were you drowsy in the hot room and shivering in the cold room? Were you thinking about how uncomfortable you were or about the task you were assigned? How do garish colors affect you? Do ugly surroundings bother you? Does furniture layout facilitate or inhibit the task to be accomplished? Can three or four chairs be easily moved so that small groups can work? Are you a left handed student with a right handed student desk?

Many physical facilities which challenge efficient use by students act as dissatisfiers. They do not motivate students to work effectively. They irritate and distract students from the task. If a student's frustration level is exceeded it is possible that a discipline problem may occur. Solving the physical facility problem may be as simple as moving a piece of furniture or substituting one piece for another.

If you are affected by adverse environmental factors you are probably using physical energy which could be better used to listen to the teacher, complete the experiment or finish the essay. In order that students work efficiently and effectively teachers should be aware of dimensions of physical environment. We will discuss three dimensions. They are security and shelter, use of classroom space and social contact.

Security and shelter

This refers to protection from physical or psychological harm by the environment. It is dangerous to assign 35 students to a room with a fire code capacity of 25. Overcrowding or the placement of students too close to each other frequently causes behavior problems. Placing a class time-out space near the exit door tempts the student in the time-out space to trip or hit students leaving the room. The student in a time-out situation should be placed in an isolated part of the room. Assigning a shy student a prominent and public seat may cause a behavior problem. Providing for private spaces in a classroom is necessary for those students who require the emotional security of occasional privacy. If the classroom is arranged so that useful social contact is encouraged while learning tasks are accomplished, discipline problems are reduced.

Use of Classroom Space

Many of the newer schools are designed in an open space arrangement called a "pod." A pod is a large space shared by three to five teachers and 80 to 150 students. Most often all teachers and students will be assigned to the same grade level. Often one of the first things that teachers assigned to a pod will do is to divide the space with furniture — file cabinets, book cases, portable chalk boards and student desks. They are making a statement about the usefulness of an open space for many teachers and 150 students. Some of the newer schools are designed with round classrooms or a part of the room that is triangular. These non-rectangular spaces are difficult to use by teachers who have not thought through the possible uses of such spaces. Although open-space designed schools can be used effectively, are these facilities being used in an efficient and effective manner?

Social Contact

Classroom seating arrangement is to a great extent the cause of different kinds of social contact. Teachers who seat students in straight rows will cause student interaction which is different than interaction among students who are seated in groups of three or four. Discussion is more difficult in a classroom with straight rows of desks. The richness of full communication is denied when one student talks to the back of another's head. Learning centers which accommodate more than one student might be designed for group work. Some teachers allow students to move freely about the room. Others do not. Both policies can be defended. Gathering places such as the pencil sharpener encourage student contact. Classroom rules should be designed to prevent problems which may result from social contact which is not useful. As you decide how to redesign the classroom which has been assigned to you it will be necessary to consider how to use space usefully while remembering that students are human and do require social contact.

Social environment

The social environment consists of all environmental factors which are not physical. The social environment is created by the relationship of students to each other, the teacher, visitors and to the physical facility. Teachers are concerned with this environmental factor, perhaps because they believe that they can control it. They also believe that changes in the social environment will cause changes in student growth. An earlier chapter described this as a belief in fate control.

Classroom Organization

Teachers who believe in fate control as well as taking charge of the classroom will attempt to carefully organize classroom activity. They consider models used by favorite teachers, models shared by colleagues and models read about in professional journals. When a teacher decides that one pattern of classroom organization is better than others it will probably be used frequently. However, there is no one best way to organize a classroom. Nor is every way of organizing a classroom equally effective. Organizing a classroom for a small group activity should be different from organization for discussion. Two different purposes are intended. The physical and social environment necessary for effective problem solving with small groups of students contrasted to discussion among students and the teacher are different. Therefore the organization must be different. If discussion is the intended process, students and the teacher must be able to see each other to capture the richness of communication. Seats grouped in one circle would be appropriate. Talking students would be hoped for. Another pattern is small group activity. Several small groups of students engaged in problem solving will operate independently of the teacher to a great extent. Students will create a "buzz of sound" in the classroom as they work interdependently.

Group and individual work

The study of human development suggests that very young children are egocentric and therefore not prone to work in groups naturally. Each of us at all ages prefers to work outside a group setting at particular times. Since one function of teaching, especially in the elementary school, is the teaching of social norms it is necessary for teachers to motivate students to engage in group work. Although individual work is to be valued, the basic building block of all organizations is the group. Most of us are group members at work, in families, at parties and in school. It is necessary to learn group skills.

When groups are formed there is a fair amount of uncertainty about goals. As groups of students work with each other throughout the school year there is less uncertainty about the agenda, values, skills and knowledge of individuals. It is critical for the teacher to clearly state the goal of the project, the process to be used and the expected time of completion. Parenthetically, a mission statement is also important for individual work. Unless a group leader is appointed by the teacher it is likely that a leader will emerge. The leader must encourage the group to organize its work. Task responsibility must be assumed or assigned to group members. Finally, an evaluation method must be devised to respond to the question "Was the goal reached?"

If groups do not carry out assigned tasks they malfunction. As this failure is understood, the group begins to look for another task. Dissatisfaction by group members causes physical movement and noise. This is often interpreted as a discipline problem by the teacher. It is necessary to carefully manage group work if the group is to be a success and discipline problems avoided.

Cooperation in the classroom

When cooperation is discussed it is frequently contrasted to competition. Both exist in classrooms. Teachers frequently create competition with questions like "Who has the highest grade?" and "Who was first today?" Other bases for competition are boys compared to girls, the "Robin Reading Group" compared to other reading groups and the best tennis player compared to others. The list is endless. While healthy competition is helpful to the developing student, much of the competition in schools is not consciously structured to assist students in developmental tasks. Illustrations of development opportunities are students competing with their own past achievement or when they cooperate on an athletic team in competition with another team.

If the basic building block of an organization is the group and if group work requires cooperative effort, teachers should teach cooperation and encourage healthy competition. Cooperative effort is required in a group task such as a science problem to be solved. As stated earlier, some uncertainty will exist at the start. If group members know each other well, individual skills will be known by the group. Leaders will be asked to take the role of group leader. Goals, objectives, process, timing and evaluation will be identified. Group members will have different ideas about what the intermediate objectives should be or how to go about the process of solving the problem. Throughout, group membership skills will be used so that a synergy is often effected. Individual members of the group must be willing to expose their ideas to student colleagues. Exposure of ideas is risky since other students may disagree! A strongly worded discussion may result. Negotiation will probably be needed. Compromise may be necessary. Although specific responsibilities must be completed on time, group members may not do so. What should the group do? At the end of the project someone will write the report of the project. Individual members who were not part of the report writing team may offer a minority report. Conflict might result. In order that students learn cooperative behavior many opportunities for cooperation should be offered to students. Repetition fine tunes group membership skills.

Cooperative learning

Recent attention to the improvement of student achievement has motivated the development of instructional methods such as cooperative learning. Cooperative learning promotes greater student achievement, helps the student to assume responsibility for learning and assists the student to develop social skills. Cooperative learning can be used with any subject area in all grade levels. To a great extent cooperative learning methods are motivational. The positive results of cooperative learning methods include:

greater academic achievement,
individual accountability,
improved relationships between handicapped students and non-handicapped students,
greater self esteem for mainstreamed students,
improved internal locus of control,
student initiated integration with other students,
respect for others,

positive interdependence,
improvement of critical thinking skills,
improved ethnic and racial relations,
elimination of ethnic and racial selfsegregation to some extent,
positive conflict resolution,
improved time on task,
increased attendance, and
a positive attitude change by teacher and student.

A cooperative learning methods list would include methods such as:

1. Group investigation in any subject area,
2. Partners. Students work in pairs to master objectives,
3. Jigsaw. Class is divided into several groups. Each group becomes expert in a topic. Each member of the expert group returns to their home group and teaches the home group.
4. Team Assisted Individualization. A combination of cooperative learning and individualized instruction.

Many other methods exist. The bibliography at the end of this chapter lists many sources of assistance for the teacher who wants to use cooperative learning.

Group Cohesion

If students are given many opportunities to work as groups and if that experience is a favorable one, each member of the group will have a strong positive feeling for the group. This is sometimes called cohesiveness. Each individual may speak in possessive terms when describing the group. They may talk about "My group in school..." The group would have developed a special set of expectations for each member, a special feeling for individuals and the group and perhaps an evaluation of their group as better than other groups.

Cohesive groups influence individual group members. The attraction of the group is a powerful force. Individuals begin to model the behavior of dominant group members. They begin to conform to group expectations. Individuals begin to help each other with tasks. Peer tutoring begins, often without teacher suggestion. Although teachers need to monitor the direction and process of the group, strong management of the group by the teacher may not be necessary.

Communication

In order for groups to operate productively, effective communication is necessary. Cohesive groups communicate within the group more effectively than groups which are less cohesive. This is so because each member has an increased sensitivity to other members. Each member may trust other members to a great degree so that to communicate is not to take a deadly risk. Members are more willing to risk because the degree of uncertainty is less and the degree of group ownership is greater.

It is often necessary to teach students how to communicate effectively. Skills such as paraphrasing, behavior description, feeling description and impression checking are communication skills which help students to understand each other more effectively, work together more productively and perhaps reduce conflict.

Paraphrasing. When a teacher paraphrases a statement the statement is rephrased in the words and thought patterns of the listener. It is not a statement which is a word for word repetition of the speaker's statement. If a student were to use inappropriate language as the immediate result of a heated discussion with you a paraphrase may be useful. You might say "You seem angry." Or if the student stated that "I hate you," and then continued with inappropriate language the teacher paraphrase above would be appropriate.

Behavior description. This is a cognitive descriptive statement of another's behavior. Evaluation of the behavior is not appropriate. A group member may state that another member only spoke once during a discussion and that is unusual behavior. Or the teacher involved with a student who used inappropriate language in class might repeat that language in an effort to describe the language rather than condemn its use because it is "dirty talk."

Feeling description. When a group member directly communicates his own feeling, an emotional state is being described. Feelings are most often indirectly communicated and therefore frequently misunderstood. It is better to describe one's feelings rather than allow those feelings to be misunderstood. A teacher might tell a student "I am angry because you and I cannot solve a problem which we share — a personality conflict."

Impression checking. This is used when a group member is confused and wants to test an understanding which may be accurate or not. It is carefully and tentatively stated since it is a test of another's emotional state. Nonverbal cues are useful. A teacher may ask a student "Are you embarrassed by John's compliment?"

SELF CHECK FOR OBJECTIVE TWO

CAN YOU: name two kinds of environment?

Describe the physical and social environment of the classroom which you last visited? Include cooperative learning if appropriate.

THE TEACHER

Do you have a favorite teacher? Why was this teacher your favorite? Because the teacher was helpful? Had a pleasing personality? Was fair? Operated an orderly classroom? Taught your favorite subject? Each of us fondly remembers a particular teacher as our favorite just as teachers remember particular students and associate those students with special events, personality traits or behaviors. Favorite teachers are often successful teachers. And, successful teachers artfully use strategies which have been shown to facilitate student learning and reduce discipline problems. Some of these strategies follow.

Planning

In another part of this book a rationale for the careful planning of lessons was offered. In order that a class achieve a particular objective using a process which is likely to work successfully, a plan needs to be created. This is the scientific side of teaching — predicting outcomes from specific behaviors. Teachers who plan will match the content to be mastered with the time allotment for that content. The class will be filled with carefully selected activities in contrast to meaningless activity or periods of time with nothing to do. Students who are asked to engage in busy work or who are given unclear directions have a tendency to supply their own direction which may be a discipline problem in the embryo stage.

Process Planning

Planning a process is as important as planning content. Process is related to student motivation. Process issues which can be planned include

1. Expecting the best from each student. Teachers get the level of growth, development and achievement they expect.
2. Be positive.
3. Use variety to prevent boredom.
4. Make assignments which have a purpose. Eliminate busywork.
5. Be lavish with honest praise.
6. Focus on the student. Use student ideas and attitudes.
7. Reduce anxiety. Fit the work to the student.
8. Plan for class cooperation.
9. Observe and evaluate student behavior continuously.
10. Eliminate or minimize disruptions. Always have an emergency filler activity which is interesting and relevant.
11. Give feedback as soon as possible. Use self-correcting materials.
12. Eliminate or reduce your stress.

Cultural Factors

To the extent teachers become aware of a culturally diverse group in their classes, they begin to plan for that group. As teachers begin to plan, questions surface.

- What cultural stereotypes exist in class?
- Is locus of control an issue?

- Has the minority group's culture changed as a result of contact with the dominant group?
- What are the major rights and responsibilities of students in the minority culture? In school? At work?
- How are roles acquired in the student's culture?
- How is language competence related to role taking?
- Is "speaking well" related to age, gender, position?
- What is the function of the native language at school, work or home?
- What is decorum?
- How is discipline valued?
- What does the culture teach about school misbehavior? Is the school responsible? The teacher? The child?
- Who has authority over whom?
- How is the behavior of children traditionally controlled?
- Does religious belief impact school behavior?
- Are cultural cult rituals present? (ashes, dress, marking, etc.)
- Is diet a cultural factor which impacts school behavior?
- What meaning does the minority culture attach to touching, smiling, eye contact, noise vs. silence, learning style, display of emotion, waiting to speak in class and punishment?
- What is the purpose of education in the minority culture?

Special approaches. Since school is a busy place, which at times resembles the performance of a three ring circus, it should not come as a surprise that teachers and students learn concurrently. Teachers learn about minority cultures; minority students learn about the dominant culture and about school subjects. Special approaches are necessary. And, some of these can be used with other students. Two dozen suggestions are below.

1. Student-to-student mentor to *show the ropes* to the minority student. Peer tutoring works too.
2. Use cooperative learning structures.
3. Opportunities to relate to learning objectives in physical styles is useful.
4. Allow *settling in* time.
5. Overteach.
6. Learn some words in the minority student language. Learn about the student's culture too.
7. Keep students involved, even if they cannot speak English.
8. Help the student to develop listening abilities.
9. Provide a non-threatening environment.
10. Focus on language meaning first, then correct errors within the context of the conversation for clarification.
11. Provide as much speaking practice as possible. But, allow a silent period before inviting students to speak.
12. Use concrete items such as pictures
13. Vary methods. Avoid student boredom.

14. Seat minority culture students in the center of the class.
15. Assign responsibilities to the student to help the student feel a part of the class.
16. In reading classes which are grouped, assign the minority culture student to a group other than the lowest group. The student needs to hear the best models, not the worst.
17. Depending on the minority culture, involve parents if appropriate.
18. Use games if possible.
19. Stress self-esteem and character building.
20. Minimize lecture. Maximize the use of role play, experiments and plays.
21. Encourage the appropriate expression of feelings.
22. Display minority culture bulletin boards and artifacts.
23. Encourage tape recording of lectures.
24. Testing procedures may require changes.

Clarity

We will consider clarity from the view of the teacher and the student. If the teacher is unclear about objectives to be taught, the class will be somewhat chaotic. If a teacher is unclear about objectives, communication of those objectives will be unclear to students. Teachers will try to hedge and side step some issues raised by students. Students will conclude that the teacher hasn't thought through the assignment or material clearly and therefore cannot explain new material so that it will be understood by them. Consequently, students will not know the material as intended by the teacher. They may react passively or perhaps become determined to learn on their own. Teachers who are unclear cause student frustration which often causes students to become aggressive. Aggressiveness is often interpreted as a behavior problem.

Transitions

Transitions should be made from one part of a lesson to another or from lesson to lesson. It's a movement from one activity to another. Teacher uncertainty can cause transitions to become sources of student behavior problems. If a teacher is uncertain about what to do next or how the present objective and the next objective are related, a pause will occur. Seconds will appear like minutes and a minute like an hour. Students, not knowing what to do next, will become restless.

Teachers must know how to make skillful transitions from lecture to discussion, question to question and discussion to closure. Clear directions for the initiation of the next activity must be given.

Students who know what teachers expect will more likely do what is expected. If teachers expect students to come into the classroom from another part of the school in an orderly manner they will probably do so. If students are expected to move to another part of the campus for physical education, an assembly or a special activity in an orderly manner, they will probably do so especially if the teacher is present.

Presence

An effective student behavior management strategy is teacher presence. If a teacher is respected by students, presence is required, not nagging. Students know the rules, especially if they have been told the rules. Teachers must be present to students in the classroom, while students are moving throughout the campus, while students are coming to class in the morning, leaving in the afternoon and during activities after school. Teachers who move around the classroom commenting on student work, who give special coaching on the playing field, who encourage students to learn how to throw a ball and who socially chat with students waiting on the bus line are present to students. However, presence is more than mere physical presence. Teachers are involved with students and students are involved with them. They have mutual respect and ownership of a special relationship which will not be adversely tested. Enthusiastic presence prevents discipline problems.

Enthusiasm

Throughout this book we have tried to motivate you to evaluate teaching as a combined science and art form. Throughout this chapter it has been implied that the ideal teacher is one who is interested enough in being a success to be sensitive to the environment, plan effectively, be clear in communicating, learn how to make transitions and to be present to students. Teaching is a complex activity about which the teacher must be enthusiastic. It is hard work physically, intellectually and emotionally. Without enthusiasm for hard work the teacher could easily begin to adopt a strategy of sliding by, of taking the easy way in contrast to the appropriate way. Enthusiastic teachers generally communicate their enthusiasm to their students. Enthusiasm is contagious. Students then acquire their teacher's enthusiasm. On the other hand teachers who do not communicate their enthusiasm or who are not enthusiastic pass that on too! Consequently, students take on the quality of the teacher — disinterest and boredom.

Teachers demonstrate their enthusiasm using methods which appeal to the senses of a student. Since teachers talk a great deal in the classroom it is necessary for an enthusiastic teacher to develop a voice quality which is controlled. The teacher should use an excited voice, a whisper, pleasant volume and ideal articulation. The enthusiastic teacher is a wordsmith attempting to fashion phrases, sentences and paragraphs as a goldsmith fashions valuable jewelry from raw material. Enthusiastic teachers use a variety of descriptive words within interesting sentences. Nonverbal speech which uses body language is often as articulate as verbal speech.

Body language includes use of facial expression as well as body use. A teacher's eyes can be a communication tool. Eyes that communicate enthusiasm are wide open or narrowed, smiling, interested and accepting. Use of facial expression can emphasize a statement. A flat expression, a smile, a grin are appropriate uses of one's face. A reasonable use of gestures flavors speech as salt seasons food. Excessive gesturing exaggerates and often appears comic and not serious.

Flexibility and Consistency

Flexibility and consistency are often viewed as opposites. Therefore, it is believed that a teacher who is consistent cannot be flexible. Equity encourages both to coexist. No classroom has two students with exactly the same set of needs. Although all students must be treated in the same way with their universal needs such as opportunity to participate in class activity, they must be treated differently since they have specific differences. Teachers are consistent when treating students with the same needs in the same way. When treating students with dissimilar needs differently, teachers practice flexibility.

Teachers often call on higher achieving students more frequently than others. They give several reasons for this. They do not want to embarrass low achieving students. They want to use time efficiently. Low achievers will take up too much class time since they are so slow and often do not know the answer. Low achieving students are not insensitive. They know that the teacher will not call on them often. Low achieving students often are not given equitable response opportunities.

Individual help for a student illustrates flexibility in teaching. Individual help consists of a teacher showing a student how to improve his work, not just a positive remark to the student.

Flexible and consistent behavior by teachers causes an equitable social environment. This is a powerful statement to young students, one which many will remember for years. Don't you remember teachers who were fair as well as those who were not? Newspapers frequently publish articles about prominent people in the community who, when asked about a significant person in their lives, identify a second grade teacher, a coach or a reading teacher. As the interview continues specific information is offered about that special teacher being kind, fair, attentive and a special person who praised each student.

Praise

It is widely believed that although many teachers are pleased with student behavior they do not express that pleasure. Or they express pleasure constantly or randomly. If student behavior is to be shaped, praise (positive reinforcement) should be used selectively to encourage students to continue desired behavior and extinguish undesired behavior. Positive reinforcement will be treated more extensively in the next chapter as part of a behavior management system. For now it is necessary for you to remember that praise, if used appropriately, will reduce the number of discipline problems for teachers.

Communicating expectations

One powerful discipline problem prevention technique is to clearly and specifically tell students what is expected of them. Most often they will comply with expected behavior. They should also know what the consequences of noncompliance are. The consequences should be stated specifically. Most students know most of the teacher's expectations and consequences. Problems occur when the student does not know or chooses to violate an expectancy.

Classroom procedures

Since teachers are managers they need to adopt businesslike procedures. They need to be prompt by starting class on time. Tests must be given when scheduled and not be rescheduled a few times. Homework must be returned in a timely fashion. Classwork should be checked on the spot if possible. Student responses which are verbal should be evaluated so that the student knows what his next steps should be. Practice should be provided for; this will help to reduce student frustration levels.

SELF CHECK FOR OBJECTIVE THREE

CAN YOU: list three teacher behaviors and their natural consequences after a 30 minute classroom observation?

INTERACTION OF FACTORS

It is widely believed that student factors, environment factors and teacher factors are interrelated as a class is being taught. A change in one factor will change the relationship since the three factors are connected. As teachers plan changes in their classrooms it would be prudent to analyze the effects of the planned change on other factors. Ask questions such as "How will a change in the physical environment such as circling chairs influence the social environment? Influence teacher behavior? Influence student development?"

Teachers attempt to avoid classroom discipline problems. When a problem is experienced the teacher either ignores the problem or makes a change in the environment, teacher behavior or both. The authors have observed teachers responding to student behavior with both kinds of changes.

One teacher who was observed was experiencing a whole class problem as well as specific student problems. The teacher was assigned 24 third grade students in a large self-contained classroom. The room was unusually well equipped and included a full bathroom with a tub! All 24 tables with chairs were grouped in rows in the center of the room. There was about a 12-15 foot perimeter of unused space around the entire room. When the teacher was questioned about the purpose of the seating plan no particular reason was given for the dense grouping of students in the center of the room. The teacher complaint was that students were constantly talking, nudging each other and playing in groups. It was suggested that students be spread apart so that each student would have some private space. The teacher used the private space suggestion. The result was that student behavior improved and teacher complaints decreased.

Another teacher used a "time-out space" next to a first grade's in-class drinking fountain. When the child with a problem was assigned the special seat in the "time-out space" most of the students in the class were available for a jab, a poke or to be tripped as they got a drink. Moving the "time-out space" a few feet eliminated the problem and caused the "time-out space" to be used for the purpose intended.

Each of these teachers changed the environment and their behavior while considering student development to avoid student discipline problems.

SUMMARY

Mere attention to student development, environmental factors and teacher behavior will not cause a classroom filled with young developing students to always behave perfectly. Although it is necessary to attend to these factors, attention is not enough. If it is possible the environment and teacher behavior must be changed to facilitate the accomplishment of objectives. It is also necessary to have a plan, a discipline plan which is customized for the class with whom you are working as well as those special students who require special help.

ACTIVITIES

1. Observe a classroom for thirty minutes. Take notes which relate to student, environment and teacher factors. List three specific observations of cause and effect. That is, identify a student factor and its consequence in the classroom, an environment factor and its consequence and a teacher factor and its consequence.

2. Using the observations above, plan corrections to identified student factors (if possible), environment factors and teacher factors which would result in greater student growth and fewer discipline problems in the classroom observed.

BIBLIOGRAPHY

Allain, V.A. (1979). *Futuristics and education*. Bloomington: Phi Delta Kappa Educational Foundation.

Balado, C.R. (1990). (Multicultural Teaching Materials). Unpublished Material.

Curwin, R.L., & Mendler, A.N. (1988). *Discipline with dignity*. Alexandria: Association for Supervision and Curriculum Development.

DeLuke, S.V., & Knoblock, P. (1987). Teacher behavior as preventive discipline. *Teaching Exceptional Children, 19*(4), 18-24.

Duke, D.L., (Ed.). (1982). *Helping teachers manage classrooms*. Washington: The Association for Supervision and Curriculum Development.

Evertson, C.M., Emmer, E.T., Clements, B.S., Sanford, J.P., & Worsham, M.E. (1984). *Classroom management for elementary teachers*. Englewood Cliffs: Prentice-Hall.

Finnegan, R. (1990). (Work Ethic Notes). Unpublished Notes.

Galbraith, J. (1974). *Designing complex organizations*. Reading: Addison-Wesley.

Glasser, W. (1986). *Control theory in the classroom*. New York: Harper & Row.

Good, T.L., & Brophy, J.E. (1984). *Looking in classrooms*. New York: Harper & Row.

Johnson, D.W., Johnson, R.T., Holubec, E.J., & Roy, P. (1984). *Circles of learning*. Alexandria, VA: Association for Supervision and Curriculum Development.

Mercer, C.D., Mercer, A.R., & Bott, D.A. (1984). *Self-Correcting Learning Materials For The Classroom*. Columbus: Merrill.

Moore, K.D. (1989). *Classroom teaching skills*. New York: Random House.

Slavin, R.E. (Ed.). (1990). Cooperative Learning [Special Issue]. *Educational Leadership. 47*(4).

Steele, F.I. (1973). *Physical settings and organization development*. Reading: Addison-Wesley.

Susi, F.D. (1989). The physical environment of art classrooms: a basis for effective discipline. *Art Education, 42*(4), 37-43.

CHAPTER ELEVEN

INTRODUCTORY CASE STUDY

CASE STUDY 11-1
AM I CONFUSED ABOUT DISCIPLINE!

Having successfully completed the senior year internship, Lynn Serert has graduated with an education degree, is state certified and has accepted a teaching position. This is Lynn's first year, the beginning teacher year. The school to which Lynn is assigned is in a community of 34,000. It is a mixed economic, ethnic and racial community. Administrative procedures in this school district do not allow school principals to become involved in the hiring process. All teachers are recruited, interviewed and hired through the school district central administration. Lynn has never met the principal of the school, does not know administrative procedures in the school, does not know if the school has a school-wide discipline plan and does not know anyone in the school.

As Lynn walks through the front door of the school on the fourth day of the year a commotion is apparent in another part of the office. Two parents are having a heated discussion with a school staff member. Eight students are seated in chairs waiting. Several other parents are waiting to see the principal. Furniture is being loaded into a truck and replacement furniture brought into the building. The building is clean, perhaps recently painted. The parking lot is filled with cars. A few of the older students are helping with starting school chores.

A staff member walks up to Lynn and introduces herself as the school counselor, Blair Petti.

Blair: Welcome to John Adams
Lynn: Thank you. It's good to be here. I'm a few days late. But, I was just hired yesterday.
Blair: Yes. We began planning week a few days ago. It's my job to get you caught up to the rest of the faculty. I'm certain there will be no problem. First, I'd like to show you around campus and introduce you to a few faculty colleagues with whom you'll be working. Then we'll inventory the room and check out supplies.

Lynn: Thanks for all the help. I'm really impressed. John Adams is well organized. And that's great for a beginning teacher who doesn't know the ropes.

Seven weeks later, after six weeks of school, Lynn makes an appointment to see Blair Petti to discuss a class problem which began as a minor incident but has escalated. Lynn's classes are going OK but there's something wrong. A few parents have phoned and expressed doubt about their child being in a beginner's class. Others have stopped in or written notes which concern their child's seat in the room, homework, low grades, and in general not acting very confident about Lynn's teaching.

Then it happened! Two students in the class got into a fight. Lynn didn't know what to do. Lynn separated the two students and verbally thrashed them. A few days later another student challenged a direction. The whole class waited for Lynn's reaction. Lynn continued class and did nothing. This process of students ignoring Lynn Serert continued. Yesterday the roof fell in. Two students were fighting as Bobby Chazz, the principal, walked past. Lynn stood by as the principal separated Toni and Robin and told them to come to his office.

Lynn: Am I in trouble! What do I do? My job is in danger. The principal wants to see me too. I feel like a student who has been sent to the principal's office. What do I do? You're experienced, what happens now?

Blair: I don't know what the principal has in mind. What do you think you should do?

Lynn: I don't know.

Blair: What could the principal be concerned with?

QUESTIONS

1. What do you think the principal is concerned about?
2. If a problem exists, what could it be?
3. What are some solutions?
4. Role play Lynn and the principal with a colleague. Act Lynn's part in an effort to rehearse the meeting with Bobby Chazz.
5. What issues will Chazz call to Lynn's attention?
6. How should Lynn respond?
7. If a plan is required by Chazz, develop one in detail.

CHAPTER ELEVEN

MANAGEMENT OF STUDENT BEHAVIOR

"Most powerful is he who has himself in his own power."

-Seneca

GOAL

After reading this chapter and completing the activities the reader will understand how to manage the behavior of students.

OBJECTIVES

After reading this chapter the reader will

1. List four expectations that schools have for students and teachers.
2. Describe three explanations of human development.
3. List and explain types of power which teachers use to maintain discipline.
4. Describe how three cultures will influence student behavior management. Include your culture as one of the three.
5. List and describe four behavior management plans.

To the untrained observer of school behavior it may appear that teachers and students behave in an organized although inconsistent manner. Some students are called on more often than others. Some are reinforced for expected responses while others are ignored. At times teachers appear to use strategies which do not produce expected results. The observer may conclude that teachers do not always systematically manage the behavior of students. Chapter Ten illustrated several suggestions which have been successful in an effort to avoid discipline problems in the classroom. Realistically, no matter how successful a teacher is in the application of those avoidance strategies, discipline problems will occur. Therefore, this chapter will focus on the systematic management of student behavior using research based knowledge which concerns the culture of school organizations, the student's cognitive, personal and moral development and student behavior management systems which have a successful history. It is also assumed that teachers have a strong belief in fate control which was extensively discussed in an earlier chapter.

THE SCHOOL'S CULTURE

Each school has expectations for the behavior of teachers, students and other persons in the school. Although each school has its own set of expectations, there is a common set of expectations for all schools. Schools expect teachers to manage student behavior and to create a positive learning environment. Schools expect students to be orderly since orderly behavior facilitates development. And schools expect all persons in the environment, including adults, to be cooperative.

Schools' Expectations for Teachers

The school's expectations for teachers is both written and unwritten. The written portion is outlined in the legal contract between the teacher and the school system as well as in the personnel handbook and in the individual school's policy booklet. Often, unwritten expectations are more compelling than those which are written although they appear vague and or/ambiguous to the teacher newly assigned to a particular school. An illustration is the written policy that teachers are encouraged to attend monthly parent-teacher organization meetings. The informal rule may be that all teachers, without exception, will attend!

One published expectation by the school system is usually titled "Code of Student Conduct." Although the student is the apparent focus, school personnel are responsible for the administration of relationships described in the code. The code explains relationships among students, home (parents) and school personnel. Student rights and responsibilities are noted. A student's right to due process in a disciplinary action is detailed. Relationships to other community agencies such as law enforcement and other state agencies are detailed. A broad framework for student behavior and control methods is stated.

Control of students

Teachers are expected to always control their students. When teachers attempt to control students they are motivated by their own needs and the needs of their students. When a mismatch between teacher needs and student needs occurs, the teacher often experiences a behavior problem in the classroom. Control of students is considered a high priority by teachers, principals and parents. When teachers do not meet the expectations of their constituencies, negative consequences occur. The lack of discipline in the classroom will cause a lack of respect from colleagues and an expressed concern by the principal. A teacher who lacks classroom control may experience an erosion of self confidence which may seriously impact the teacher's ability to be effective. It is important that each teacher have a well developed plan for preventing deviant behavior by students.

Facilitation of student growth

Teachers are expected to help students to grow physically, intellectually and emotionally. This implies that student academic achievement and out of school behavior should demonstrate growth. This is expected of all students although each enters school with different capabilities and motivations for learning. And each student has a vast number of out of school experiences which influence learning. Experiences such as television, being a latch-key child, level of family support, poverty, child abuse and others may impact student behavior in school. In spite of these factors a teacher is held responsible for student physical, intellectual and emotional growth.

Schools' Expectations for Students.

Schools expect students to become what they were not; students are expected to change.

Growth

Students are expected to grow intellectually, emotionally and physically. All planned school behavior is expected to result in growth. School behavior which does not directly result in growth is considered unnecessary by some school observers. Some educators strongly suggest that students not interact with each other, not engage in independent activity and act subservient to the teacher. This expectation for growth proposes that students behave within narrow parameters. Other educators suggest independent activity for students, group work and a cooperative and interactive relationship with teachers. This expectation considers activity, noise and movement which accompanies it normal and acceptable. Both suggestions impact perceived student discipline.

Performance

Students are expected to perform at high levels on standardized tests, the physical education field, in plays, contests and creatively as individuals. Students are expected to take into account the consequences of their activity on the reputation of the school. An illustration is a class trip to the zoo. Student discipline will reflect on the school although their behavior is social and not academic.

SELF CHECK FOR OBJECTIVE ONE

CAN YOU: list four expectations that schools have for students and teachers?

THE STUDENT'S ABILITY TO RESPOND
TO THE SCHOOL'S EXPECTATIONS

Often the school's expectations for students appear unrealistic. Students are expected to achieve less than they can; students are expected to achieve more than they can. Students are excused from a missed assignment because of a family emergency or a minor illness. Kindergarten students are expected to know what is moral, just or fair. Each student is expected to behave appropriately. Frequently, school expectations for students do not consider what is known about student development. This part of the chapter will address personal, cognitive and moral development. A brief commentary on each area of development will be offered the reader so that a groundwork for further concept development will be present. If you would like a more complete understanding of development, we suggest that you read articles and books such as in the chapter bibliography. The work of Erikson, Piaget and Kohlberg will form the basis for the explanation of personal, cognitive and moral development.

Personal Development

Erikson's explanation of human development is positive and hopeful. He believes that development is continuous from birth until death, that earlier missteps can be changed and that growth is impacted by the culture in which one lives. The environment of the developing person will make available to that person a variety of situations which may be used as growth facilitators. While Erikson refers to these situations as crises, Sheehy softens such experiences, referring to them as passages. Nevertheless, each human must pass through each of eight (8) stages which Erikson identified. They must be experienced in order from the first to the eighth. It must also be remembered that many children are in day care facilities while other students are in schools and colleges during the first six stages.

The eight stages of personality development according to Erikson are:

1. Trust vs. Mistrust, the infant should trust his caretakers (0-1½ years),
2. Autonomy vs. Doubt, the child should begin to develop independence by testing his environment (1½-3 years),
3. Initiative vs. Guilt, a child should be encouraged to successfully initiate testing his abilities (3-7 years),
4. Mastery (accomplishment) vs. Inferiority, the elementary school student should have many successes as a result of effectively chosen projects (7-12 years),
5. Self-identity vs. Role Confusion, the early adolescent begins to define self through internal and external evaluations (12-18 years),
6. Intimacy vs. Isolation, the high school graduate moves to a new role as worker or college student and uses that experience to risk new relationships or to play it safe and not risk new relationships (18-30 years),
7. Generativity vs. Self-absorption or stagnation, the mid-aged adult who

believes that he is not making a contribution to the next generation will stagnate (30-60 years) and

8. Integrity vs. Despair, a person who is satisfied with his life accepts responsibility for it and does not blame someone else for his failures (60 plus years).

Cognitive Development

Piaget has suggested a reasonable explanation of cognitive development. His description of cognitive growth includes stages, invariable sequencing, interaction with the environment as a facilitator of growth and the presence of overlap while the person passes through four stages. Although a child may be processing stage two material he may also be processing stage one material. There are four stages which describe how the person begins to process information. They are:

1. Sensorimotor, an infant who must physically interact with the environment to understand it (0-2 years),
2. Preoperational Thought, children begin to develop a symbolic system of object reference — language (2-7 years),
3. Concrete Thought, elementary school students' thought is literal and logical although difficulty with abstract thought is present (7-11 years) and
4. Formal Thought, persons think abstractly and are not bound to images of their prior experience (11-16+ years).

Moral Development

The development of moral thought will be explained using the description of Lawrence Kohlberg. Kohlberg, like Erikson and Piaget, used a model

TABLE 11.1 THREE VIEWS OF HUMAN DEVELOPMENT	
Personality Development (Erickson)	Trust vs. Mistrust Autonomy vs. Shame Initiative vs. Guilt Mastery vs. Inferiority Self-Identity vs. Role Confusion Intimacy vs. Isolation Generativity vs. Self-Absorption Integrity vs. Despair
Cognitive Development (Piaget)	Sensorimotor Preoperational Thought Concrete Thought Formal Thought
Moral Development (Kohlberg)	Preconventional Morality Conventional Morality Postconventional Morality

which relies on an invariant sequence of stages of development which is dependent on activity or experience. Without activity, development is severely hampered. Therefore, it is necessary for teachers to structure simulations and experiences for their students in the area of moral development. It is suggested that such exercises be chosen from those at one stage higher than the student's current moral behavior stage. To consider a model of moral reasoning or thought the same as a model of moral behavior may be imperfect, although the two may be positively correlated. This is so because a person may possess a high ability to reason about moral behavior while he may choose to not behave at the same high level.

Kohlberg's work is closely related to that of Piaget since moral reasoning is dependent on the ability to reason in a general manner. Therefore, a student's inability to reason at Piaget's formal thought stage may prevent the student from reasoning about universal ethical principles. Kohlberg's moral reasoning model has three stages, each with two parts. They are:

1. Preconventional Morality, the child's judgement is dependent on a perception of the physical consequences of action and needs satisfaction (0-9 years),
2. Conventional Morality, the student acquires a reference group, wants to please others and is loyal (9-15 years) and
3. Postconventional Morality, thinks abstractly and independently and forms a conscience (15 years upward).

Erikson's description of personal development is similar to Piaget's view of cognitive development and Kohlberg's explanation of moral development. All three believe that development occurs in stages which are ordered. No one can skip a stage. The development of persons is relatively culture free, that is, all persons in all cultures experience personality, cognitive and moral development in stages which possess an invariant order. All three believe that development is enhanced by experience. In this sense the more experience the better; persons who have fewer experiences will have greater difficulty developing than those with a greater number of experiences.

SELF CHECK FOR OBJECTIVE TWO

CAN YOU: describe three explanations of human development?

TEACHER POWER

Teachers use various forms of power to create a positive learning environment. Power is frequently defined as the ability to cause someone to do something that they ordinarily would not do, or to cause someone to not do something that they ordinarily would do. Hollander and Hunt's explanation of power has five levels: coercive, reward, knowledge, legitimate and referent. Some teachers use all five. To a great extent the choice of which power to use is the teacher's. They may choose to use one, all, or a few in combination.

Coercive

Fear of the consequences of violating an expectation is the motivator of coercive power. An illustration of coercive power used in the classroom occurs when a teacher punishes a student for talking out in class by keeping him after school.

Reward

It is the positive reinforcement of a behavioristic model. Without the reward the student will not act as the teacher directs. An illustration of reward power used by a teacher is a classroom that uses classwide reinforcement of no homework over the weekend if all students do their homework Monday through Thursday.

Knowledge

Teachers possess knowledge that students must acquire. That knowledge may be related to objectives to be tested in history, reading or spelling. Teachers may share or withhold this knowledge. This can be used to change student behavior as they plan to study for a test, choose a book or play a game.

Legitimate

A teacher possesses legitimate power because of an appointment as a teacher by the district school board. Students know that "the teacher" is, or at least should be, in charge and therefore will consider a behavior change when it is requested by the teacher. If a person who is not known to students walked into the classroom and requested that students stop talking and listen to a lecture about to be delivered they would probably think, "Who are you?"

TABLE 11.2
TYPES OF POWER

Referent Power	Most effective. A student modeling a teacher's behavior is an illustration.
Legitimate Power	Power as the result of an appointment. Teachers are appointed by school boards.
Knowledge Power	A form of power based in superior knowledge by one person.
Reward Power	Related to praise and positive reinforcement.
Coercive Power	The least effective form of power. Fear is the basis of this form of power.

Referent

Referent power is the most forceful level of power available to anyone. It is the level of power that your favorite teacher still has over you although you may not have been in the presence of that person for years. When referent power is in use students refer to their teachers with the thought "I wonder what Ms. Johnson would want us to do in this situation?"

SELF CHECK FOR OBJECTIVE THREE

CAN YOU: list and explain types of power used by teachers?

THE STUDENT'S CULTURE

The student's culture should influence how the chosen discipline plan will be individually applied. Culture will influence how discipline procedures will be accepted by students. It is necessary for teachers to be aware of and understand the culture of the student. Otherwise misunderstandings will occur. Misunderstandings can escalate to the level of a problem if allowed.

Minority culture students need to learn more than English as a second language. The student needs to learn what is expected in a new and complex culture. This includes school routines, customs and social relationships. And, cultural learning is pervasive and long lasting. Because a student has lived in this country for several years does not mean the dominant culture has been accepted and the minority culture rejected.

Latin American Cultures

In Latin American cultures smiling may be used as a method to hide embarrassment. If a teacher corrects a student and the student smiles in response the teacher may misunderstand and inappropriately respond. Eye contact is indirect when being corrected. This is considered a sign of respect. A teacher may demand "Look me in the eye when I speak to you young man!" Students work better in small groups and under teacher direction. If an activity demands self-direction and the student has little experience in this mode the teacher may believe the student to be off task and disinterested. Since these students are polychronic they believe there is no need to wait for one's turn to speak or stay in line at the cafeteria. And, students may resist discipline methods being applied to them.

Haitian Culture

Haitian students are frequently members of one parent families. One parent may still be in Haiti or the Bahamas. Therefore, contacting the working parent may be difficult. Haitian parents also believe education to be the school's responsibility and delegate full authority to the school. Therefore, students will be confused when a teacher demands to see the student's parents.

Haitian children are not given decision making rights. Independent activity as required by Reality Therapy and Teacher Effectiveness Training will be foreign. They may find it difficult to operate independently since they were trained in the "listen and do" method. Many Haitian children have experienced recent fractured school schedules. And, they may not have much experience in middle class school activity.

Vietnamese Culture

This culture prizes education because it is a major step to job opportunity and social class enhancement. Violation of school rules is viewed as a violation of the moral code. This tends to make the Vietnamese student hard working and competitive. Because they are polite and modest the Vietnamese student will be quiet and passive in class. This description is that of a student who will respect teachers and will not violate class rules and procedures. They rarely question the teacher.

SELF CHECK FOR OBJECTIVE FOUR

CAN YOU: describe how a student's culture impacts the choice and use of a discipline plan?

CHOOSING THE APPROPRIATE DISCIPLINE STRATEGY

It is important for teachers to consider as many elements that impact discipline as can be identified before committing themselves to the choice of a discipline strategy. In the previous chapter many ways to prevent discipline problems were suggested. Each of these was related to the climate and culture of a classroom. Three important factors were identified: the student, environment and teacher. These factors may be related to several discipline systems that are commonly used to manage the behavior of students in a classroom. The remainder of this chapter will discuss the interrelationship of student development, power used by teachers, freedom allowed students by teachers and the appropriate discipline system to be used.

The work of Sprinthall and Sprinthall suggests that the choice of a behavior management strategy should consider students' development. Although students' development should be considered, other factors such as those imposed by the students' environment must be considered. Other environment factors include the district's and school's policies, teachers' needs for law and order in the classroom, course objectives, culture of the student and the amount of freedom to be allowed to solve problems and make decisions. Three factors should be considered in selecting a model for maintaining classroom discipline. They are the degree of freedom to be allowed students to solve problems and make decisions; the student's personality, cognitive and moral development stage; and the power level to be used. This is illustrated in figure 11.1. As the student matures in development and as the

FIGURE 11.1

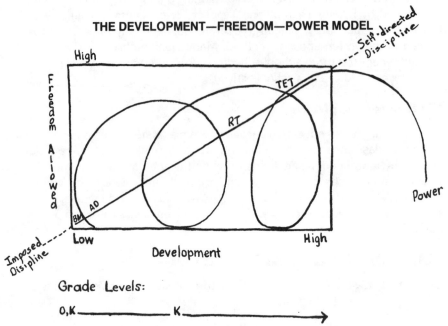

school allows students greater freedom, the choice of a behavior management strategy will change. The power level to be used varies with the environment and the student's development. Four models will be illustrated and associated with four currently used classroom behavior management strategies. They are:

Model One; Behavior Modification
Model Two; Assertive Discipline
Model Three; Reality Therapy
Model Four; Teacher Effectiveness Training

This explanation assumes that people pass through development stages in an invariant sequence and the least allowable levels of freedom precede the greatest allowable levels of freedom. It should also be assumed that not all students reach the greatest levels of development or freedom to make decisions and solve problems.

FOUR MODELS OF BEHAVIOR MANAGEMENT

Model One Illustration: Behavior Modification

Model One assumes the least freedom allowed to students and the least development of the student. Although it would appear that only very young children, typically grades K-4, are associated with this Model it is possible to experience a situation in a classroom of older students that would strongly suggest that freedom should be curtailed while reversion to a prior developmental stage is being demonstrated by a student, group of students or class. Therefore, Model One discipline practice may be appropriate at all ages depending on the situation.

It should be noted that most children in Model One are probably in Erikson's first two stages and possibly in the first part of his third stage. Observation of children proceeding through these stages of personality development notes them testing their environment and their trust of others. They also test themselves in an effort to develop competencies and self concept. Unreasonable restraint of a child's testing will result in a child's feeling of guilt in contrast to competence. Saying "NO!" too frequently tends to promote guilt. Remember, a child's judgment is dependent on the physical consequences of actions. Therefore, a behavior management strategy which relies on a student's perception of actions causing physical consequences is appropriate. This must be balanced with a teacher's ethical behavior to not harm the child physically or psychologically.

Many teachers have discovered behavior modification to be most effective with young students. Reward power is used in behavior modification; coercive power should be used much less frequently. Positive reinforcement should be used because it is effective, as they seek pleasure and avoid pain. Rewards such as free time, no homework over the weekend, brief periods at learning centers or computers and permission to do homework in class may be used as rewards.

To a lesser extent negative reinforcement and punishment can be used. Behavior-modification advocates believe that positive reinforcement is the most powerful of the three. Negative reinforcement and punishment (especially) are less powerful motivators and therefore should be less attractive to the teacher who wants to be effective.

Behavior modification can be used with anyone at any stage of development if the student continues to remain engaged. However, it is most appropriately used with students who either cannot operate at higher stages of development or who choose to operate at low stages and continue to accept little freedom to solve problems and make decisions. Several procedures are included within the behavior modification strategy. An incomplete list includes positive reinforcement, negative reinforcement, punishment, contracting, modeling, token economy, satiation and extinction.

Positive reinforcement

It is used when a teacher rewards a student for desirable behavior such as being quiet during a short speech by student peers. The reward may be a social reward such as "Thank you" or a physical reward such as candy or a popcorn party or perhaps no homework over the weekend.

Negative reinforcement

It is illustrated by the student who couldn't be quiet during the speech and was placed in a time-out space by the teacher. A time-out space is a part of the classroom in which the student is separated from classmates in such a way that the student cannot see them, they cannot see the student and the teacher can observe the student with a discipline problem. Since the student does not usually want to be apart from classmates the teacher may decide to return the student to the class when he begins to be quiet in the time-out space. An unpleasant experience (time-out space) is being removed so that the student will behave as the teacher desires.

Punishment

This should be avoided as a behavior management strategy although there is disagreement about its effectiveness. Punishment may be physical or nonphysical. Physical punishment may be against state law, school district policy or individual school policy. Physical punishment may also cause injury to students; this should be avoided. Physical punishment also sends students a subtle message. "If one is big enough he can get his own way." This is an invitation to additional physical violence and is illustrated by the administrator who regularly uses corporal punishment on students referred for fighting. Non-physical punishment may be harsh such as a teacher who yells and screams or one who issues desists such as "Mary, please stop talking to John." Mild desists are more effective than harsh punishment.

Contracts

Some student situations require that a contract be struck between concerned parties. These may include peers, parents, teachers and the student in question. It is more effective to have a written contract than a verbal contract, one which is signed by the concerned parties, and a copy for each person. The contract should cover what the student will do, the date of task accomplishment, the positive consequence for the accomplishment as well as the negative consequence for non-accomplishment. Someone should be named as the monitor of contract proceedings and as the person who is going to reward the student. The person who gives the reward need not be the teacher. An illustration of contracting may be the student who is having difficulty doing homework on time who will be rewarded with pizza at a local restaurant if his homework is on time each day for four days; if it is not on time he will be restricted to the family house and yard for a weekend. The only exception to the restriction is going to religious services with the family one time during the two days; this cannot include a social hour.

Modeling

Behavior modeling is sometimes thought of as imitation although a previous part of this chapter referred to reference power in a similar manner. A teacher or a peer may act as a model for a student who is having difficulty with appropriate use of language. The student may be removed from his chosen work group and assigned to a group of students who demonstrate the desired behavior, appropriate use of language. The purpose is to have the student model the group's behavior.

Token Economy

Token economy is used by teachers who must change the behavior of an entire class and choose an elaborate system of desired behaviors and comparable rewards. As the title suggests, a token economy is designed with behaviors and a currency. The desired behaviors cover a wide range of academic and social behavior. Students who demonstrate the desired behaviors are rewarded with printed currency — play money. Class currency can be redeemed for items such as free food coupons to McDonalds, Burger King, a hula hoop, kite, sled, a pair of skates, shirt pocket radio, doll or game. Many parents will cooperate and assist the teacher to purchase the items in the class' token economy. Class currency is used as tokens with which students can purchase desired products. A student also may buy extra time at a learning center, free time to read a special book or a weekend free of homework if his achievement in that course is appropriately high. Teachers sometimes display pictures of available items to be bought and their prices in class currency on the wall of the classroom. In this manner the student is

---

TABLE 11.3
BEHAVIOR MODIFICATION STRATEGIES

Positive Reinforcement	Related to reward power. A reward is given to a student if he complies with a teacher's wish.
Negative Reinforcement	Related to coercive power. A teacher removes a reward which the student is receiving in an effort to have him change his behavior.
Punishment	Related to coercive power. An unpleasant consequence is applied by the teacher to the student in an effort to change his behavior.
Contracts	An agreement among student, teacher and parent in an effort to meet specific expectations and rewards.
Modeling	Related to referent power. Teachers create a positive model for their students to imitate.
Token Economy	A positive reinforcement strategy which makes use of immediate rewards such as currency which can be redeemed for prizes.
Satiation	When this occurs a teacher rewards an undesirable behavior to the extent that the student becomes bored with it.
Extinction	Behaviors which are ignored and not rewarded cease.

constantly reminded of the token economy's rewards. This is a powerful technique, especially for students in the lower developmental stages.

Satiation

An undesired behavior and the accompanying reward may become so aversive to the student that behavior is changed. Suppose a student has a habit of whispering to a friend who sits in the next seat. It doesn't matter what is happening in the class at the time. The class might be discussing a current class problem, a student may be talking or the teacher may be talking. The whispering student continues to whisper. The teacher would insist that the student whisper continuously for 30 minutes. This will be a long time for the whispering student. While the student is whispering the teacher would reinforce the whispering. At some point in this exercise the student would tire of whispering and stop. Too much of what he previously valued (whispering) was experienced. He is satiated.

Extinction

Extinction is practiced by teachers who ignore the misbehavior of particular students when they do not harm themselves or other students. This is more effective if teachers can persuade students to ignore the misbehaving student too. If the student who is using inappropriate language receives no attention it is likely that he will discontinue its use. He will not be positively reinforced although he was reinforced previously by student giggles and teacher reprimand.

Model Two Illustration: Assertive Discipline

Students with whom model two strategies are used should be allowed more freedom than those with whom model one is used since the student has developed to a greater extent. Model two student discipline should not be used in a pre-school setting. However, it can be used with all other age groups. This includes students assigned to grades kindergarten through high school. It also can be used with groups of adults who never develop to the extent to which they are capable. They sometimes choose to remain in a relationship, personal and professional, which does not facilitate their development and consequently allows little freedom in decision making and solving interpersonal problems. The most appropriate use of the model two illustration, assertive discipline strategies, is in grades K-8.

Students with whom assertive discipline strategies could be used are probably in the following Erikson stages of personality development: the latter part of initiative vs. guilt, mastery vs. inferiority and self identity vs. role confusion. Most students will leave high school at the end of this last stage. Students in these stages will explore their environment and personal relationships with others in an attempt to identify goals, plan for their accomplishments and successfully achieve them. While testing competency the student

When the teacher's behavior management system works well, students acquire more freedom in the classroom. The right behavior management system is one which matches the students' cognitive, personal and moral development with the class-room's demands.

evaluates self achievement in an effort to articulate a perception of self. If the self is integrated, self identity has been achieved and role confusion avoided. Students with whom model two strategies are used successfully are spread across a cognitive continuum. Some have just begun to acquire language competency while others have great facility with language. They think liter-ally, intuitively, logically and inferentially. Less developed students are bound to concrete images; more developed students can think symbolically.

A student in early model two will attempt to maximize pleasure while minimizing pain; others in the later part of the model will act according to a conscience. Since model two discipline procedures are most appropriate with students in the initial part of the model, most students will seek pleasure, avoid pain, try to please others and be loyal to self and group. A result of the development level of these students is that legitimate, reward, and coercive power are most appropriate. Coercive power appears to be used most frequently as an unpleasant consequence which is understood as threatening by the student. Therefore, it is appropriate to choose a strategy for the model two student which considers the student's goal to seek pleasure and avoid pain within an organized set of rules and consequences.

Assertive discipline is only one model two strategy which can be used.

Since it is a prevalent method it will be used as an illustration of a model two behavior management strategy. Assertive discipline's assumptions, methods and goals are related to those of behavior modification. Both discipline methods can be used with the same population, except young children who would have difficulty with elements of each. Consequently, it is necessary for the teacher to consider the developmental stage of the student before choosing a discipline strategy. Another element which demands being attended to is the environment in which students will be working. What degree of freedom to make decisions and solve problems will be allowed students? What power type can be used with them? If assertive discipline is to be used, little freedom will be allowed. All types of power will be used. Yes, this includes coercive power as a negative consequence which the student dislikes if the student does not conform to stated rules of behavior.

There are five components to assertive discipline behavior management strategy. They are:

1. Know your assumptions and act them out,
2. A statement of rules should be formulated,
3. A statement of consequences which will be experienced by students should they choose not to follow the rules should be made,
4. Teachers should reinforce student behavior which conforms to the stated rules and
5. Cooperation among teacher, student, school administration and parents should be designed into the strategy. If used appropriately this strategy is not aversive; it is a positive experience for both the student and the teacher.

Assumptions

There are three assumptions which teachers make when using assertive discipline. They are:

1. No student should prevent a teacher from teaching,
2. No student should prevent himself from learning and
3. No student should prevent another student from learning.

Rules

Teachers should know exactly what they expect from students. It is necessary to communicate these expectations to the class. Teachers are sometimes unclear about what they expect; they sometimes communicate unclear expectations to students. From the teacher's view the result is a behavior problem. Teachers should examine those student behaviors which they need in order to teach. Student behaviors which are generally necessary are:

1. Students should follow directions,
2. Students should be on time to class and
3. Students should bring necessary materials to class

These necessary behaviors suggest three rules which are:

1.   Follow directions,
2.   Be on time and
3.   Bring necessary materials.

There should be few rules, perhaps five at the most. Rules should be explained to the class and published on a poster in the room. If there were 45 rules students and teacher would not attend to them; they would forget many of the rules. If the rules were not made public how would students know what the rules are? And consequently, how would they be able to follow the rules?.

If you can't think of rules for your class ask yourself which student behaviors bother you. Make a list of these. Convert them into rules. An illustration of a student behavior which bothers most teachers is inappropriate talking in class. The rule which would follow is "Raise your hand to talk."

Consequences

Without consequences many students have no reason to follow rules. Therefore, consequences must be designed for those students who do not follow rules. The consequences must be few, be clear, be undesirable from the student's view. The teacher must be comfortable applying them. The consequences must be explained to the students; they must be made public. They could be printed on a poster and displayed in the room.

A method of notification of rule infraction must be used. A method which works is below:

1.   When the student breaks a rule the first time his name is written on the board,
2.   The second time he breaks a rule a check mark is placed next to his name and
3.   The third time he breaks a rule a second check is placed next to his name.

No verbal explanation of why his name is written on the board is offered to the student. They generally know why and feign ignorance. The result of an explanation might be disruption of the class.

Often, placing the student's name on the board quiets the entire class. No one wants to have his name on the board because of the social and teacher designed consequences. A chart with the following consequences could be used.

1.   Name on the board — 15 minutes after school,
2.   Name and one check — 30 minutes after school and
3.   Name and two check marks — see the principal.

In schools where staying after school is not possible because of bussing or other reasons, creative teachers can think of many consequences which will make students uncomfortable. One is eating lunch apart from friends and perhaps with the teacher. Students will follow the rules in an effort to avoid pain and discomfort. This behavior is related to low level personal, cognitive and moral behavior. It is a discipline plan which assumes low level freedom and one which thus far uses coercive power.

A teacher must choose consequences which can be comfortably enforced. The teacher may not want to stay after school with his misbehaving students every afternoon. If he does not want to stay in with them at lunch every day he must become creative. It is possible for five teachers to cooperate and stay in one day a week rather than every day. A teacher may believe that every student needs a break from the routine at lunch and does not want to keep student in a "lunch club." Consequences which students want to avoid and teachers are comfortable enforcing should be designed. Consequences must be applied to the student as soon as possible; next week is too late because the student will possibly forget the connection between the consequence and rule breaking. This connection is necessary so that the student learns that the consequence and the behavior are to be avoided.

Classroom situations occur that suggest that teachers should not write the student's name on the board, then go through the one check, two check process. These are severe student behaviors. Fighting with injury is one; another is sexual harassment by students. The student should be sent to the principal immediately — with an adult if possible.

Teachers share students with other teachers. Often students move from one space to another; in some schools teachers move from class to class. When a student has five or six teachers a day the potential for testing assertive discipline is present. This is especially true if teachers give warnings rather than consequences with the first rule infraction. Teachers who use a warning fracture assertive discipline. They encourage students to break one rule a class period, go to the next class and break a rule without a consequence being applied and do it again throughout the day. There should be no warnings since problem students view warnings as teacher weakness to be tested. Teachers who warn are teachers who threaten; frequently they are teachers who do not back up their threats; they only warn.

Teachers who share students with other teachers need a tracking system so that students who do not follow the rules come to the attention of the principal. A discipline card can be used for this purpose. When a student breaks a rule he is asked for his discipline card if it is the second period or later. If it is the first period he is given a discipline card. The broken rule is noted on the card. Other infractions are also noted throughout the day. The student's last period teacher is responsible for referring to the principal. If a student loses or destroys a discipline card, he is treated to the maximum consequence. Another method which works is analogous to the absent student list. The names of students who break rules are placed on a list and submitted to the principal. At the end of the school day they report to him. He administers the consequences.

Another teacher response to a discipline problem is related to the teacher's use of a support system. Teachers can agree to accept students with discipline problems from widely diverse grades. The student with a problem is sent to a well run classroom in a grade that is four or five grades higher or lower than that of the student with a behavior problem. Students are sent with a full period's work to do. They should not participate in the host class' activity and be seated apart from students in the host class. In that way a fifth grader will be sent to a first or second grade and conversely a first grader to a fifth grade. The student will probably be somewhat uncomfortable in a strange environment apart from his friends.

Another technique that allows a fast response is simple. Place an audio tape recorder on the desk of a student who insists on being verbally disruptive while other students are participating in classwide activity. The teacher places an audio tape recorder on the disruptive student's desk with the record function activated. The student is informed that the recording will be played during a parent conference. The student's reaction is usually disbelief and silence. Other students near the audio recorder usually become quiet.

Positive reinforcement

Always reinforce the appropriate behavior of students. When students follow class rules they must be reinforced so that their rule following behavior continues. Reinforcement can be either individual or classwide. Individual reinforcement takes place when particular students follow class rules. Each student should be praised every day, especially in K-3 grades. Older students should be praised carefully since peer pressure sometimes directs them to overtly reject the praise with a smart verbal or facial remark. Positive notes should be sent home when students follow the rules of the class. A teacher should send home two handwritten notes a day. In this way all students will receive a note periodically while the teacher will not find the process a burden. Positive notes can be used at all levels. A professor of accounting at a state university who sent a positive note to the parents of one of his students was recognized in a recent newspaper article. If teachers carefully observe their students they will find a positive behavior which can be commended in a note.

A second reinforcement method is classwide. The entire class will enjoy a form of praise as a reward for the class following rules. The teacher may do this in an overt manner or in a somewhat private process. The overt manner works best since praise will be frequent, public, whole class and individual. The overt method uses a small jar and a hundred or so marbles. When a student responds to a question, follows a rule or when the entire class has been effective in its work for a short period of time the teacher can drop a marble or a few marbles in the jar. The noise of the marble(s) being dropped in the jar will reinforce the class immediately. When the jar is filled that day or at the end of the week the teacher rewards the entire class with a popcorn party, a monster bread surprise, no homework over the weekend or that night or another valued reinforcer. Young students require daily jar full reinforcement; older students can wait a week.

Cooperation with school administrators and parents

The most effective use of a discipline plan requires the cooperation of all individuals who are involved. If assertive discipline is to be used effectively school administrators and parents should be notified that it will be used in the classroom. Teachers should share a copy of the plan with the principal as it will be used in the classroom. The teacher should also send home a copy of the plan. Teachers should reinforce administrators, colleagues and parents when they experience cooperation. A positive note to the principal, a colleague or parent is one way to praise cooperation. Praise will insure continued cooperation.

If a teacher secures the cooperation of administrators and parents it is more probable that support will be forthcoming if a thorny situation presents itself. Severe or continued deviant student behavior should be called to the attention of parents. It may be necessary to call a parent at work. It may be necessary to send a student to the principal. A contract with a disruptive student and his parents may be appropriate. If a thorny situation presents itself, support will be forthcoming if the teacher is known and respected by the parent and principal. If the teacher is unknown or if the discipline plan is unknown, administrators and parents will be cautious when asked for support.

Model Three Illustration: Reality Therapy

A model three environment allows students a medium amount of freedom to make decisions and solve problems. The developmental level of a student in model three is also medium, not at the lowest levels but not at peak levels. Students with whom model three strategies are being used are probably in upper elementary school, middle and junior high school and high school.

In order that model three strategies function effectively students must be developed to the degree that they can make decisions and solve interpersonal problems using inductive and deductive thought at a beginning level. Past problems may have taken place in an environment which is familiar to the student. New responses in new environments may be necessary. Students

---

TABLE 11.4
FIVE COMPONENTS OF ASSERTIVE DISCIPLINE

Assumptions	Teachers make assumptions about student and teacher assertiveness.
Rules	Classroom rules should be published.
Consequences	The consequences for not complying with classroom rules should be made explicit to students.
Reinforcement	Whenever possible students should be praised.
Cooperation	All persons concerned with discipline in schools should cooperate.

will risk again if they were a success in a prior risk. Praise and success are both important. Students in this model level will begin to struggle with value questions such as fairness and loyalty. The student's cognitive and moral ability to consider fairness is tempered by loyalties — to peers, to adults, to a developing conscience and to values such as fairness. Nevertheless, they have the ability to begin the struggle, the need to struggle and the right to struggle in order that they can grow. Although students with whom model three strategies can be effectively used are spread over a wide age and grade range, students at the lowest levels are best served with models one and two strategies.

Power forms which are most effective with model three strategies are knowledge, legitimate and referent. Knowledge and legitimate are the most appropriate of the three. Coercive power should not be used with model three strategies. Reward is somewhat inappropriate. There should be no punishment by the teacher in model three strategy use. Rewards should be internally generated by the student.

It is possible that you are wondering if a student exists with whom a model three behavior management strategy can be used? No coercion? No reward? Why should a student not cause behavior problems? Perhaps an illustration of a model three strategy and the possible students it might work with will help to answer these questions.

Reality Therapy is a well known behavior management strategy that is appropriate to illustrate model three. Reality Therapy was developed by William Glasser, a psychiatrist. He suggested that individuals with problems be assisted to solve their problems in a caring manner which is personal. Parenthetically, a student who is the focus of the application of a behavior management strategy is having an interpersonal problem. Glasser's view is that each individual is responsible for identifying and solving his own problems as well as being responsible for the consequences of his behavior. Reality therapy requires the teacher and the student to be dispassionate and rational in the analysis of behavior, discuss the analysis and develop a plan to solve the problem. The method, together with illustrations of each step, is below.

Let's assume that a student in a classroom where the teacher is using Reality Therapy is experiencing a problem. The teacher would use the following process:

1. The teacher should be personal. The student should be addressed by name. The teacher would communicate concern with the student as a unique individual, one who is different from every other human. The teacher may say "Juan and Bill, what are you doing?" (They were fighting.)
2. Teachers should not treat this problem as necessarily related to the student's past behavior, his sibling's behavior, that of his peers or the history of his parent. The teacher should stay in the present.
3. The student is then questioned further in an effort to help the student

make a value judgement about unacceptable behavior. An illustration may be:

"Juan, how did punching Bill help you?"

"Bill how did punching Juan help you?"

Students will try to rationalize their behavior with comments such as:

"He started it."

"I won the fight."

Additional questions need to be asked.

"If punching helped why does your problem still exist?" Or,

"If the fighting helped, why are we having this talk?"

The student should be helped to evaluate his behavior using the criteria of:

(a) Is the behavior helpful to you?

(b) Harmful to you?

(c) Helpful to anyone else?

(d) Harmful to anyone else?

The student must make a judgement about his behavior from his frame of reference. Using skillful questions the teacher should help the student to make this value judgement. The teacher should never make the value judgment for the student.

4. The student must then make a plan to help him to change his behavior. It must be his plan since he will be psychologically committed to it. He would be less committed to a plan which the teacher made. The plan can be either oral or written. The authors of this book suggest a written plan with a copy for the teacher and a copy for the student. The student should sign the plan. The plan should include the natural consequences of the plan being carried out as well as not being carried out. If Juan's plan is to stay apart from Bill for one week so that they will not fight, and if they are together and do fight, a natural consequence would be placing each boy in an isolation space for one day. The purpose of placing both boys in an isolation space is to give them time to think about the problem and perhaps develop a better plan. Should one or both of the boys be injured in the fight both boys should be referred to the nurse and to the principal

---

TABLE 11.5
REALITY THERAPY STEPS

1. Be personal.
2. Stay in the present.
3. Ask the student to make a value judgement.
4. Ask the student to make a plan to correct the problem.
5. Get a commitment from the student.
6. Follow up and accept no excuses for failure.
7. Use no punishment if the plan does not work.
8. If the plan does not work place the student in a quiet space so that the student can think of a plan which may work.
9. Recycle the process.

immediately.

5. The teacher must get a commitment from the student. At times a handshake is enough. Other times a written plan and a signature is necessary.

6. The teacher should monitor the student carrying out the plan. Teachers should be available for follow-up if that is necessary. Juan and Bill should be observed to be certain that they are staying away from each other, if this is the plan. The teacher should not accept excuses.

7. There should be no punishment, only the natural consequences of a plan not being carried out. There should be no physical punishment.

If this series of steps does not work with a student, the student should be placed in an isolation space so that he has time to think. Some students will be difficult to work with. This plan should not be used with them. They may not be developed enough cognitively, morally or personally. Or, a prerequisite for the use of Reality Therapy may not be present, a positive student-teacher relationship.

Model Four Illustration: Teacher Effectiveness Training

The use of Teacher Effectiveness Training (TET) assumes the student to be in an environment which will allow a high level of student freedom to make decisions and solve problems in recognition of the student's high level of development. Referent power is the most appropriate type of power to be used at this level. Coercive power should be avoided. TET may be used with those elementary and middle school students who have developed personally, morally and intellectually as well as with students of greater chronological maturity. Besides the developmental characteristics of students with whom model four behavior management strategies are being used, *optimum* use of model four discipline strategies requires well developed communication skills by both the student and the teacher. Both persons should be effective problem solvers who are skillful in paraphrasing, behavior description, feeling description and impression checking. Each of these communication skills were defined and illustrated in chapter ten.

The personality of students at the model four level is more integrated than not. Consequently they are willing to take high risks with new relationships. Since they are cognitively capable of formal and abstract thought they are able to consider abstract concepts such as justice. They continue to develop a conscience.

Teacher Effectiveness Training (TET), developed by Thomas Gordon, will be used as an illustration of a model four strategy. Central to Gordon's method is trust in the individual to exercise power to identify the problem, accept ownership of the problem if the problem is his, discover a solution to the problem and carry out that solution. The teacher's role is to facilitate the student's behavior in a nondirective manner.

Gordon states that three methods are generally used when teachers respond to student problems. The first is authoritarian; the teacher asserts his position of power over the student. Behavior Modification and Assertive Discipline are authoritarian strategies. The second is permissive whereby the student assumes power and the teacher is passive to the extent that students assert that they will get their way. This method exists when a student nags at a teacher (or parent) to get his way. No win-no lose, the third method, assumes a position that neither the student or the teacher should have power over the other and that a no power, no lose strategy is to be used. Related to this is an analysis of the problem to determine ownership. Is the problem the student's? Or the teacher's? Or, does a third party own the problem?

Gordon's method also requires the use of well developed communication skills. Those who use the method optimally must communicate. They must listen as well as hear the other's statement. Hearing is a physical whereas listening is an intellectual—emotional act. It requires the message from another to be heard, to be filtered through the listener's emotional state and intellectual history. "I messages" rather than "You messages" are to be used.

"I am angry" is an "I message."

"You are so clumsy and stupid!"
"You make me so frustrated." These are illustrations of "You messages."

"I am so mad at you because you spilled paint on the carpet" is an illustration of a "You message" which is disguised as an "I message."

A key element is self-responsibility. The student is responsible for his problems. Teachers are responsible for theirs. Some problems are not to be owned by either the teacher or student.

The following six steps of Gordon's method form the core of a no win-no lose, problem solving method.

1. Identify and define the problem. Using active listening and "I messages" the teacher facilitates the student in the statement of the problem. Eliciting and probing questions are used. This step also includes the assumption that the student has accepted ownership of the problem. The student would state that he was smoking in the school building after skillful listening and perhaps some questioning by the teacher. The student's initial remark may have been "I am so mad at the Principal for making dumb rules."

TABLE 11.6
TEACHER EFFECTIVENESS TRAINING

1. Identify and define the conflict. Whose problem is it?
2. Generate alternative solutions.
3. Evaluate each alternative solution.
4. Choose the best solution.
5. Action plan the chosen solution.
6. Evaluate the carried out solution.

2. During the second step the teacher assists the student to list possible solutions to the problem. Since the problem is smoking in school the student may generate solutions such as
   a. stop smoking,
   b. smoke away from school or
   c. continue to smoke in the building but don't get caught
3. The third step requires the teacher to assist the student to evaluate alternate solutions. The outcome of the solution must be considered since a possible outcome of continuing to smoke in the school building may not be acceptable by the teacher since this may violate a fire code, the state school code, the school district policy and parental wishes expressed in a school policy handbook. The teacher must express the inability to support the choice of that decision with an "I message." The student should also use "I messages" in this conversation.
4. Step four involves the choice of the best alternative.
5. This step involves both student and teacher in creating ways to action plan the chosen solution.
6. The last step is one in which both teacher and student evaluate how the solution worked. They look at the results of the implemented solution, the timing of the implementation and if necessary a recycling of step two, generating alternative solutions through the last step, evaluation.

Although TET is not an illustration of Models One or Two, structuring a positive learning environment is suggested. Prevention of disruption should be undertaken, perhaps in ways suggested in chapter ten. Modeling appropriate behavior is considered important. Should the student not respond to TET, Gordon suggests that he be given time to think about the problem in a quiet space. The authors of this book suggest that if TET is not working with a student other models of discipline strategies should be considered. Perhaps the student's developmental stage was misjudged.

SELF CHECK FOR OBJECTIVE FIVE

CAN YOU: list and describe four behavior management plans?

SUMMARY

This chapter described the impact of student developmental stage, amount of freedom to be allowed and power type on the choice of a behavior management strategy. Teachers should not use a preferred behavior management strategy because they used it at another school successfully or because it suits their personality. Teachers should choose a strategy which corresponds to the characteristics of their students and school policy. The choice of a management system should not be a capricious act.

Four models were identified. An illustration of each model was described. The description was complete enough for a choice to be made and a behavior management program installed in a classroom.

ACTIVITY

This activity will require the student to observe a classroom for one hour. The student should examine and analyze the environment structured by the teacher, teacher behavior and student behavior. Notes should be taken.

The second part of this activity requires the student to develop four plans for this class. They are:

1. A Behavior Modification plan,
2. An Assertive Discipline plan,
3. A Reality Therapy plan and
4. A Teacher Effectiveness Training plan.

When creating the behavior modification plan name the student for whom the plan is created unless you are creating a token economy for the entire class.

An Assertive Discipline Plan should be designed for the entire class.

Write a script for a Reality Therapy plan for one student in difficulty that you have observed.

Write a scenario for one student for the TET option.

BIBLIOGRAPHY

Canter, L., & Canter, M. (1976). *Assertive discipline.* Santa Monica: Canter and Associates.

Carter, J. (1989). The "champions" program—behavior improvement in physical education. *Journal of Physical Education, Recreation and Dance, 60*(5), 66-67.

Galloway, C. (1976). *Psychology for learning and teaching.* New York: McGraw-Hill.

Gordon, T. (1976). *P.E.T. in action.* New York: Bantam.

Henkel, S. (1989). The teacher's edge to pupil control. *Journal of Physical Education, Recreation and Dance, 60*(1), 60-64.

Lunenburg, F.C., & Schmidt, L.J. (1989). Pupil control ideology, pupil control behavior and the quality of school life. *Journal of Research and Development in Education, 22*(4), 36-44.

Render, G.F. (1989). Assertive discipline, a critical review and analysis. *Teachers College Record, 90*(4), 607-630.

Schneider, G.T., & Burgos, F. (1987). The microcomputer: A decision-making tool for improving school discipline. *NASSP Bulletin, 71,* 104-112.

Sheehy, G. (1976). *Passages.* New York: Dutton.

Sorensen, A.S. (1986). A student monitored classroom management system for the physical sciences classroom. *Clearing House, 59*(7), 305-309.

Sprinthall, R., & Sprinthall, N. (1987). *Educational psychology, a developmental approach.* Reading: Addison Wesley.

Weber, W., Roff, L., Crawford, J., & Robinson, C. (1983). *Classroom management, reviews of the teacher education and research literature.* Princeton: Educational Testing Service.

Wolfgang, C., & Glickman, C. (1980). *Solving discipline problems.* Boston: Allyn and Bacon.

CHAPTER TWELVE

INTRODUCTORY CASE STUDY

CASE STUDY 12-1
WHAT KIND OF TEST SHOULD I GIVE?

Jan Trixel is a first year teacher in a new suburban school. Most of the faculty are young and have little teaching experience. Many of the teachers have their teaching degrees from a local university which has a fine reputation. Jan is troubled about evaluating student performance.

Students who attend this school are from varied cultural, economic and racial groups. Many are bussed to the school. Very few walk to school. Others catch rides to school from parents who are on the way to work or from older brothers or sisters. Student motivation and achievement is as diverse as their background. Jan has decided to talk to a more experienced teacher who has acted as Jan's mentor in the beginning teacher program.

JAN   "I have a problem with my social studies class."

SEAN   "Oh, that class is a problem isn't it?"

JAN   "But this isn't the usual discipline problem with that group. It's almost time to give them their first test of the year and I don't know what to do. I've taken the testing class at the university and I know how to write test items and all that stuff. But, I don't know what to do with this group.

SEAN   "What do you mean?"

JAN   "The class is so diverse."

SEAN   "How?"

JAN   "They are so different. Different from other classes I've observed while in college and different from the class I taught when I was an intern."

SEAN   "How are they different?"

JAN   "Some students don't seem to want to come to school while others are so eager to learn. Some read at grade level while others are below grade level. When I've used oral questioning some students jump out of their chairs to respond while others go to sleep. They don't care. I'm afraid they won't take the test or won't do their best.

And, I can't appeal to the parents of my uncooperative students. They aren't available.

What do I do now?"

WHAT SHOULD JAN DO?

1. Should the test be rescheduled? Until Jan's students are motivated to take the test?
2. Should a more experienced teacher's test be used?
3. Should several tests be written for this group so that each student is appealed to at the proper motivation and achievement level?
4. Should Jan write one test which appeals to each student? How?
5. Could Jan ask the students to help write the test? How would this be helpful? Harmful?
6. Should evaluation include a written test only? Or, should other types of measurement be used. What kind?
7. How should Jan begin to plan for this test?
8. What is the purpose of this evaluation. End of semester grades?
9. Should grading of this test be different for each group, the achievers, the unmotivated, different cultural groups?

CHAPTER TWELVE
PLANNING FOR EVALUATION AND TEST ITEM CONSTRUCTION

"How little do they see what really is, who frame their hasty judgments upon that which seems."

-Southey

GOAL

After reading this chapter the student will appreciate evaluation and understand how to measure student progress.

OBJECTIVES

After completing this chapter students will

1. state why student progress is evaluated,
2. describe the relationship of evaluation and decision making,
3. design a table of specifications,
4. write a wide variety of non-essay items for each objective in a table of specifications,
5. write a matching format item,
6. write a cloze format item for a content area such as history,
7. write a cloze format item for a reading class,
8. write essay items in each of four Bloom Cognitive Taxonomy levels and combination of levels: application, analysis, synthesis and evaluation,
9. create and use an essay response scoring sheet and
10. design observation checksheets, oral tests and portfolio evaluations for student behavior.

As teachers plan instruction they must concurrently plan evaluation procedures. Evaluation of student work is necessary so that students and teachers know which next instructional experiences are necessary. Evaluation is important enough to be planned as lessons and units of instruction are planned.

Some of the questions which teachers ask themselves when planning for instruction are: Which strategy should be used? Which procedure? Which item type? When? The discussion which follows should help you to answer many questions about planning for evaluation.

THE ROLE OF MEASUREMENT AND EVALUATION

Six groups of people are interested in the results of testing of student progress. They are students, parents, teachers, counselors, principals, and citizen-taxpayers. Each group has a special interest in the results of testing and evaluation although some overlap of concern exists. Their concern manifests itself in three areas—instruction, guidance and administration.

Instruction

Students and teachers are concerned about the success of the student with a particular objective and the student's next steps toward the accomplishment of other objectives. Teachers may spend as much as 30 percent of their time evaluating instruction. When the results of testing are less successful than hoped for, students and teachers examine test items and objectives taught. If they do not match, students question the teacher. Teachers clarify and refine their objectives, instruction and testing procedure. As students and teachers engage in the process of learning and teaching, parents request information about the process and results of school activity.

Guidance

If parents and teachers suspect that a student possesses a special aptitude or ability they refer the student to the school counselor. Some students are talented musicians, dancers, artists or unusually gifted learners. Others possess learning disabilities, underdeveloped vision or hearing and undisciplined physical behavior. Some special characteristics of students are helpful; others are restrictive. School counselors often request assistance from school psychologists who test the student's special characteristics with academic and perhaps psychological instruments. The next step in the process is staffing. The staffing meeting frequently includes the student's teachers, parents, counselor, school administrator, school psychologist and sometimes the student himself. An administrative result of the staffing may be a different program for the student.

Administrative

Administrators are concerned with achievement. They use testing and grades information as a quality control procedure. Since grades and report cards are computerized, administrators have access to individual student grades, school-wide grades and district-wide grades. They also have access to the school district's standardized test scores. This information is sometimes used to make judgments about the need for a program, the effectiveness of a program and the effectiveness of school personnel. When it is discovered that a particular program is needed and funds are not locally available, school systems may write a proposal to a government agency or a foundation for the funding which is necessary. Funding agencies require that the school district's need be documented with data. Testing results are useful for this purpose since they can provide required data. Whether or not the program is funded the school district can share its progress with the public through an effective public relations program.

SELF CHECK FOR OBJECTIVE ONE

CAN YOU: state why student progress is evaluated?

MAKING DECISIONS USING EVALUATION

It can be inferred from the discussion above that evaluation information will be used in different ways to make educational decisions. The need for answers and consequently questions which must be asked is the focus of evaluation.

Teachers are both questioners and decision makers. They become questioners when they observe students who cannot read on grade level, who write creatively or who have not adequately developed small muscles. When needs are present and resources are available teachers determine how a program can be developed to meet the needs of students. Programs should include testing and evaluation strategies which measure the progress of students as they master objectives. Short quizzes or tests administered on a daily or weekly basis give the student and teacher feedback so that both know what to do next. The analysis of feedback is necessary so teachers can make corrections in their instructional strategies. Corrections may take the form of special tutoring for individuals or groups as well as reteaching a block of content to the entire class. At the end of a course or semester a final evaluation is often conducted. The question the teacher asks is "Have strategies used been successful?" That is, "Have students mastered course objectives?" And, "Should other strategies be considered?"

Measurement Driven Instruction

Each of us has probably experienced a test review when an important test was about to be administered. Teachers schedule daily, weekly and unit tests.

Teachers consider these tests as a measure of student achievement which may suggest reteaching content not mastered. School districts schedule annual testing of students as a quality control strategy. Administrators and teachers often consider this process to be an annual audit and very important. Therefore, test review is essential.

What should be reviewed? Content taught? Or content assumed to be on the annual achievement (audit) test? And if test scores are lower than hoped for should the curriculum be changed to assure higher test scores? Should instruction be driven by all tests or some tests?

The True Curriculum

What is the true curriculum? Is it different from the curriculum? And, which curriculum should be evaluated using teacher made tests?

When the science curriculum requires a field trip to a lake, what is experienced by the student? The content of an experiment conducted? The thinking process which led to proven or disproven hypotheses? Does the student only experience what is anticipated to be on the test of science? While some course objectives are not achieved, unanticipated objectives are achieved. And, how does the teacher evaluate the student's intellectual closure? This is especially difficult since students frequently do not share personal closure and feelings with teachers.

Teaching is difficult work. Since evaluation is central to teaching, evaluation is also difficult work. It is improbable that an annual test or an unsophisticated series of teacher made tests will adequately assist students and teachers as they make effective teaching and learning decisions.

These questions and others are asked preliminary to making decisions about programs and individual educational objectives. Program objectives, teaching and testing should be congruent. Although many of the ideas which follow this part of the chapter can be used in the construction of standardized tests, they will be used in demonstrating how teacher made tests are written.

SELF CHECK FOR OBJECTIVE TWO

CAN YOU: describe the relationship of evaluation and decision making?

TESTING OBJECTIVES

Chapter two of this book demonstrated the need for objectives as well as how to write and use objectives in teaching. In this chapter we will use objectives as a management tool because teachers are managers of curriculum, time, activity and testing. And, we will focus on how objectives are used to manage testing.

As you remember from chapter two, formal objectives consist of four parts—the condition, identification of the learner, the behavior and the criterion for acceptable performance. They help to clarify testing content and process. The content of testing consists of what was taught. The process consists of how testing will take place.

The following is a list of axioms related to classroom testing.

1. All objectives should be tested with two test items.
2. No question on a test should cover content not taught.
3. Testing should take place frequently and not only at the end of the chapter, book or semester. Frequent testing provides feedback which enables students and teachers to respond to the question, "What should be accomplished next?"

To make the relationship of course content, objectives and test items clear, a tool called a table of specifications is used.

A Table of Specifications

A table of specifications assists a teacher to make clear which objectives should be tested and how they should be tested. It's a planning tool which enables a teacher to construct more effective teacher made tests. And, it tends to increase the validity and reliability of tests.

Two sample tables are illustrated below. Although the content is specific,

---

FIGURE 12.1
A TABLE OF SPECIFICATIONS

COGNITIVE LEVELS

CONTENT OBJECTIVES	Knowledge	Comprehension	Application	Analysis	Synthesis	Evaluation
Determine the main idea in a paragraph						
Identify the order of events in a paragraph						
Identify cause or effect stated in a paragraph						
Distinguish between facts and opinion in a paragraph						

tables can be constructed for any content area and at any educational level. The Bloom Cognitive Domain and "objectives for basic skills in writing" are used in the table of specifications illustration in Figure 12.1.

FIGURE 12.2
AN ITEM TYPE SELECTION TABLE

	Short Answer	Fill In	T F	MC	Problem	Essay / Other	Time Emphasis
Identify or write a grammatically correct sentence							
Classify pictures and shapes under appropriate headings							
Spell words needed through grade two							
Capitalize the first letter of the first word of a sentence							

Figure 12.2 makes use of frequently used test item formats. Both figures use educational objectives. Teachers examine check marks made in the cells of each table to determine the comparative use of each objective and each test item format. Teachers have a tendency to teach and test at the lowest levels of the Cognitive Domain. They also tend to use favorite test item formats, perhaps essay or true-false. These somewhat unconscious behaviors should be identified and evaluated using the criterion of appropriateness.

The use of tables as in Figures 12.1 and 12.2 sharpen teacher planning and test construction behavior. The teacher becomes aware of objectives taught and tested; cognitive, affective or psychomotor domains worked with; and the importance of objectives compared to other objectives for the day, week or year. They also become aware of test item types used.

Once the teacher is aware of which objectives are to be taught and tested, which item types are most appropriate, test items can be written. They will be either essay or non-essay. The testing process should be a planned, orderly process which focuses on concepts and information compared to trite bits of content.

Organizing Testing

One effective procedure for constructing test items is as follows:

1. Purchase a few packs of 5 x 7 index cards.
2. Write the objective at the top of the card.

3. Write only one objective on one card.
4. Immediately below the objective write the name of the book and page number from which the objective is taken. If the objective is taken from a source other than a book note that source. This will be helpful when reference to the source of the test item is asked by the student.
5. Begin writing test items. Start with a short answer item. Follow that with its answer.
6. Next, write a completion (fill-in) item, TF, multiple choice and other appropriate type items for the same objective. Note the answer to each.

Another effective procedure uses a microcomputer. Many teachers are integrating computer use into the curriculum. Students learn writing, reading and other subjects using computers. Teachers have discovered computers to be a powerful administrative tool in the classroom. One administrative use is in test item writing.

Special test item writing programs have been designed for classroom teachers. Many are item specific and menu driven. The program will prompt test item writers through writing an item.

Teachers may also use a word processing program to write test items. The first method illustrated above used 5 x 7 index cards. If the teacher substitutes a piece of computer paper for the 5 x 7 index card the method will work. A variety of test items can be written for each chapter. When a chapter test is to be given a unique computer file for that test is created. Test items to be used on the test can be copied to the new computer test file. No retyping of the test is required. Test items not used on this test can be used at a later time. Or, if a teacher is testing two or more sections of the same course different forms of the same test can be easily created with very little typing. And, test writing computer programs which randomly scramble test items exist. Test security is enhanced when using multiple forms of a test.

Test items should assist teachers to identify students who have mastered educational objectives and those who have not. Some objectives can be tested with non-essay items.

WRITING NON-ESSAY OR OBJECTIVE ITEMS

General rules

The following general rules apply to writing all non-essay items:

1. Never use items which are intentionally tricky. If the student evaluates the item as tricky the face validity of the test will be compromised. Face validity is related to the student's perception of the fairness of the test and probability of success.
2. Do not double score items. Be certain that there is only one answer. This will reduce student and teacher stress after the test. Eliminating double scoring will increase validity and reliability of tests. Do not ask for opinions. They are easily double scored by students.

3.   Do not give students too much or too little information in the item. Too much information results in giving away the correct response whereas too little information forces the student to guess. Neither will enhance the discriminatory power of the test.
4.   Do not give students a hint. This is related to giving students too much information.
5.   Keep the reading level somewhat below the student's assigned grade level unless the test is one of reading. Students who do not read at grade level will not be tested on the content of history, spelling, mathematics or social studies. Instead, their reading level will be tested.
6.   Ask one question with one item. Items which have two questions confuse students. They do not know which part to answer, especially if the parts do not have the same answer.
7.   Try to avoid using absolutes such as always and never. Students frequently assume that an exception can be found to the always and never items. Therefore, the item is flawed.

Associated with general rules are procedures which make non-essay item writing more effective. They are:

1.   Vary test item formats used. Using one format makes the test boring to students.
2.   Group all items of one format together. Do not try to group content.
3.   Non-essay items can be easily written at the lowest three levels of the Bloom Cognitive Taxonomy—knowledge, comprehension and application. Try to write items on all three levels.
4.   Write the correct answer next to the item so that it will be available for scoring and questioning by a student.
5.   After using the item on a test write the item's power to discriminate and item analysis information near the item on the 5 x 7 card.
6.   Items can be written with a wide variety of content and at all grade levels.
7.   Non-essay items can be written with maps, graphs, figures, drawings and tables.

Short Answer Items

First, examine the objective at the top of the 5 x 7 card. Write an item which requires a very short response, perhaps a word, a numeral or a short sentence, but never an essay. Examine the samples below.

1.   Who was the first solo transatlantic airplane flier?
2.   Which country produces more cars than any other?
3.   Given a circle with diameter=5 what does Circumference=?
4.   Say the words on the cards which I hold up.

These questions are easy to write. They minimize guessing. They can be used to vary item types on a test so that the test is not boring to students.

They cannot be scored with an optical scanner as T—F and multiple choice items can be scored. They can test a great amount of content in a short time.

Completion Items

Examine the objective at the top of the 5 x 7 card. On the same card as you have written a short answer item write a completion item. If possible with a minimum of effort convert the short answer item to a completion item. Examine the samples below.

1. One word that rhymes with cat is _____ .
2. An agogie is a _____ .
3. We can eat _____ in place of meat when trying to eat a balanced meal.
4. _____ is the man who discovered America.
5. A _____ tells us what we can and cannot do.

The rules for writing successful completion items are related to the examples above. First, do not give students a grammar hint as in the second and fifth items. The blank is preceded by "a" which suggests that the correct answer does not begin with a vowel which would have required "an." Use only one blank in each item. More than one blank unnecessarily complicates some items. Place the blank at the end of the sentence. This procedure allows the student to read the question two times instead of three, once to generate the answer and once to check the generated answer. If the blank were at the beginning of the sentence the student would probably read it two times to generate the answer and once to check the answer. The fourth and fifth items violate this rule. Students often judge as obscure those items which concern footnote information as item two might.

Two-Choice Items

See the examples below for samples of a two-choice format

1. Circle the cities below if they are in California.

    Fort Worth   San Francisco
    Orlando   Harworth
    Stamford   Minerva

2. Put an X through all even numbers.

    0   12   47   7   6   31   1   9   74

3. Put an X through all words below which are blends.

    grow   man   flip   when   boy

4. See FIGURE 12.3 for an illustration of a two-choice format used in a kindergarten or first grade. The student is instructed to color the shape which is related to the word to the left of the shapes on the page. Besides

evaluating the concept of ordinality, ability to color and willingness to stay in the lines is evaluated.

Note that in the first item the student is not asked to circle the California cities, underline the Florida cities and cross out the Texas cities. That would be unneeded complexity for the student when taking the test and for the teacher when scoring the test.

You now have three types of questions for one objective written on one card. A familiar type of two-choice classification question is a true-false question.

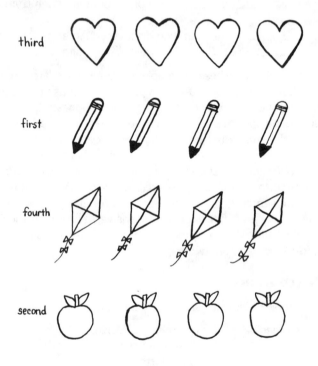

FIGURE 12.3

True-False Items

General rules for writing other non-essay items are applied to the True-False format. Absolutes such as always and never should be avoided when writing the T-F item. The true-false item is easily written, easily responded to and easily scored. A great amount of content can be tested in a short time. Examine the samples below.

1. A circle and a triangle are the same.

2. The four stages of a butterfly's life are: egg, caterpillar, cocoon and butterfly.
3. The perimeter of a 3 foot long square is 12 feet.
4. Never administer CPR on the roadway.
5. The plural of man is mans.

Students have developed many biases from experience with teacher made tests. The fourth item uses an absolute. If this is a true statement an exception can probably be found. Another is that sometimes teachers place more true items than false on a test and they sometimes place T-F items on a test so that a pattern of responses such as T FF T FF T FF exists. To not reinforce such bias a teacher should first write the true version of the item on a 5 x 7 card and then write the false version. The second step is to use a coin to randomly assign the T or the F version. If the coin is flipped and comes up heads the T version is used. If it comes up tails the false version is used. This will give the true and false version an equal chance to be used and to develop a random pattern of responses on the test. Students should be told about this process so that they will not spend time trying to psychologically assess the teacher and the test.

A type of T-F item requires the student to mark the false items F and to rewrite the statement so that it is true. This eliminates guessing to a great extent. This also requires more time than the standard T-F item and consequently less content is covered in the same amount of time as a standard T-F item test.

The teacher now has five different types of items for the same objective on one 5 x 7 card. The T-F item can be converted to a multiple choice item.

Multiple Choice Items

General rules for the writing of non-essay items apply to the multiple choice format. Examine the following multiple choice items as illustrations of general rules as well as others specific to the multiple choice item. Are they all constructed without flaws?

1. Which of the following is untrue?
   a. Basketball uses a five man team.
   b. Cricket is uniquely an American game.
   c. Bowling is a lethal sport.
   d. Swimming provides excellent cardiovascular exercise.
2. The name "John" is
   a. an adjective.
   b. an adverb.
   c. a noun.
   d. a verb.

3. On the map below X marks the place where
   a. our state capitol is.
   b. our city is located.
   c. the highest mountain in the state is located.
   d. the city with the most people is located.

FIGURE 12.4
STATE MAP

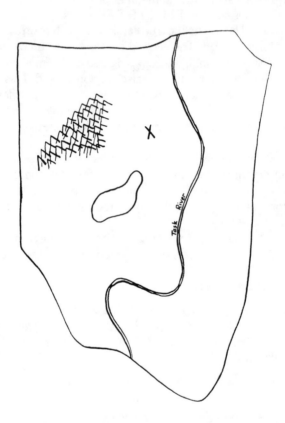

Note that in the first multiple choice item the stem "Which of the following is untrue?" is stated negatively. The stem should present a positive statement. It is also double scored (Two options are correct). The second stem is a positive statement. The options a,b,c and d have one correct answer. Options which are incorrect are called distractors. Options should be about the same length. Students generally believe the longest option is the correct one. Every distractor must be plausible. Otherwise students will eliminate the implausible ones; the item will not discriminate adequately.

The central thought must be in the stem and not in the options. An example of an incomplete stem is below.

4. A man
   a. is the current president of the USA.
   b. is the current president of NOW.
   c. plays the lead in Annie, a stage play.
   d. was recently named Sheik of Canada.

This question is not only a problem because of the incomplete stem but also because option c is improbable considering the title of the play. Option d is also not plausible since Canada does not have sheiks. A clue has been given to the student.

Student bias about the placement of the correct answer among options a, b, c and d states that if in doubt chose option c. One way to avoid this is to randomly place the correct answer with the use of a deck of playing cards. Assign option a hearts, b diamonds, c spades and d clubs. Shuffle the cards. Turn the top card. If it is a heart place the correct answer in option a, if a diamond use option b and so on. Thus, the teacher avoids the overuse of a particular option as well as avoiding a pattern of option use as in the T-F item type.

It is the judgment of the author that four options should be used. Exactly four. The reason for this is that additional options reduce the probability of the student guessing the correct answer to a small extent, and it is difficult to write plausible options. If four options exist, a student has a chance of guessing the correct answer one out of four or .25. If five options are used the chance of guessing is reduced to one out of five or .20. If six options are used the guessing chance is one out of six or .17. Compare the following:

   four options—.25
   five options—.20
   six options—.17

All of the above, none of the above, a and b, neither a or b, a nor b should not be used unless the course is a logic course. Examine the options "neither a or b" and "neither a nor b." Do they present the same meaning? Is this a logic course? Examine the multiple choice item below for an interesting violation of this latest rule.

5. The burning hot Chilean desert, Atacama, is in the northern part of the country. It is also
   a. very dry.
   b. very high in altitude.
   c. being exploited by oil companies.
   d. close to Bolivia.
   e. a and b.
   f. a and c.
   g. a and d.
   h. a, b and c but not d.
   i. neither a nor b.

This is an extreme example of what could become an interesting logic examination and not one in social studies.

This is an appropriate time to discuss exceptions to procedures which concern writing multiple choice items. First, some authors believe that if the test writer wants to attempt to test students at the higher levels of the Bloom taxonomy the use of one option such as "none of the above" is permitted. Try not to use the "none of the above" family of options frequently since students perceive such options as very difficult and perhaps unfair. Second, it is possible to test students with non-essay items at the higher Bloom Taxonomy levels if the writer is experienced and skillful. Begin writing multiple choice items in the knowledge, comprehension and application levels.

Matching Items

Matching items can be used if a relationship is the basis for the content. Relationships such as states and their capitals and pictures and words which identify the pictures are appropriate. This item format should not make use of more than about ten items in each column because longer columns force students to examine a column of 20-25 choices before choosing the presumed correct response. This is an inefficient use of time. Examine the matching items below for a sample of the two rules suggested.

For 1-3 below match column one with column two. Items in column two may be used once, more than once or not at all. Place the letter response in the blank next to the numeral.

Column One   Column Two

_____ 1. Atacama   a. music accent
_____ 2. Agogie   b. not a word
_____ 3. Amex   c. a desert

For items one through six below match column one with column two. Items in column two may be used once, more than once or not at all. Place the letter response next to the numeral.

Column One   Column Two

_____ 1. chip   a. yellowish brown
_____ 2. prince   b. severe
_____ 3. taunt   c. a broken piece of china
_____ 4. flash   d. jeered or mocked
_____ 5. amber   e. king's son
_____ 6. stern   f. brief light

Cloze Items

Cloze items have the potential for wide application although testing of reading is a common use. When using cloze items for reading comprehension testing, every fifth or seventh word is omitted from the paragraph being used.

However, when testing the content of a course such as test item writing, key words should be left out. Examine the sample below.

The _____ item has the potential for wide application although testing of reading is a common use. When using the _____ item for the testing of reading comprehension every _____ or _____ word is omitted from the paragraph. However, when testing the content of a course such as social studies _____ words should be _____ .

Cloze items can be modified by supplying students with several possible responses at the bottom of the paragraph. This variation of the cloze item format is somewhat similar to the multiple choice item format.

SELF CHECK FOR OBJECTIVES THREE—SEVEN

CAN YOU:
1. design a table of specifications?
2. write a wide variety of non-essay items for each objective in a table of specifications?
3. write a matching format item?
4. write a cloze format item for a content area such as history?
5. write a cloze format item for a reading class?

WRITING ESSAY ITEMS

Essay items, as commonly written, can be confused with the short answer format. Many essay items are written without enough information for the student. The result is student confusion. A few procedures, if used, can eliminate most confusion which centers around the nature of the item. Examine the inappropriately written essay items below.

1. Who is your hero and why?
2. Contrast Hitler and Stalin.

The first item asks for a name and a brief explanation. The second item's response is difficult to predict. A few words or several pages may be written.

General Procedures

Appropriately written essay items use the following procedures:

1. Items should be written using the 5 x 7 card method.
2. Each item should be written clearly.
3. Students should be supplied with enough detail.
4. Students should be given response instructions such as the
   a. points to be covered,
   b. length of response in words, pages or time allotment,
   c. evaluative criteria to be used by the teacher and the
   d. number of points allocated to the item.

5.   Write the essay item at a reading level somewhat below the assigned grade level of the student.

Each of the above inappropriately written questions violates the third and fourth general procedure.

It's possible to test content with non-essay items at the Bloom Cognitive Taxonomy levels of knowledge, comprehension and application. Knowledge can be most efficiently tested with non-essay items. The test writer can target the content so that specific feedback is possible. A great deal of content can be tested in a short time with a non-essay test. Essay test response scoring is influenced by several variables which are not related to the content. Non-essay tests are less susceptible to outside influence. For the same reasons teachers should consider testing comprehension and application with non-essay tests.

Application Level

Application can be tested by both essay items and non-essay items depending on the content. Mathematics application can be tested using the short answer format as well as the essay format. The short answer format in the question

$$x = 5 \times 6 + 3 \times 2 + 1 - 6 \times 3$$

is as efficient and effective as a word problem used in another setting. The mathematics word problem is an item in essay form that most often does not require an essay response.

It is necessary to know how to write effective application level essay questions. The following procedures are helpful when writing application level items:

1.   Present a problem situation.
2.   Require that students act on the problem.
3.   Students should never have seen this problem.
4.   The student's response should be rooted in knowledge and comprehension of the content.

Examine the following example of an application level essay item.

> You have just visited the city fire department. A fireman has come to our class and explained fire safety in our school and in your home. With one other student list the principles of fire safety which you both know. Both of you should take these listed principles and examine this classroom for fire safety rules which are broken. After examining this room try the same kind of examination in your home. List fire safety rules which are broken at home. Then write a paragraph on how your home can be made more safe from fires. Please write about one page. Your handwriting and spelling are important. Look up words which you want to use and do not know how to spell. Your paragraph is due on Monday.

Analysis Level

Analysis level items use the procedures below.

1. Students should work on this question for the first time.
2. Ask students to identify elements, relationships and principles.
3. Compare or contrast are appropriate instructions.
4. The response should be based in the student's knowledge, comprehension and application of the content.

Examine the item below for an illustration of the above procedures as well as general procedures for writing essay items.

> In the 1800s when cities were being built and populated, many good reasons existed for the location of those cities. Consider why Chicago and New York became large cities. In this century reasons for the growth of cities are not the same as in the 1800s. Consider Atlanta and Denver. Write an essay comparing the reasons that cities such as Atlanta and Denver are rapidly growing in this century while cities such as Chicago and New York grew in the 1800s. Please write about one page. Both handwriting and spelling count for 2 points each of this 50 point item. You should use no more than 40 minutes to write the paragraph. After forty minutes are up you will be allowed to use your dictionaries for 10 minutes to look up all words which you are unsure of.

Synthesis Level

Synthesis level items involve the creative spirit of the student, often putting together new and unique combinations. The following procedures will assist the teacher in writing synthesis items effectively.

1. Students should work on a problem to be solved.
2. Students should work on this problem for the first time.
3. They should create new and unique thought (for them).
4. Their response should be based in knowledge, comprehension, application and analysis of the content.

Examine the following synthesis level essay item as a model.

> You are a member of 75 men, women and children who have been banished to the remote island of Znofobia as the result of political activity in your native land of Somfobia. Your group tried to persuade the ruling junta that a democratic form of government would be in the best interests of Somfobia. Consequently, the group was banished. The group also decided to try democracy on Znofobia. All members, other than young children, have been assigned to small groups of four to develop a model democratic state for the island. Your group's task is to create a model of

democracy for Znofobia's 75 citizens. Please write an essay describing the model. You have one hour on each of Monday, Tuesday and Wednesday to think, talk about and make notes concerning the model. Each person in the group will make copies (with the Learning Resource Center copier) of the notes before leaving school on Wednesday. At home on Wednesday night each person should sketch a democratic model for Znofobia. On Thursday the group will have one and one-half hours to write a group essay describing the group democratic model for Znofobia. Make copies for each person to study Thursday night. On Friday the final model should be written. The group will have time to negotiate differences on each of the five days for this project. Use all the knowledge you have read about. This is the final exam for this part of the course and is worth 40% of the grade. You should use a computer in the computer lab to word process, spelling check and grammar check the report. Word processing skills count for 15% of the group grade.

Evaluation Level

Evaluation level essay items give the student an opportunity to make a judgement with support. The following procedures, when used, will facilitate that purpose.

1.   Students should work on the problem for the first time.
2.   They should be given a situation to evaluate.
3.   They should state detailed support for their position or judgement.
4.   Their response should be based on knowledge, comprehension, application, analysis or synthesis of the content in question.
5.   Students should be told that their response to the essay item will be judged on consistency and logic as well as external standards of excellence.

The following item should be examined as an illustration of an evaluation level essay item:

> Some people believe that rules are important, especially in schools and families. Do you believe that rules are important? In a paragraph tell why you believe that rules are important in the classroom or why they are not important. Be sure to state why you believe rules are important or not important. Be certain to check your spelling with a dictionary before you hand in your paragraph.

Essay items are more often written at a combination of Bloom levels rather than one level only. Some common possibilities are:

1. creating a solution and evaluating it,
2. analyzing a performance and evaluating it,
3. analyzing a performance, creating a better solution and finally evaluating the solution created.

Combined Levels

The item below illustrates a combination item compared to a single Bloom level item.

> Describe three (3) uses of a five pound sack of white sand. Consider each use of the sand that you have named attempting to decide whether there would be a better way to accomplish that purpose. If so, describe the better way. Your essay will be scored on the basis of judgement and analysis demonstrated (20 points) and language use and spelling. The essay is due at the end of the first hour of this class period. We will have a class discussion during the second hour.

The major shortcoming of this type of essay item is that each part is contingent on the previous part(s). If the analysis is faulty it is possible that the creation of a better method will be faulty (analysis-synthesis). If the new method is not creative it is possible that the evaluation of that method will be faulty (synthesis-evaluation). However, it is necessary to remember that the combination essay item is used frequently.

Essay Response Scoring

Well written essay items are more effectively scored than those which are written vaguely or ambiguously. Teachers who give students evaluative criteria have students who know what is expected and therefore are more likely to meet the expectation. Teachers expect essays to include appropriate content and language use. If these expectations are conscious and used in scoring, the student will be treated fairly. An essay response scoring sheet can be used to accomplish fair scoring of essay questions. Other ways to insure fair scoring of essays include reading the essay while not reading the student's name. This is called reading the essay blind. It is possible to be either biased in favor of or against a student. This bias may influence the student's grade. Another method used to insure fair treatment is to write an ideal response to the item and measure each response to that criterion. Finally, it is sometimes necessary to ask a colleague to read an essay that one of our students wrote. The colleague then acts as a judge. If more than one colleague is asked to read the essay they are a panel of judges. All judges would use a scoring sheet such as the one below.

Evaluation of students should include all aspects of their performance. Verbal interaction in a group setting is one of the many student behaviors to be measured.

Essay Response Scoring Sheet

Criterion:	Points	Points Earned
Content	65	
Organization	10	
Originality	10	
Language Use	10	
Spelling	5	
Total points	100	

Development Impacts Student Performance On Written Tests

While an older student can be expected to write lengthy papers a very young student has not developed appropriate motivation or skills. Earlier in this chapter an application level essay item was used as an illustration. A visit to the city fire department was part of the scenario. This test item could be modified so that two second grade students who have begun to express written thoughts could respond with a short phrase or series of phrases for each part of the item. The teacher would prompt students through parts of the entire item.

Older students, in pairs, could be expected to write sentences without prompting. And, oldest students in the school would be required to write complete and correct paragraphs without prompting.

SELF CHECK FOR OBJECTIVE EIGHT AND NINE

CAN YOU:
1. write essay items in each of the top four Bloom Cognitive Taxonomy levels and combination of levels?
2. create and use an essay response scoring sheet?

OTHER EVALUATION TECHNIQUES

Essay and non-essay tests cannot be used to evaluate all student behavior. Courses such as physical education and home economics make use of performance evaluation in addition to essay and non-essay evaluation. During a lesson teachers must know which skills and concepts have been mastered. Oral questions can be used for this purpose. Teachers often need to document a particular student's behavior. This need can be met with the use of a behavior checklist. Behavior checklists use a series of behaviors listed and a degree of performance continuum. Two performance checklists are displayed below.

Behavior Checklist

Rating scale: 1=behavior present
0=behavior absent

____ moved to a new task without teacher direction
____ worked on a task without teacher presence
____ carried a task beyond stated requirements
____ used learning center as part of work activity
____ organized work schedule without teacher help
____ used classmates as a legitimate source
____ assisted classmates legitimately
____ made accurate evaluation of own work

Sample Reading Checklist

Rating Scale: 1=presence of behavior
0=absence of behavior

____ letter recognition
____ beginning consonants
____ beginning vowels
____ ending consonants
____ ending vowels
____ short vowel sounds
____ long vowel sounds
____ identify lower case letters
____ identify upper case letters

Oral Tests

Although most students immediately think *written test* when tests are discussed, oral tests are extensively used in schools. A version of the Socratic questioning method discussed and illustrated in Chapter Four can be used to mix lecture with oral test questions. Teachers frequently use oral questions to test students' knowledge. Oral tests are used in all subject areas and all grade levels. Spelling bees are used as oral examination in schools as well as at the national level. The use of the quiz show format in classrooms is another form of the oral exam. And, oral exams and essay exams are related. To a great extent the student is in control of the response.

Oral exams give the student who responds an opportunity to gain confidence and self esteem while responding. Only one student at a time can be quizzed and therefore the oral exam is inefficient. Each student gets a different question thus making the exam susceptible to being unfair.

Students often do not share their thoughts and experiences with teachers unless asked (an oral test). A student interview is an illustration of an oral test. The content of the interview should be structured in advance by the teacher. A list of broad questions should be written. Notes should be taken while the student speaks unless the student objects.

Another type of oral test could take place at the end of every class. Broad questions such as "What is the most important concept/idea/skill/thing that you have learned today?" A whip format could be used so that answers are encouraged to be brief, unique and broad. The entire class could be covered in five or ten minutes. And, the teacher could have a general idea about what was learned.

Oral tests are appropriate and inappropriate. They generate information which frequently cannot be generated any other way. But, like the essay test, they possess reliability and validity problems. Their use publicly embarrasses some students. Self-esteem is lowered as well as raised. They take too much time.

Portfolio Evaluation

Artists, stage performers, athletes, and radio and television personnel use portfolios to document the result of their work. During a job interview, which is a form of an oral test, they will frequently demonstrate competence with a portfolio. The portfolio may contain photos, oil paintings, videos of a performance and articles written. The portfolio of a young student is often shared with parents at a parents' conference. The teacher and student have accumulated the student's work to share with the parent.

Often the portfolio is used as justification of a judgment, an award made, a low grade or a decision to retain the student in the present grade. Can the portfolio be used to assist students to judge (evaluation) their own work, to engage with the teacher in a strategy to improve skills, to generate a grade and to report to parents?

Portfolio evaluation is not as neat as a non-essay test evaluation. It cannot be scored by a machine. Thus, it will take more time to make a judgment. Why use portfolio evaluation? First, process can be evaluated. In writing, art, music and physical development, early stages of skill can be evaluated so that the next instructional steps can be decided. Serious golfers videotape their swing so that after evaluation, improvement can take place. Serious education students videotape their classroom performance so that after evaluation, lessons can be improved. Second, if the portfolio contains a broad collection of student work a judgment about the growth of a student can be made, not a judgment about the English student, the math student and the physical education student. Fragmentation is less likely to occur since student behavior themes will surface. The student's thinking process, motor coordination and interpersonal skills may be consistent across subject areas.

ANALYSIS OF TEST RESULTS

Students often focus on test grades as the outcome of a test. Teachers should focus on the grade as a global indicator of success while focusing on specific indicators of success. A specific indicator of success is the level of student mastery of objectives tested. The level of success is suggested by test item results. While item analysis provides helpful information to test item writers, analysis of test results provides helpful information to teachers.

Each test item's response for each student must be analyzed no matter which type of test item is used. It is easier to analyze responses generated by machine scored tests than by oral tests, essays and portfolios. If student responses are not analyzed how will the teacher know the next step to be taken with a whole class or an individual?

Machine scored tests

If computer sheets are used a manual system or a microcomputer program can be used to analyze results. Both will provide

1. the percent of the class which responded correctly to each item and
2. the percent of the class which chose each option.

Analysis will reveal groups of items which suggest whole class, group and individual reteaching of a concept or the application of a concept.

Non-machine scored test items

Items such as essays, oral tests and portfolios are scored using an ideal response which has a listed outline for the response content and preferred process. As teachers match ideal response to student response, discrepancies are noted. These form the knowledge base for analysis and consequent reteaching of concepts and application of concepts.

SELF CHECK FOR OBJECTIVE TEN

CAN YOU: design observation checksheets, oral tests and portfolio evaluations for student behavior?

CHOOSING AN EVALUATION PLAN

Now that you know several ways to measure student achievement and behavior which should a teacher use? Five ways are non-essay written tests, essay written tests, oral testing by teachers, teacher observation of student behavior and teacher assessment of student products. In order to choose an appropriate evaluation process it is necessary to compare the variety of methods. Although the concepts of validity and reliability are discussed in Chapter Thirteen the figure below assists a teacher to choose an appropriate evaluation process.

FIGURE 12.5
FEATURES OF TEACHER CREATED EVALUATION METHODS

	Type of Information	Validity	Reliability	Ease of Administration	Cost
Non-Essay Written Tests	Lower levels of cognition. Some affective information.	Higher	Higher	Easier	Low
Essay Written Tests	Higher levels of cognition. Written communication ability. Affective information.	Lower	Lower	Difficult	Higher
Oral Tests	All cognitive levels. Oral communication ability. Affective information.	Lower	Lower	Easier	Higher
Teacher Observation of Student Behavior	Application of knowledge. Values and attitudes. Moral reasoning. Psychomotor Skills.	Lower	Lower	Easier	Moderate
Teacher Assessment of Student Portfolio	Process outcomes. Less fragmented assessment. Growth and Development.	Lower	Lower	Difficult	Higher

A review of the comparison above may lead a teacher to administer non-essay written tests and exclude other ways to generate information about students. The kind of information in which schools are interested is covered. Validity and reliability are high. Non-essay tests are easy to administer and cost is low. Sounds perfect! If other methods to evaluate are considered it will be noted that many types of information will not be generated by non-essay tests. One illustration is higher levels of cognitive behavior. Since it is necessary to have a full view of student growth it will probably be necessary to use many ways to evaluate student behavior although each is deficient. If a teacher forms an evaluation design which includes all evaluation methods it is more likely that evaluation will be effective.

SUMMARY

Evaluation of teaching is not an add-on activity. Evaluation should be a part of each activity. It should be planned to happen before, during and after the lesson. Although evaluation has philosophical, ethical and legal bases none were discussed in this chapter. This chapter provided the student with other issues related to evaluation. Issues such as who is concerned with evaluation and how to write a test were discussed.

We also shared with you a system of writing tests and test items. It began with writing tables of test item specification and item type specification. Then a rational process of test item writing was explained. Objective and non-objective test items were discussed. Other types of evaluation such as instruments, observation formats, oral tests and portfolios were illustrated.

ACTIVITIES

To complete many of the following exercises it will be helpful to have a teacher's edition of a textbook commonly used in schools. Therefore, go to your college library or learning resource center and withdraw a textbook in a content area with which you are familiar.

1. Using the objectives you have found in the teacher's edition create a table of specifications. Use the Bloom Cognitive Domain. Write six objectives in short form.
2. Next, purchase a package of 5 x 7 cards. Write one objective from the table of specifications at the top of the card. Then, write one each of the following item types for the objective at the top of the card:

    1. short answer format,
    2. completion format,
    3. two-choice classification format,
    4. one true version of the true/false format,
    5. one false version of the true/false format and
    6. one multiple choice item

Write the answer to each of the items above next to it on the card. Also write the page number from which the objective was taken.

3. Repeat this for the second and third objective written in the table of specifications.
4. Write a matching item for the fourth objective.

5. From a student or teacher's edition of the textbook choose a suitable paragraph of between ten and fifteen lines to design a cloze item for a content area such as social studies.

6. Continue to use the 5 x 7 card method using a new card. Write an objective at the top of the card. Write the page number from which the objective was taken. Then write an application level essay item (Bloom's Taxonomy) on the card. Below the item in outline form, write the ideal response to the item.

7. Continue this process with a new card for each of the following Bloom Taxonomy levels:
   a. analysis essay item,
   b. synthesis essay item,
   c. evaluation essay item,
   d. analysis and synthesis essay item,
   e. analysis and evaluation essay item and
   f. analysis, synthesis and evaluation.

8. Design one performance checklist in a content area such as reading or physical education with between seven and ten items and an observation rating scale.

9. Write a test for one week's work out of the student or teacher's edition of the textbook. Design a table of specification and an item type selection table. Write a variety of non-essay items for this test. Prepare an answer sheet. If possible prepare the test to be optically scanned.

10. Using the textbook which you used for the exercise above, choose a brief section which can be completed by students in one class period. Write a list of questions to be used with the lesson. The purpose of the questions should be evaluation.

11. Choose a content area with which you are familiar. From a unit plan in the course design an assessment of a student portfolio. Choose activities which demonstrate mastery of objectives at different competency levels. Choose many varied objectives, some of which require cognitive abilities while others may require psychomotor activity. Try to vary the media used to demonstrate competence. Try not to use paper and pencil activity only. Write a set of statements which indicate goals of the portfolio evaluation as well as criteria which may be used to judge student activity. Remember to include a requirement for self evaluation by the student.

BIBLIOGRAPHY

Airaisan, P.W. (1988). Measurement driven instruction: a closer look. *Educational Measurement: Issues and Practices, 7*(4), 6-11.

Brossel, G., & Ash, B.H. (1984). An experiment with the wording of essay topics. *College Composition and Communication, 35,* 423-425.

Buckle, C.F., & Riding, R.J. (1988). Current problems in assessment—some reflections. *Educational Psychology, 8*(4), 299-306.

Cangelosi, J.S. (1982). *Measurement & evaluation.* Dubuque: Wm. C. Brown.

Cooper, T.H. (1988). A study of three option and four option multiple choice exams. *Journal of Agronomic Education, 17*(2), 101-104.

Freilich, M.B. (1989). Frequent quizzing, the final exam, and learning: is there a correlation? *Journal of Chemical Education, 66*(3), 219-223.

McKensie, D.L., & Padilla, M.J. (1986). The construction and validation of the tests of graphing in science. *Journal of Research in Science, 23*(17), 571-579.

Mundrake, G.A. (1988). Testing and evaluation: the academic payroll. *Business Education Forum, 42*(8), 3-4.

Shinn, M.R. (1989). *Varying the difficulty of testing materials: implications for curriculum based measurement, 23*(12), 223-233.

Stufflebeam, D., Foley, W.J., Gephart, W.J., Guba, E.G., Hammond, R.I., Merriman, H.O., & Provus, M.M. (1971). *Educational evaluation & decision making.* Itasca: F.E. Peacock.

Torrance, H. (1986). What can examinations contribute to school evaluation? *Educational Review, 38*(1), 31-43.

Wainer, H. (1983). On Item Response Theory and Computerized Adaptive Tests. *Journal of College Admissions, 27*(4), 9-16.

Wise, S. (1988). Applications of item response theory to partial credit scoring. *Applied Measurement in Education, 1*(4), 279-378.

CHAPTER THIRTEEN

INTRODUCTORY
CASE STUDY

CASE STUDY 13-1
PARENTS, PARENTS, PARENTS!

Lee Cyr and Jean Kara are teachers at Midtown School, an urban education center in a city which is a patchwork of different cultures, economic levels, political beliefs and races. Pat Preola is a student in one of Jean's classes. Pat's parents have inquired about a report card which was recently issued. They are also concerned about Pat's standardized test scores. The scores tend to indicate that Pat's school work is below his aptitude. Jean is also concerned about Pat's work in class. It seems as if Pat is either not attending or is learning disabled. Jean doesn't know which is true. This is especially so because Jean is not a trained teacher of learning disabled students. Jean has asked Lee Cyr to a meeting which includes Pat's parents and Phyl Hanna, a teacher of children at risk.

Jean has explained to members of the team that Pat's parents have received one note home about each three weeks. It's the school policy to send two positive notes home per class each day. The purpose is to link teachers in the school with parents and students. Also, Pat's standardized test results have been sent home. The following information was included in those reports.

1. State Student Achievement Tests:
   - Reading Comprehension .... 60th percentile
   - Listening Comprehension .... 40th percentile
   - Written Language .... 40th percentile
   - Social Studies .... 50th percentile
   - Science .... 70th percentile
   - Mathematics .... 90th percentile
2. Kuhlmann-Anderson Test .... 50th percentile
   (Group Intelligence Test)
   Wechsler Intelligence Scale .... 90th percentile
   (Individually administered Test)

It's 3:05 PM and all persons who were invited to the meeting are making small talk and waiting for Mr. & Mrs. Preola who apparently are a few minutes late. The teachers have shared Pat's testing information, portfolio of work and teacher observations.

When Mr. & Mrs. Preola arrive Jean greets them, introduces them to the remaining members of the staff and starts the meeting.

QUESTIONS:

1. Should an agenda have been prepared in advance of the meeting?
2. Who should have contributed to the agenda?
3. What should be on the agenda?
4. Should other persons be invited to the meeting?
5. Is more information needed before Jean responds to items 2-4 on this list? What information?
6. Since the meeting has started what should Jean observe (look for)?

CHAPTER THIRTEEN
EVALUATION, TESTS AND TEACHING

"Men are not to be judged by their ... appearance, but ... by their works."

-J. Mason

GOALS

After reading this chapter students will
1.   understand students' test data and
2.   understand how to communicate test data.

OBJECTIVES

After studying this chapter students will
1.   list external factors which influence test scores (include student culture),
2.   define types of validity and reliability and describe each with an illustration; include the correlation coefficient relationship,
3.   explain norm and criterion referenced measurement,
4.   describe and interpret two types of standardized tests and
5.   role play teachers communicating grades to parents.

Teachers and school districts, like *smart systems* which use artificial intelligence, require information about past results to make better decisions about future strategies. Teachers use teacher made tests to measure learning. After grading and evaluating test results teachers can decide the next steps of instruction. School districts administer standardized tests to measure the success of programs in content areas such as reading and mathematics. The results of those tests will suggest changes to school districts and teachers.

FACTORS WHICH INFLUENCE TEST SCORES

Although a teacher follows procedures intended to insure fair, valid and reliable testing, other factors do influence testing. One is the method used to administer the test. Was the test given on an overhead projector, a TV monitor, written on the board or was each student handed a piece of paper? Each influences test outcomes. Students closer to the board and TV monitor see the instructions and test items more clearly. Consequently, they will probably finish faster and perhaps respond more accurately. Was there a disturbance in the room? This affects some students. How did the examiner read the instructions? What time of the day was the test administered? Was the test announced or was it a surprise? How does the examiner respond to students who violate honesty rules?

Besides administrative variables which influence test scores, students invent special methods of taking tests which work for them. Some students believe that speeding through a test is the best way. Others believe that slow and careful is the best strategy. Students believe that teachers choose "True" and "C" more often than "False" and "A,B,D" as response options. Others believe that the longest option in a multiple choice set of options is probably correct. Some believe that coaching helps. They ask friends to coach them for the SAT and ACT. Others take SAT and ACT preparation short courses. Some students believe that retaking the standardized test will insure a better grade. Others believe that one must be cool. Anxiety is a factor. Some anxiety will probably be helpful while too much anxiety will debilitate the student. Factors that exist in the formal and informal testing environments influence the validity and reliability of the test.

Culture of the Student

When a student's culture is identified as a factor which impacts a test score, the student's use of language frequently comes into focus. One method which would help to treat the student fairly while obtaining valid and reliable test scores is to have a native speaker of the student's language administer the test verbally. If the student reads English fluently, although at a slower pace, extra time can be given. If the test is non-standardized, an open book test might be considered.

Since other subtle cultural factors impact test scores teachers must understand the student's cultural background to test equitably. Parenthetically, all students whose cultural background impacts test scores were not born in another country. Some native born American students live in another culture with adults whose culture impacts the student.

If a test is timed so that few students finish (a speed test), the culture of the student may impact the test score. For example, Hispanic students are polychronic while Anglos are monochronic. American culture views time more precisely while Hispanic culture treats time less precisely. If a short 20 minute test was the announced time allotment for a test, Hispanic students may interpret 20 minutes as 20 or 30 or 40 minutes. The interpretation would lead to a test taking strategy which is more leisurely resulting in fewer test responses and a less valid test for that student. A test without a time restriction (a power test) may be more appropriate. And, in some cultures tests are only one way to evaluate learning while in American culture tests are the primary method.

Successful test taking requires extensive experience in middle class American culture. Native born American students who do not have a middle class culture experience will have difficulty with tests. Motivation, test language and test scenarios are variables from a longer list which impact a test score. Perhaps allowing students who have difficulty taking tests an unlimited amount of time is the most reasonable response.

Group or Individual Tests

Standardized tests are generally administered in groups. A whole class will take an achievement or aptitude test. These tests are generally used to screen students for special programs. If a student is highly successful or unsuccessful, individual testing is indicated. Perhaps the unsuccessful student was unmotivated, unable to understand the directions or read the language of the test or has a learning or cultural disability. Individual testing is then required.

SELF CHECK FOR OBJECTIVE ONE

CAN YOU: list factors which influence test scores?

Validity and Reliability

Generally, test validity relates to how effectively a test satisfies the purpose for which it was written. A test of history which is written on a reading level above that of students who take the test measures reading to a greater extent than history. That test may not be valid. Several types of validity exist.

Face Validity

The student's first impression of the test determines its face validity. If a student believes the test to be fair, that it measures content covered in class, it has face validity.

Content Validity

Content validity is concerned with the test's ability to measure the universe of content studied. Unless the test measures a small amount of content, such as a daily quiz might measure, tests do not measure the entire universe of content of a particular unit or semester. Most tests measure a sample of all objectives studied. Content universe is another way to express all the objectives studied in a particular unit or course. For a test to possess content validity it must measure a representative sample of the content universe.

Predictive Validity

The principal function of predictive validity is to predict the future success of students in a particular skill or cognitive area. Basketball shooting could predict the success of prospective basketball players. Reading readiness tests may predict the future success of first grade reading students. Tests of manual dexterity may predict the success of typists. Grade point average of students may predict their success in college.

Concurrent Validity

A test possesses concurrent validity if its scores correlate highly with scores of another test over a long period of time. Many education programs require prospective students to take either the SAT or ACT exam as an entrance examination. One implication is that the scores of the two tests correlate highly over time. It is assumed that each test has concurrent validity when compared to the other.

Construct Validity

Construct validity is concerned with the measure of a psychological construct such as rigidity. The construct validation of a test is the analysis of test scores compared to the psychological constructs as manifested by those tested. The scores of a test of rigidity would be compared to the behavior of students.

Most teacher made tests do not have computed validity coefficients. Standardized tests have published validity coefficients. If a standardized test is being considered for use and validity coefficients are not available because they do not exist there are three options. Compute the coefficients. Do not use the test. Use the test without coefficients. We suggest that you consider standardized tests with the highest coefficients. A high coefficient is one which is more than +.70. It may be necessary to use an instrument which has a lower coefficient because its coefficient is the highest available. Other reasons given for the use of tests with coefficients lower than +.70 are availability of the test and cost of the test.

Teachers should be concerned with the validity of tests which they write. Although they may decide to not compute validity coefficients, they can write tests which are as valid as possible. One way to increase the face and content validity of the test is to be certain that no test item tests an objective which was not part of the unit or course being tested. Writing a few of the easier items of the test as the first few items helps students to judge the test as one which they can take successfully.

Reliability

A term sometimes confused with validity is reliability. Generally, a test is reliable if it consistently measures what it measures. If a student takes a test of mathematics three times with three different forms of that test and obtains the same score or close to the same score each time, the test has high reliability. Some tests have high reliability with low validity. An example of this occurs when a teacher of first grade reading asks each student to throw a softball overhand. Based on the skill level observed the teacher attempts to predict the reading readiness of individual students. While each student will probably throw the ball each of five tries equally well, thus indicating high reliability, the predictive validity of this test is probably low.

A concept related to reliability is regression toward the mean. The mean is the arithmetic average of a group of scores. If a golfer entered a hole in one golf tournament and achieved a hole in one which carried a prize of $1,000, what is the chance of the same golfer swinging the same club at the same time of the same day of the week on the same golf green and getting a second hole in one if the prize was a new convertible? Very slim! Suppose you were to test 30 students with a test of reading and arrange the scores from highest to lowest. What are the chances that students who score 100% would get 100% on a second test of the same material? What are the chances that the lowest scoring students will obtain 5% and 10%? If the average score was 70% both the lowest scores and the highest scores will regress toward 70%. This is called regression toward the mean (the average score).

Teachers often question student behavior and make decisions which result in new programs for those students. These new programs are designed to meet the needs of low achieving students. Before students begin the program a test is given. The program is then applied to the students. Finally, students are retested. Often, low scoring students achieve higher scores on the second achievement test. Teachers frequently conclude that the program caused the higher score. The cause may have been a regression toward the mean. Therefore, it is prudent for a teacher to treat evaluative information with respect while searching for true meaning.

Teachers are concerned with the reliability of standardized tests and teacher made tests. You should consider the use of standardized tests which have the highest coefficients, at least +.85. Tests which lack high reliability should not be considered for use. If a test does not consistently generate very similar scores we do not know what it tests. It may test other factors such as who administered the test and time of the day the test was administered.

Teacher made tests should be reliable too. If you write two or three forms of the same test, computing concurrent validity and reliability over a few years of use is possible and is not difficult.

The results of standardized testing provide much information about the students who took the test, their teachers and the school. It is often the teacher's responsibility to properly interpret and transmit test results to parents.

CORRELATION COEFFICIENT

Wouldn't it be wonderful if teachers could administer a simple test to children, before they entered kindergarten, which would determine without error which reading program would be best for each child? Or, does a test exist which will predict a student's success in band? And, why couldn't a simple test be designed to identify which children will become drug abusers so the school could construct a special drug prevention curriculum for them? And, if these tests were possible could they be made valid and reliable? Validity and reliability of a test, when expressed numerically, uses a relationship called correlation and is expressed as r = a number from +1.00 to –1.00. Sometimes it is useful to know the relationship between two distributions of data or the strength of relationship of those data. A discussion of correlation is appropriate now so that validity and reliability concepts are more meaningful.

If the school system in which you teach was experiencing a resource shortage and could only include students at high risk in special programs not every student would be included in a drug abuse prevention program. A paper and pencil test is selected by a committee. It is administered to all students. Those who have a tendency to abuse drugs are included in the treatment group. If such a test does not exist one needs to be designed.

If a test is to be designed the following steps would be taken. A group of students who have a history of drug abuse behavior would be identified.

Juvenile records would be searched. Personal observation would corrobo-
rate court records. A severity (of drug abuse behavior) score is assigned to
each student's drug abuse behavior. These scores are listed from low to high.

The creation of a paper and pencil instrument is the next step. Items are
written. They must distinguish between drug abusing students and those who
do not abuse drugs. The items are tried out with groups of students who do
not abuse drugs. Students who abuse drugs should take the same test. Their
scores will then be compared to those of non-abusers. The test should
discriminate between the two groups. A representation of the relationship
between possible drug abuse scores and drug abuse instrument scores is
below.

FIGURE 13.1

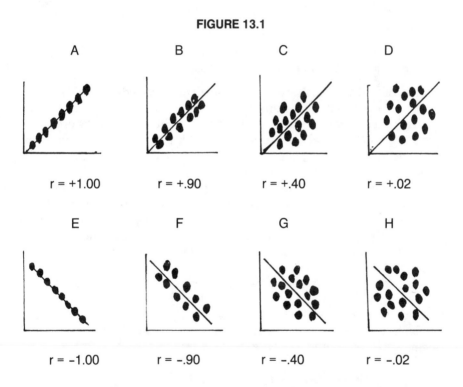

A indicates a perfect (correlation) positive relationship, +1.0, that is, a high
  drug abuse test score is accompanied with a high tendency to abuse drugs
  while low test scores are related to low drug abuse.

B indicates a strong (correlation) positive relationship, +.90, that is, it's highly
  probable that a high drug abuse test score will accompany a strong
  tendency to abuse drugs while a low test score will be accompanied by a
  low tendency to abuse drugs.

C indicates a moderate (correlation) positive relationship +.40, between test results and the student's abuse of drugs.

D indicates virtually no (correlation) relationship (+.02) between the test score and the student's tendency to abuse drugs.

E indicates a perfect negative (correlation) relationship between the test score and drug abuse. This means that a student who has a very low test score has a high tendency to abuse drugs and a student who has a very high test score has a very low tendency to abuse drugs.

F indicates a strong negative (correlation) relationship (-.90) between the test score and drug abuse tendency.

G indicates a moderately negative (correlation) relationship (-.40) between the student's drug abuse test score and the tendency to abuse drugs.

H indicates virtually no (correlation) relationship (-.02) between the test score and the student's tendency to abuse drugs.

The correlations which are the highest are most valued. In the illustration above it doesn't matter if the correlation is positive or negative, students who have a tendency to abuse drugs can be identified. Students with the predicted greatest tendency to abuse drugs later in their lives would be identified as students at risk and would be assigned to a special drug abuse resistance program.

If students were administered a music aptitude instrument and a group of them scored high in music aptitude, a guidance counselor would invite them to a counseling session. The test score would be discussed in relationship to opportunities at school to enhance the test documented aptitude. Perhaps registration in a special music class or joining the school band would be appropriate.

When kindergarten students are tested before their fall class assignments, some may fall into a group which would learn reading best while using a phonics program and others a whole language program. Kindergarten students whould be assigned to the reading program which would be best for them.

SELF CHECK FOR OBJECTIVE TWO

CAN YOU: define types of validity and reliability and describe each with an illustration?

DESCRIBING QUANTITATIVE INFORMATION

Assume that a group of students has been tested using a test which is as valid and reliable as could be designed. Test items used on the test reflected objectives taught. The possibility of external factors influencing test scores was reduced as much as possible. Therefore, a valid set of test scores should exist. How should this set of test scores be used? What purpose does this set of scores serve? How can this set of scores be interpreted? Who will interpret the set of scores? Parents are concerned with the achievement of their children. Students are concerned too. Teachers need to know the achievement level of their students.

Students ask each other "Whatjaget?" Parents ask their children about test scores. If the scores are very high or very low the parent will often ask how the remainder of the class scored. Teachers compare students to each other.

Norm and Criterion Referencing

Norm referencing

One way that a test score can be interpreted uses a reference group which may be the class in which a student is a member. A larger group such as all students in the student's grade group or in a school district may be used too. For teacher made classroom tests the class group is likely to be the reference group. This comparison group is called a norm group and the method being used is called norm referenced measurement. When norm referenced measurement is used a particular student's grade is compared to the norm group's grades.

When a parent asks how other students in the class did on a test, a norm referenced question is being asked. A comparison of test scores is being made.

Criterion referencing

A second way to interpret test scores is to compare a particular student's grade to the total possible points. If a student achieved a 94 out of 100 possible points the student would probably judge that he was successful. In this instance the student is comparing his performance to all correct answers on the test. The criterion for acceptable performance for each item on the test is a perfect answer for that item. This method is called criterion referenced measurement. When a parent helps a student with a homework assignment which is to correct all missed items on a test, the parent is concerned with criterion referenced measurement. When a student is completing a mathematics assignment and checks each answer with those given in the back of the book, the student is concerned with criterion referenced measurement.

The question "Whatjaget?" is more than likely a criterion referenced question. Later, the child's answer may be compared to class grades; at that time norm referenced measurement is being used.

To better understand a student's test score, uncomplicated statistical procedures may be performed on a group of scores. They are the frequency distribution, range, mean, mode, median, and standard deviation.

SELF CHECK FOR OBJECTIVE THREE

CAN YOU: explain norm and criterion referenced measurement?

Uncomplicated Statistical Procedures

Frequency distribution

A frequency distribution of a set of scores shows how many of each score exists for a test. Assume that the following scores were generated by a teacher who gave a test:

11, 11, 11, 11, 10, 9, 8, 5, 5

Examining the scores reveals four 11s, one 10, one 9, one 8 and two 5s. This is the frequency distribution of the set of scores. It is usually expressed as:

scores	frequency
11	4
10	1
9	1
8	1
7	0
6	0
5	2

There are nine scores in this group of scores. We used a small number of scores so that examination of the scores could remain uncomplicated.

Range

The range of this set of scores is expressed in two ways. One uses the least score-greatest score such as 5-11. The second way uses the difference between the least score and the greatest score which is 11 minus 5 equals 6. The range of this distribution of scores can be expressed as either 5-11 or 6. Using both ways to express the range is more helpful since the teacher would then know the least score and the greatest score as well as the difference. To illustrate, if a range of six is known the teacher does not know if the least score was 5 and the greatest score 11 or if the least score was 92 and the greatest score 98 if in both cases the total possible score was 100. Two different judgments could be made about the achievement of the nine students whose scores are being examined.

Mean

The mean of a set of scores is the arithmetic average of the scores. If the set of scores above is added the sum is 81. There are 9 scores. Eighty-one divided by nine is 9. The mean is 9.

Mode

The mode of a set of scores is the score which appears most frequently. Since there are four 11s the mode is 11.

Median

The median is the score which is the midway score in the distribution of scores. Since there are nine scores the fifth score is the midpoint score in the distribution. Examine the frequency distribution above. Counting from the score of 11 to that of 5 the fifth score is 10. There are four 11s. The fifth score is 10. Counting from the score of 5 toward that of 11 the fifth score is 10.

When describing a particular student's score, the mean, mode or median is used as a reference. The mean is used most often. In a typical class the teacher may state the average score in an effort to encourage students to compare their score to the average score. This is a norm referenced suggestion. Therefore, the teacher of the class of the nine scores above may state that the class average (mean) was 9 and ask each student to compare his grade to the average (mean) or imply the comparison task. Five students scored above the mean, one scored at the mean and three scored below the mean.

Standard deviation

The standard deviation can be used to compare one student's scoring position with that of another student. Or it can be used to compare a student's score on one test to the same student's score on another test. The standard deviation and the range are used in a similar manner. They describe how a particular set of scores is spread or how the scores vary in comparison to the mean. The range of the above set of scores was expressed as 5-11 or 6. The range can be easily changed with a new score such as zero (0). The new range would be 0-11 or 11. Therefore, the range is said to be somewhat unstable. A better expression of the spread of scores is the standard deviation. It is more stable and more useful. The standard deviation is used with the bell or normal curve.

Curves, A Visual Representation of Scores

Skewed curves

From an examination of the nine scores above it can be observed that the scores tend to group at the end with the greater scores. This set of scores if placed on a curve would be identified as skewed. Since they group near the greater scores it is called a negatively skewed set of scores. If the tail points to the left, the curve is called negatively skewed.

If most scores group near the lower scores, the curve would be called a positively skewed set of scores. The tail would be pointing to the right. See figure 13.2.

FIGURE 13.2
SKEWED CURVES

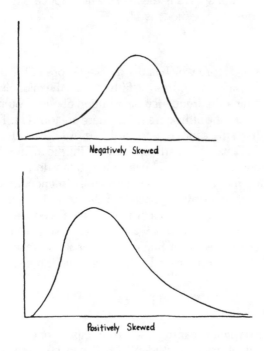

Negatively Skewed

Positively Skewed

A conclusion which may be drawn from a negatively skewed set of scores is that your students mastered most of the objectives and very few students did not. A positively skewed set of scores might lead you to the conclusion that few students mastered objectives taught and either the objectives should be retaught, the teaching strategy was inappropriate or perhaps objectives taught are not appropriate for this group of students. Teachers with consistent positively skewed scores frequently state that they have a "low group." This could be translated to inappropriate objectives for this group.

Leptokurtic and platykurtic curves

If the scores grouped in the middle of the possible range, the curve would be called leptokurtic. If the scores were evenly spread throughout the possible range of scores the curve would be named a platykurtic curve. A leptokurtic curve represents scores which are grouped in the middle with few, if any, high and low scores. A platykurtic curve represents a set of scores which is almost evenly spread throughout the possible range. There are about as many low, high and average scores.

FIGURE 13.3

LEPTOKURTIC AND PLATYKURTIC CURVES

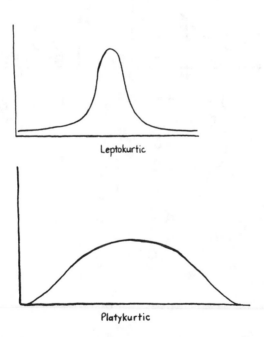

Leptokurtic

Platykurtic

Bell or normal curve

The curve and set of scores which is used for standardized test interpretation is called the normal or bell shaped curve. Many of the assumptions necessary for the use of this curve are not present in a typical classroom of 25 or 30 students. There are too few scores. However, we continue to use the normal curve because it is convenient to do so.

FIGURE 13.4

BELL CURVE

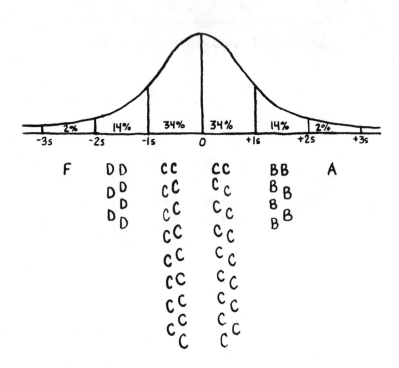

Examine the normal curve for vertical lines with the numbers -3s, -2s, -1s, 0, +1s, +2s, +3s below them. These are indicators of the six standard deviations. Although an infinite number of standard deviations exists, over 99% of the scores in a normal distribution are contained in six. Therefore, six are used. Also note the letter scores below the horizontal line. These are test scores. The numbers which are percents indicate the portion of the total scores which is in that band. The first positive standard deviation contains about 34% of the scores, the second positive standard deviation contains about 14% of the scores and the third positive standard deviation contains about 2% of the scores. This explanation is true for the negative half of the normal curve.

The curve's shape frequently reflects the distribution of the skill or knowledge tested. When teachers discuss their classes with each other they make statements such as "This year, my class is unusually gifted in reading." Or, "I don't know what's wrong with my class. There are no leaders. They are all the same."

STANDARDIZED TESTS

The bell curve is helpful in the interpretation of student scores on standardized tests which are administered in schools. Although teachers do not construct standardized tests they do administer them and use the results.

The kinds of tests which teachers administer can be divided into two types, standardized and non-standardized. Non-standardized tests are often called teacher made tests. Standarized tests are written by testing specialists who work with content area specialists. Standardized tests are created by organizations which specialize in large scale testing, universities and state departments of education. Before standardized tests are used they are administered to many groups of students in an effort to reduce the number of flaws in the test and standardize the testing and scoring process. The result is a test which can be administered to many different groups of students whose scores can be compared to each other. It is estimated that 16 standardized tests are taken by the time a student graduates from high school. That is an average of about one and one-third standardized tests a year.

Aptitude Tests

Scholastic aptitude tests are often called intelligence tests. They are used by educators to measure the probable future success of their students. Other aptitude tests exist. They include tests which measure aptitudes such as arithmetic and reading readiness, artistic, clerical, creative, mathematical, mechanical, musical and sales.

Since the purpose of aptitude tests is to predict future success they should have high predictive validity. They should also be highly reliable. It is necessary that aptitude tests validly predict future success because schools use them as a basis for selection and placement decisions.

"Roundup" is a rite of spring in many school systems. Future kindergarten students and their parents are invited to school to participate in a "roundup" of next year's students. Students and parents are introduced to kindergarten teachers and school resources. Teachers and counselors have the opportunity to readiness test next year's kindergarten students. The success of next year's placements depends on the validity of the readiness test.

While teachers use standardized tests to help predict the future success of their students it is also necessary to use teacher judgment which is non-standardized and probably does not have published validity and reliability data.

Achievement Tests

A second type measures achievement in a particular content area. Standardized achievement tests are survey tests which measure a set of objectives which are common to students throughout the nation. The objectives measured may be *all* those which are taught in the school district in which you teach. The test may measure *most* of the objectives taught in your school district. Or, the test may measure *none* of the objectives taught in your school district.

Standardized achievement tests of elementary school reading and mathematics have high content validity. Other academic areas have less content validity. This is because reading and mathematics curricula have greater content and skill sequence uniformity throughout the United States. There is less content validity in high school achievement tests since there is greater variation in high school curriculum than in elementary curriculum throughout the nation. One criticism of the administration of nationally standardized achievement tests in high school is what is measured is what has been retained from elementary school more than what is learned in high school.

Standardized achievement tests are constructed by large testing organizations and some states' departments of education. A strategy which can be used to improve the achievement level of students includes state-wide testing. Consequently, state departments of education have searched for published standardized achievement tests which closely approximate standard curricula in the state. Assuming the nonexistence of such a test a state department of education is motivated to create such a test. Tests which have been written for a particular state's curriculum have greater potential for content validity than those which are written for national consumption because test items which are included in the test closely approximate those objectives which are taught in the state.

Achievement tests which are national in scope are useful. They provide the opportunity for comparison of local achievement to national norms which are defined by a wider experience than those of a single state. Educators can purchase comparison data which are those of student groups that are similar to their students. Illustrations are data of sparsely and densely populated areas.

Standardized achievement tests are also used for quality control, student and parent information and student diagnosis. When using achievement tests for instructional purposes it is necessary to include data from other sources such as observation of student behavior, data of non-standardized tests and student background. Culture free tests probably cannot exist since tests are administered using language and language is permeated by culture. The student's level of ability to read the language of the test will influence the test outcome. The teacher's interpretation of test results must take into account the student's culture.

Interests, Attitudes, Values and Personality Tests

Tests of interests, which are preferences of one activity compared to another, are important as students begin to search for an occupation. But, student interests change. The Strong-Campbell Interest Inventory and the Kuder Occupational Interest Survey are two instruments which are used with older students. Interests tend to stablize in the late teens and change little after age 25.

Self-report tests of attitudes, values and personality are subject to faking. Disguised techniques and lie scales are used. Another difficulty exists with projective techniques. Although they are not easily faked they possess unique assessment difficulty. One difficulty with these tests is that some individuals act differently than their responses on the test.

Non-standardized or Teacher Made Tests

Although standardized tests are widely used other tests are also used. These are written by the teacher who teaches the course. (The construction of teacher made tests was the subject of the previous chapter.) Considering resources which are available to teachers it is not possible for teachers to standardize tests which they administer although it is estimated that teachers spend as much as 30% of their time evaluating instruction.

FORMATIVE EVALUATION

Teachers need to know how sequences of instruction should be changed, if content should be modified or if students should be reassigned to other work or classes. This type of evaluation is a tool of instruction and is called formative. Teacher made tests which are administered daily are formative and give teachers information which is necessary to make better instructional decisions.

SUMMATIVE EVALUATION

Although the present level of standardized testing is opposed by groups of educators and parents, they are useful as a tool to determine the general effectiveness of a program. When tests are used at the end of an instructional unit or course for this purpose the process is called summative. Summative evaluation is used to determine the extent to which students have mastered course objectives and if the course or program should be modified or not continued. Summative evaluation is not used by teachers to make instructional decisions while teaching the course.

INTERPRETING TEST RESULTS

Besides reporting the results of standardized tests as a percent correct or a number of the total items correct, other expressions of test results are used. They are reported using the language of the normal curve. The report can include standard deviation scores, percentiles, T-scores and stanines.

FIGURE 13.5
EXPANDED NORMAL CURVE

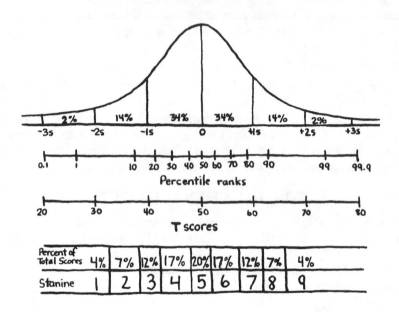

Standard deviation

Scores reported between the first negative and the first positive standard deviations are described as average (68% of the scores). Those reported between the first and second positive standard deviations are above average (14% of the scores). And those between the second and third positive standard deviations are very high scores (2% of the scores). Scores reported between the first and second negative standard deviations are described as below average (14% of the scores). Those scores between the second and third standard deviations are very low (2% of the scores).

Percentiles

If percentiles were used to report scores and a particular student scored at the 99th percentile, that student scored higher than 99% of those students with whom he is compared. If the student scored at the 50th percentile he scored better than half and worse than half of the students with whom he is being compared.

T-scores

T-scores are sometimes used to describe student scores. Please examine the normal curve and the T-scores on the curve. The T-scores' midpoint is 50 and each T-score represented is different from the one next to it by ten (10). This is so because in T-score measurement a standard deviation of ten (10) is assumed. Note that the difference between 50 and 60 is 10 or one (1) standard deviation. The difference between 50 and 70 is 20 or two (2) standard deviations. The difference between 20 and 50 is 30 or three (3) standard deviations.

Stanine

Another expression of a student's score is the stanine. Note in the word stanine the word "nine." The entire continuum of scores has been divided into nine parts with the fifth stanine in the center position. Scores in the ninth stanine are highest and in the first stanine lowest.

Expression of student scores such as standard deviation, percentile, T-score and stanine are useful since student scores on different tests can be compared. If Manuel, a student in your class, has a reading score of 89 percentile and a social studies score of 50 percentile what can be concluded? The two scores are divergent enough to suspect that Manuel, a proficient reader, is not successful in social studies for reasons other than his reading ability. After examining your notes on unusual student behavior during standardized test day you conclude that Manuel was not ill nor apparently upset. Other options can be considered. Was Manuel motivated in social studies? What are his teacher made test grades?

Standardized test scores for students are helpful when educators tentatively group students for instructional purposes. If students are going to be grouped, test information, school achievement indicated by grades, motivation level and other factors are considered. Numbers act powerfully during grouping discussions. They allow groups of students to be differentiated. Groups may be cut at the 90th, 75th and 60th percentiles.

SELF CHECK FOR OBJECTIVE FOUR

CAN YOU: describe and interpret two types of standardized tests?

ITEM ANALYSIS OF TESTS

Each time a test is administered an item analysis should be performed. An item analysis of a test can be described as a "test of a test." Test performance is measured. Standardized tests are routinely item analyzed. Nonstandardized tests should also be item analyzed.

An item analysis will examine student performance on the test. The number and percent of students who responded correctly to each item will be noted. The option, A-B-C-D, which was selected will be listed for each item. A list for the class and for individual students can be prepared. And, the performance on each item will be compared for the successful and unsuccessful students.

An item analysis assists test item writers to continue to use items which discriminate between students who have mastered objectives tested and those who have not. It also enables rejection of nonfunctioning items and improvement of items. Miskeyed or double scored items will be noted. Items which are ambiguous will surface. Items which are too easy or too hard will be obvious.

The purpose of an item analysis is to improve the testing process, not diagnose mastery of objectives. However, items can indicate which objectives were not mastered adequately. Teachers can make planning decisions based on this data.

Electronic optical scanning equipment enables this process to be less cumbersome. Computer programs exist which allow bubble-in computer test forms to be optically read, the data transferred to a desktop computer, then item analyzed.

COMMUNICATING TEST RESULTS, GRADES AND EVALUATION

What are the purposes of grades? Is a grade a communication? To whom? And, how accurate a communication?

Grades

Grades communicate student achievement to the students themselves, their parents and to others who have a need to know those grades. A test grade has the potential of being an accurate communication if the test was written effectively and if scoring methods used are objective as those suggested in a previous chapter. Report card grades have the potential of abuse since factors other than academic ones can be factored into the final grade. The student's personality, behavior, sibling's behavior, and parental reputation can be factored into the report card grade.

Grades are communicated in a variety of schemes. Some use Pass or Fail. Others use letters such as A,B,C,D,E. And numbers such as 90,80,70,60 and 50 are used. While Pass/Fail and A,B,C,D,E suffer from presumed inaccuracy, number grades are assumed to be more precise than justified. In an effort to bridge this dilemma plus and minus have been appended to the letter grades.

There are many factors which are the basis for grades.

1. *Achievement* is most often used as a basis for the assignment of grades. Student achievement on tests and units of content are compared to ideal student responses. The grade which is issued reflects the comparison.
2. Student *behavior* is observed by teachers; in early elementary school this is the major basis of a student's grade. Behavior observation is formal or informal. Informal observations rely on teacher memory of objectives and student mastery of objectives. Formal behavior observation systems rely on behavior checklists (discussed in the previous chapter). Checkmarks are substituted for letter or number grades.
3. Students are sometimes administratively assigned to ability groups for instruction. *Achievement on ability groups* is consequently used as background for the issue of grades. The result is students assigned "A" whose achievement is academically comparable to students in other groups receiving "B."
4. *Effort* is valued by educators. Consequently, grades often reflect an "effort" factor. Students who try hard receive a higher grade than students who do not try as hard as they could.
5. Goal oriented persons are directed toward *improvement* in knowledge, attitude and behavior of students. Teachers factor improvement into grades. This is especially true in elementary school when motivation of the student is an issue.
6. It is in the nature of most students to compare their achievement to other students' achievement. Some teachers use a comparison system when assigning grades. *Student to student comparison* can easily be achieved using the properties of the bell shaped curve. Grades can be assigned using the language of "T-scores, percentiles and stanines." This method is used in reporting standardized achievement scores to teachers, parents and students.
7. It is common for teachers to negotiate contracts with students for improved academic and social behavior. It is less common for *teachers to contract with students for report card grades*. The contract is a familiar form of agreement in schools. A series of academic and behavior contracts could become part of a report card grade contract.

Grading methods are incorporated into grade reports on tests and report cards. Illustrations of some of the grading methods are below. Report cards which are not represented are those which are in a language other than English. Should report cards in other languages be created? Why?

Although grades result from a variety of flawed behaviors they are an uncanny and accurate predictor of success in later school experiences including college. On the negative side grades and grading tend to influence self esteem. Students who are assigned to high and low achieving groups know the implications of those assignments. Students who receive lower grades tend to think of themselves as academic losers. In an effort to avoid grading of students for life as eggs are graded, schools that are sensitive to the self esteem issue are taking steps to change the process. One change is the behavior checklist used in early elementary grades.

Teachers who sympathized with parents' confusion developed a report which is a list of objectives to be mastered in a particular grade or course. Lists used were inclusive and long. This method has survived in some kindergarten and grade one classrooms. The list of objectives to be mastered and the student's mastery level tells parents (more accurately) about the progress of their child using a statement which is more direct and less riddled with other information. An illustration of a kindergarten report is below. This illustration is incomplete since the entire report would be lengthy.

STUDENT REPORT
KINDERGARTEN
USA SCHOOL DISTRICT
199_

STUDENT NAME _____

TEACHER NAME _____

Student is able to:	Achievement Level
State her/his name	___
State her/his age	___
State phone number	___
Recognize the eight basic colors	___
Name the eight basic colors	___
Follow one step oral directions	___
Follow two step oral directions	___
Repeat nursery rhymes (less than six lines)	___
Recognize upper and lower case alphabet letters	___
Name upper and lower case alphabet letters	___

Achievement Levels:
4—Achieves objective consistently without error.
3—Achieves objective consistently with little prompting.
2—Achieves objective inconsistently.
1—Has not achieved objective.

The report above eliminates the vague communication of "A," "B," "C," "Satisfactory," "Unsatisfactory" and "Needs Improvement." The use of numbers such as 90, 80, 70 in a report card implies precision which does not exist. Possibly the most precise reporting statement is the use of a statement of objectives and the level of mastery.

STUDENT REPORT
GRADE THREE
USA SCHOOL DISTRICT
199_

STUDENT NAME _____

TEACHER NAME _____

QUARTER	1	2	3	4	AVG
ART	—	—	—	—	—
LANGUAGE					
COMPOSITION WRITING...............	—	—	—	—	—
GRAMMAR USE	—	—	—	—	—
PENMANSHIP.........................	—	—	—	—	—
READING SKILLS......................	—	—	—	—	—
SPELLING	—	—	—	—	—
MATHEMATICS					
COMPUTATION	—	—	—	—	—
PROBLEM SOLVING	—	—	—	—	—
MUSIC	—	—	—	—	—
PHYSICAL EDUCATION	—	—	—	—	—
SCIENCE	—	—	—	—	—
SOCIAL STUDIES	—	—	—	—	—
STUDY SKILLS..........................	—	—	—	—	—
FOLLOWS DIRECTIONS	—	—	—	—	—
PARTICIPATES..........................	—	—	—	—	—
RESPECTS OTHERS	—	—	—	—	—
WORKS INDEPENDENTLY	—	—	—	—	—

Achievement Levels:

4—Above Expectation
3—Satisfactory
2—Below Expectation
1—Unsatisfatory

Days Late	—	—	—	—	—
Days Absent............................	—	—	—	—	—

TEACHER NOTES:

The report card on page 279 is one frequently used in elementary grades. It is less descriptive than the kindergarten report card above but more descriptive than those used by the typical secondary school.

Secondary school report cards are frequently computerized. The card below can easily be computerized. It makes use of many symbols which require a code description and translation on the card.

USA SECONDARY SCHOOL DISTRICT REPORT CARD

STUDENT NAME _____ STUDENT NUMBER _____

SCHOOL _____ DATE _____

Subject   **Teacher**   **Quarter Identification:** _____

		Level	Grade	Behavior	Absence
Comp 4	Anocrom	____	____	____	____
Math 3	Finnell	____	____	____	____
PE4	Bassett	____	____	____	____
Psych	Skinnet	____	____	____	____
Science	Blinkno	____	____	____	____
SocStu	Krather	____	____	____	____

CODES

Grade Level: 3=above level; 2=at level; 1=below level

Grade: A=Excellent; B=Good; C=Average; D=Pass;
        F=Fail; W=Withdraw; I=Incomplete

Behavior: S=Satisfactory; U=Unsatisfactory

Absence: Number of classes missed this grade period

Parents are the ordinary consumers of report card information. Considering the number of elements which teachers use as a basis for reporting grades it's easy to conclude that parents are sometimes offered a confusing communication called a report card. The card includes a list of academic subjects and social behaviors (known as "conduct"). As you reexamine the seven factors which are the basis for grades think of your experience as a student who received a report card. Were your grades a result of your academic achievement? Your behavior? Your academic achievement compared to your ability? Your effort? Your improvement? A comparison of this period's achievement to that of the last reporting period? Your achievement compared to that of other students in your group? Or, did you contract for grades? Or, did your single grade include a few of these such as combined academic achievement, behavior, effort, improvement and a comparison to your classmates' achievement? Are you confused? So are many parents. They frequently do not know what report cards communicate. They use report cards as a rough indicator of academic and behavioral change. When obvious changes occur many parents call school and request a parent conference.

Parent conferences

Besides communicating with parents with written reports, parent conferences are requested by parents and educators. Parent conferences take place before or after school on the school campus. It is not unusual for a parent conference to take place in the student's home.

A parent conference is an opportunity to communicate with parents; this method is more personal than sending home a report card. To effectively conduct a parent conference it is necessary to communicate effectively. Effective communication is transactional. It is not one way. The teacher, parent and child (perhaps) take turns talking and listening. The teacher should not do all the talking. Remember, the purpose of the conference is to give parents information, get information from parents and if necessary negotiate a child-parent-teacher relationship.

Don't alarm parents unless it is appropriate. When faced with a letter or a phone call from the school most parents will react with alarm. If they are alarmed before the conference they may be defensive during the conference. And defensive parents sometimes become angry. Teachers should not become angry. They should structure the conference so that parents do not become angry. Prepare for the conference so that it is a rational meeting.

When preparing for the conference write an agenda. Clarify the agenda when the parents arrive. Ask the child's parents if they would like to add to the agenda. In this way hidden agendas will be minimized. Follow the agenda. Try not to topic hop. Bring several of their child's work samples to the conference. Look for positive samples of their child's behavior. Try to be encouraging. Ask parents how they feel about their child's progress in school. Establish a relationship which will lead to further cooperation and will facilitate the student's growth.

Some suggestions which the teacher might make are short term contracts between student, parent and school; the use of a family council when dealing with thorny issues and the use of positive reinforcement by the parent with the student.

While discussing the school's hopes for the child, teachers should be sensitive to the information being given by parents. This is especially true if the conference is being held at the student's home. Try to understand the environment in which the child is living. Is the environment a rich one? Are there many books in the house? Does the family subscribe to magazines which facilitate growth? What kind of music is listened to? Does the child live in a house or a home? Be sensitive to family values, discipline and parental ideas about education. How is the child treated by his parents, his siblings and other members of the family if it is an extended family? Try to take information, give information and initiate a relationship which will be helpful to the child, parents and teacher.

SELF CHECK FOR OBJECTIVE FIVE

CAN YOU: role play teachers communicating with parents?

SUMMARY

When teachers give tests, teacher made or standardized, it is necessary to give meaning to the scores which result. Scores alone are meaningless! A reference framework is necessary to make sense of the meaningless. This chapter was written to help you to make sense of test scores. Factors external to the test which affect test results were discussed. Validity and reliability were explained. We suggested caution when interpreting test results. The numbers are so seductive! Don't be misled by the apparently unquestionable nature of numbers. More frameworks followed, norm and criterion referencing. Finally, curves were presented. The bell curve, although occurring infrequently in small groups was identified as the curve of choice when interpreting test results. Last, the conference as a communication with parents and others was discussed. Conferences were described as either opportunities or pestilence — opportunities if the teacher is prepared and pestilence if all goes wrong.

This chapter introduced you to test results interpretation. It was not intended to be a full explanation of measurement theory or statistics. For a more extensive explanation please see the bibliography.

ACTIVITIES

1. Using the following test scores compute the
   a. frequency distribution
   b. range
   c. mode
   d. mean and
   e. median

6,9,4,13,6,12,11,4,6,11,6

2. If the set of scores above were plotted would the resulting curve be bell shaped, skewed, platykurtic or leptokurtic? Why?
3. Write a five minute speech which you will give to a school PTA describing external factors which influence test scores. Be certain to use language and examples which non-professionals will understand.
4. With two student colleagues plan a role play which involves a teacher trying to explain to parents why their child failed this year.

BIBLIOGRAPHY

Brueggemann, L.V. (1987). What teachers should know about test wiseness. *Reading Horizons, 27*(3), 159-163.

Canady. R.L., & Hotchkiss, P.R. (1989). Its a good score; just a bad grade. *Phi Delta Kappa, 71*(1), 68-71.

Ebel, R. (1972). *Essentials of educational measurement.*Englewood Cliffs: Prentice-Hall.

Hopkins, K., & Stanley, J. (1981). *Educational and psychological measurement and evaluation.* Englewood Cliffs: Prentice-Hall.

Moran, J.D. (1988). Measuring creativity in preschool children. *Journal of Creative Behavior, 22*(4), 254-263.

Mehrens, W.A., & Kaminski, J. (1989). Methods for improving standardized test scores: fruitful, fruitless or fraudulent? *Educational Measurement: Issues and Practice, 8*(1), 14-22.

Mulkey, L.M. (1989). Using two instruments to measure student gains in reading achievement when assessing the impact of educational programs. *Evaluation Review, 12*(5), 571-587.

Nitko, A.J., & Hsu, T.C. (1984). A comprehensive microcomputer system for classroom testing. *Journal of Educational Measurement, 21,* 377-390.

Tuckman, B. (1975). *Measuring educational outcomes, fundamentals of testing.* New York: Harcourt Brace Jovanovich.

index